I0092290

# Deconstructing Peace

# About the Peace and Security in the 21st Century Series

## *Series Editor:* Charles Hauss, Alliance for Peacebuilding

Until recently, security was defined mostly in geopolitical terms with the assumption that it could only be achieved through at least the threat of military force. Today, however, people from as different backgrounds as planners in the Pentagon and veteran peace activists think in terms of human or global security, where no one is secure unless everyone is secure in all areas of their lives. This means that it is impossible nowadays to separate issues of war and peace, the environment, sustainability, identity, global health, and the like.

The books in this series aim to make sense of this changing world of peace and security by investigating security issues and peace efforts that involve cooperation at several levels. By looking at how security and peace interrelate at various stages of conflict, the series explores new ideas for a fast-changing world and seeks to redefine and rethink what peace and security mean in the first decades of the new century.

Multidisciplinary in approach and authorship, the books cover a variety of topics, focusing on the overarching theme that students, scholars, practitioners and policymakers have to find new models and theories to account for, diagnose and respond to the difficulties of a more complex world. Authors are established scholars and practitioners in their fields of expertise.

In addition, it is hoped that the series will contribute to bringing together authors and readers in concrete, applied projects, and thus help create, under the sponsorship of Alliance for Peacebuilding (AfP), a community of practice.

## Titles in the Series

*Military Chaplains in Afghanistan, Iraq, and Beyond: Advisement and Leader*
    *Engagement in Highly Religious Environments*
Edited by Eric Patterson

*Security 2.0: Dealing with Global Wicked Problems*
Charles Hauss

*Drug Trafficking and International Security*
Paul Rexton Kan

Combating Criminalized Power Structures: A Toolkit
Edited by Michael Dziedzic

*Criminalized Power Structures: The Overlooked Enemies of Peace*
Edited by Michael Dziedzic

*Ethics for Peacebuilders: A Practical Guide*
Reina C. Neufeldt

*Forging Peace in Southeast Asia: Insurgencies, Peace Processes, and Reconciliation*
Zachary Abuza

*Civil Society, Peace, and Power*
Edited by David Cortright, Melanie Greenberg and Laurel Stone

*How to Resolve Conflict: A Practical Mediation Manual*
James E. Gilman

*Making Peace with Faith: The Challenges of Religion and Peacebuilding*
Edited by Michelle Garred and Mohammed Abu-Nimer

*Human Security: Theory and Action*
David Andersen-Rodgers and Kerry F. Crawford

*The Ecology of Violent Extremism: Perspectives on Peacebuilding and Human Security*
Edited by Lisa Schirch

*Truth and Reconciliation Commission Processes: Learning from the Solomon Islands*
Karen Brounéus

*Choosing Peace: Agency and Action in the Midst of War*
Bridget Moix

*New Directions in Peacebuilding Evaluation*
Edited by Tamra Pearson d'Estrée

*For the Sake of Peace: Africana Perspectives on Racism, Justice, and Peace in America*
Edited by Charles L. Chavis Jr. and Sixte Vigny Nimuraba

*Building Peace in America*
Edited by Emily Sample and Douglas Irvin-Erickson

*Narrativized Strategic Choice*
John P. DeRosa

*Unsettling Empathy: Working with Groups in Conflict*
Björn Krondorfer

*Beyond Mediation: Exploring Indigenous Models, Narratives, and Contextualization*
Daniel Njoroge Karanja

*Human Security and Agency: Reframing Productive Power in Afghanistan*
Nilofar Sakhi

*Deconstructing Peace: The Contested Politics of Post-Conflict Northern Ireland and Bosnia and Herzegovina*
Patrick Pinkerton

# Deconstructing Peace

## The Contested Politics of Post-Conflict Northern Ireland and Bosnia and Herzegovina

Patrick Pinkerton

ROWMAN & LITTLEFIELD
Lanham • Boulder • New York • London

Published by Rowman & Littlefield
An imprint of The Rowman & Littlefield Publishing Group, Inc.
4501 Forbes Boulevard, Suite 200, Lanham, Maryland 20706
www.rowman.com

6 Tinworth Street, London SE11 5AL, United Kingdom

Copyright © 2021 by Patrick Pinkerton

*All rights reserved.* No part of this book may be reproduced in any form or by any electronic or mechanical means, including information storage and retrieval systems, without written permission from the publisher, except by a reviewer who may quote passages in a review.

British Library Cataloguing in Publication Information Available

**Library of Congress Cataloging-in-Publication Data**

Names: Pinkerton, Patrick, 1982– author.
Title: Deconstructing peace : the contested politics of post-conflict Northern Ireland and Bosnia and Herzegovina / Patrick Pinkerton.
Description: Lanham : Rowman & Littlefield, [2021] | Includes bibliographical references and index. | Summary: "This book interrogates the peace process by developing and applying concepts from the philosophy of Jacques Derrida, applying this novel analysis of the contested post-conflict political situations. The approach will both examine how this political context has developed, and provide a means of moving beyond it, through a 'deconstructive conclusion' which targets historical narratives of the conflicts, while simultaneously disrupting their contemporary political consequences. This provides a fresh interpretation of how the entrenchment of division in Northern Ireland and Bosnia and Herzegovina transpires, an examination of the ways in which this reification of division fails, and a means of moving beyond the dysfunction produced by this failure. This study provides a key contribution to both peacebuilding and Derridean scholarship within IR, through bringing a new critical perspective to the peacebuilding literature, and by demonstrating the utility of Derrida's key ideas through their application to fresh empirical terrain. This theoretical approach will demonstrate how Derridean concepts can be utilised to provide deep understandings of the real-world events under discussion, as well as allowing political interventions to be made into these processes" — Provided by publisher.
Identifiers: LCCN 2020058095 (print) | LCCN 2020058096 (ebook) | ISBN 9781786614070 (cloth) | ISBN 9781786614087 (ebook) ISBN 9781538153345 (pbk)
Subjects: LCSH: Derrida, Jacques. | Peace-building—Northern Ireland. | Peace-building—Bosnia and Herzegovina. | Peace-building—Philosophy. | Conflict management—Northern Ireland. | Conflict management—Bosnia and Herzegovina. | Northern Ireland—Politics and government—1998– | Bosnia and Herzegovina—Politics and government—1992–
Classification: LCC JZ5584.N75 P56 2021 (print) | LCC JZ5584.N75 (ebook) | DDC 941.60824—dc23
LC record available at https://lccn.loc.gov/2020058095
LC ebook record available at https://lccn.loc.gov/2020058096

*For Bronagh*

This is impossible, but no one has ever said that deconstruction, as a technique or a method, was possible; it thinks only on the level of the impossible and of what is still evoked as unthinkable.

—Jacques Derrida
*MEMOIRES for Paul de Man*, 135

# Contents

# Acknowledgements

This book is in part an adaptation of my doctoral thesis, but the bulk of the argument and analysis has been developed in more recent years. For the material that has been adapted from my thesis, I must acknowledge the support given to me during my PhD studies at the University of Manchester, particularly by my supervisors Maja Zehfuss and Cristina Masters. Some material in chapters 1, 3, 4 and 6 is reproduced from the article 'Deconstructing Dayton: Ethnic Politics and the Legacy of War in Bosnia and Herzegovina', published in the *Journal of Intervention and Statebuilding* 10(4).

The development of my argument over the last four years has benefitted from numerous conference presentations, including at the October 2017 Millennium Conference held at the London School of Economics, the 2017 and 2019 British International Studies Association conferences held in Brighton and London, respectively, and the October 2019 *Beyond 'Sectarianism'?* workshop held at the University of Cambridge. I would like to thank the organizers of these conferences and all those participants who commented on my papers and presentations, particularly the discussants at the LSE and Brighton, Andrew Hom and Laura McLeod, and the convener of the Cambridge workshop, Emanuelle Degli Esposti. I also received substantial feedback from colleagues in the School of Politics and International Relations at Queen Mary University of London. I would like to thank Jean-Francois Drolet, Clive Gabay, Kimberly Hutchings, Jef Huysmans, Andro Kitus and Elke Schwarz for the detailed and encouraging comments they provided on drafts of the manuscript.

# Preface

Even though I was fortunate enough to avoid being directly affected, growing up in Belfast in the late 1980s and early 1990s meant the Northern Ireland conflict was formative to my childhood. I would wait for my Granny to collect me from primary school next to on duty British Army soldiers, and I still remember the day one squaddie let us look through the scope of his automatic rifle. There was nothing strange to me about knocking over my toy street set and saying 'the IRA have bombed it' before sending in toy firefighters to rescue the stricken inhabitants. I caused much amusement for the rest of my family by asking 'who is this Sinn Féin person anyway, why is he never on the news', and for years I thought the joint address by the UK and Irish prime ministers in 1993 was called the 'Downing Street Decoration' (not 'Declaration'): Why else were the two men standing in front of a well-decorated Christmas tree?

While I was aware of the Northern Ireland conflict for as long as I can remember, the wars in the former Yugoslavia also made a strong impression on me from an early age. Without knowing the differences between these organizations, I remember hearing news reports about debates between the UN and NATO over who should take the lead role in the latter stages of the war in Bosnia and Herzegovina. I have stronger memories still of the war in Kosovo, particularly the NATO air campaign there, which was perhaps the first time I became properly engaged with a major event in international politics.

When I started studying International Relations at the University of Manchester, Northern Ireland and the Balkans were two topics I always looked out for. Would they come up in my module readings lists? Were there entries in the indexes of my textbooks on them? How did academics account for the violence, explain the success of the peace processes, or characterise their contemporary politics? The similarities were striking: tropes about 'ancient hatreds', the 'weight of history', and 'long memories' were prevalent in the more salacious accounts; while categories like 'ethnic conflict', 'ethno-national competition', 'inter-communal violence' and 'consociation-alism' were scattered throughout the drier, more scholarly works. Whatever the terminology, the common trends seemed to be an exceptionalisation of these two political spaces and a portrayal of the people there as atavistic, pre-modern and innately prone to violence. How could these accounts be so common, I asked myself, and what impacts have these representations had on the conflicts and the post-conflict politics of these two places?

The present book is the culmination of this interest. After writing a doctoral thesis on the international administration in post-conflict Bosnia and Herzegovina, and an article on the politics of memorialisation in post-conflict Northern Ireland, I decided to tackle the two cases together, to see where an extended reflection on them would take me. While my scepticism of comparative analysis of the two cases remain, the period in which I was writing this book did present one undeniable similarity that has strongly marked the development of my argument: the general state of dysfunction into which the two polities descended in the last few years. As I will describe, Northern Ireland was without a devolved government for three years from January 2017, while Bosnia and Herzegovina went without a state-level government for fourteen months from October 2018. The challenges and opportunities of writing while these crises unfolded has left an indelible impression on the book, and it will be fascinating to see how future political developments reinforce or reconfigure the arguments put forward here.

Patrick Pinkerton
London, March 2020.

# List of Abbreviations

| | |
|---|---|
| AIA | Anglo-Irish Agreement |
| ARBiH | Army of the Republic of Bosnia and Herzegovina |
| BiH | Bosnia and Herzegovina |
| CoE | Council of Europe |
| DFM | Deputy First Minister |
| DPA | Dayton Peace Agreement |
| DUP | Democratic Unionist Party |
| EBM | East Belfast Mission |
| EC | European Community |
| ECHR | European Convention on Human Rights |
| ECtHR | European Court of Human Rights |
| EU | European Union |
| FBiH | Federation of Bosnia and Herzegovina |
| FM | First Minister |
| FRY | Federal Republic of Yugoslavia |
| GFA | Good Friday Agreement |
| HDZ | Croatian Democratic Union |
| HV | Croatian Army |
| IFOR | Implementation Force |
| IMF | International Monetary Fund |
| JNA | Yugoslav People's Army |
| MEP | Member of the European Parliament |
| MLA | Member of the Legislative Assembly |
| NATO | North Atlantic Treaty Organisation |
| OHR | Office of the High Representative |
| OSCE | Organization for Security and Co-operation in Europe |
| PBP | People Before Profit |

| PIRA | Provisional Irish Republican Army |
| PM | Prime Minister |
| PUP | Progressive Unionist Party |
| RS | Serbian Republic |
| SAA | St Andrews Agreement |
| SBiH | Party for Bosnia and Herzegovina |
| SDA | Party for Democratic Action |
| SDLP | Social Democratic and Labour Party |
| SDP | Social Democratic Party |
| SDS | Serb Democratic Party |
| SFRY | Socialist Federal Republic of Yugoslavia |
| SNSD | Alliance of Independent Social Democrats |
| STV | Single-Transferable Vote |
| UK | United Kingdom |
| UKUP | United Kingdom Unionist Party |
| UN | United Nations |
| UNHCR | United Nations High Commissioner for Refugees |
| UNPROFOR | United Nations Protection Force |
| US | United States |
| UUP | Ulster Unionist Party |
| UWC | Ulster Workers' Council |

# Chapter 1

# Introduction

## *The Problems of Peace in Northern Ireland and Bosnia and Herzegovina*

The Good Friday Agreement (GFA)[1] and the Dayton Peace Agreement (DPA)[2] are rightly celebrated as landmark achievements in the pursuit of peace. Agreed in April 1998 and November 1995 respectively, the deals ended conflicts in Northern Ireland and Bosnia and Herzegovina (BiH) that had, in the former case, endured at a low level of persistent violence for nearly thirty years and, in the latter case, escalated to a horrific intensity across three and half blood-soaked years. The events leading up to the signing of the agreements have been the subject of countless academic inquiries, popular accounts and documentaries, and the events marking prominent anniversaries have been major international occasions, attended by former politicians, heads of government and other assorted dignitaries (Balkan Insight 2015; BBC News 2018). More importantly for this current study, the GFA and DPA continue, in the third decade after they were agreed, to shape and influence political debate in Northern Ireland and BiH, whether through operating as the basis for the political institutions in both polities, through providing an oft-cited 'spirit' that is evoked to encourage further compromise or efforts at reconciliation, or through provoking challenge and calls for reform or renegotiation. The prominence of these peace agreements, and the contrasts that can be drawn between the present situations and the rampant and endemic violence that proceeded them, means that Northern Ireland and BiH are often put forward as paragons of successful peacebuilding and examples that can be followed in other cases of inter-communal conflict[3].

However, both Northern Ireland and BiH have suffered persistent political dysfunction in the years since the signing of the peace agreements. The devolved institutions created by the GFA have been suspended on numerous occasions due to disagreements between the major parties, most recently for three years between January 2017 and January 2020 (BBC News 2020). The multi-layered political institutions created by the DPA, often commented upon due to their complexity (Nardelli, Dzidic, and Jukic 2014), are persistently in a state of crisis. After the most recent general election in October 2018, it took until December 2019 for a state-level government to be formed (Kovacevic 2019b). This dysfunction has been the subject of a strand of critical conflict studies and peacebuilding literature which emphasises the shortcomings and limitations of the agreements in both cases. While recognising the relative success of the peace deals brokered by outside mediators in managing a transition to peace, such approaches highlight the endemic political problems that still plague both countries, with this dysfunction often connected to the consociational political settlements created by the peace agreements. The common arguments tend to proceed as follows: rather than viewing the hardening of opposed identities in Northern Ireland and BiH as a consequence of inter-communal violence, outside mediators have accepted these identities as drivers of the conflicts; the proposed solutions therefore seek to contain and accommodate stable, self-enclosed and conflictual groups, whose existence is presupposed from the outset, through political structures based on mandatory coalition, power-sharing and mutual veto; this, in turn, operates in the post-conflict period to reify and entrench division, by empowering political parties who represent one identity, while failing to provide incentives for compromise or reconciliation; parties operating across the divide are therefore marginalised, political debate fractures along the fault-lines mobilised during the conflict, and politics is reduced to 'war by other means', with conflicts that once played out in violent terms being displaced to other arenas of contestation (such as culture, education or memorialisation).[4]

The critical peacebuilding literature is therefore well aware of the shortcomings of contemporary peacebuilding practice in places like Northern Ireland and BiH, and much effort has been dedicated to providing the conceptual tools to overcome these limitations. The present book intervenes into these debates in the conflict and peace studies literature. As suggested by the brief outline given above of the critical strands of this literature, the entrenchment of division through peacebuilding endeavours has long been recognised and diagnosed as a damaging side-effect of dominant peacebuilding practice, which must be analysed and understood in order to produce more meaningful forms of peace. The present study of the Northern Ireland and BiH cases differs from this literature by exploring the *instability* and *contingency* of this entrenchment of division, rather than viewing it as something fixed or frozen in place through the peace agreements. Drawing on the philosophy of Jacques Derrida, I highlight the ways in which the reification of division proceeds alongside the simultaneous *failure* of such reification. By examining the presence in Northern Ireland and BiH of *both* a divisive politics *and* a politics that challenges and subverts the entrenchment of division, I side-step the need for academics to generate models of 'better' peacebuilding measures which can overcome the reification of division, as such reification is seen as an inherently unstable process.

The central argument of this book is that the peace agreements in Northern Ireland and BiH embody contradictory understandings of the conflicts, and that these contradictions are transmitted into the contemporary politics of both places. The peace settlements *simultaneously* understand the conflicts as arising from the existence of innately opposed and irreconcilable groups who must be *accommodated* by appropriate political structures, *and* as political conflicts based on grievances that can be *transformed*. Rather than arguing that the peace agreements simply freeze divisions in place, I explore how both the formal electoral politics and informal political spheres of artistic, cultural, judicial and protest movements already contest these divisions. To use the Derridean terminology employed in the book, that is to say that the peace agreements, and the political systems they inaugurated, are *already in a process of deconstruction*. Furthermore, by exploring how the peace agreements transmit specific understandings of the history of the conflicts into contemporary politics, I argue that completing the deconstruction of the peace agreements, in order to allow the politics of Northern Ireland and BiH to move beyond their persistent states of dysfunction, requires unravelling these historical narratives *alongside* contesting their contemporary political consequences. I suggest a means of enacting this through a 'deconstructive conclusion', which challenges the historical understandings of the conflicts *at the same time* as challenging the consequences of these in the contemporary period. This book therefore provides a fresh interpretation of *how* the entrenchment of division in Northern Ireland and BiH transpires, an examination of the ways in which this reification of division *fails*, and a means of *moving beyond* the dysfunction produced by this failure.

My decision to analyse both the Northern Ireland and BiH cases is driven by recognition that the conflicts have been understood and engaged with in similar ways, both in academic texts and in the accounts of those engaged in the peacebuilding endeavours, and that this has had similar consequences for the post-conflict politics of both places. This means I do not engage in an extensive comparative analysis of the conflicts in Northern Ireland and BiH. Indeed, a quick glance at the key features of the conflicts, and the post-conflict situations, reveals more differences than similarities. 'The troubles' in Northern Ireland was a near thirty-year, low-level conflict largely contained within one small region of Europe, resulting in less than 4,000 deaths; while BiH was the site of an intensive war, lasting less than four years but part of a wider series of conflicts around the destruction of a major European state, resulting in over 100,000 deaths, acts of genocide and massive population displacement. There is also a clear difference in the current political status of the two places. Northern Ireland remains a sub-national region of the United Kingdom (UK), while BiH is a sovereign state in its own right, after seceding from the Socialist Federal Republic of Yugoslavia (SFRY) in April 1992. This is important to recognise, even if only as a factor in how I will describe the two cases. While BiH is a 'country' in the sense of being a sovereign state, Northern Ireland is only a 'country' in the UK context, in which all four constituent parts (England, Northern Ireland, Scotland and Wales) are referred to as 'countries', despite lacking any international political recognition as such.[5] These facts remain contested, of course, with Irish Nationalists seeking a sovereign united Ireland, and some Bosnian Croats and Bosnian Serbs seeking closer ties with the neighbouring Croatian and Serbian states.

Yet, the current status quo in both places has led to clear variations in the peacebuilding measures employed. The UK government holds sovereign authority in Northern Ireland, but has accepted that the Irish government are an integral party to all peace negotiations. While international mediators such as former United States (US) senator George Mitchell, retired Canadian general and diplomat John de Chastelain, and ex-Finnish prime minister (PM) Harri Holkeri played crucial roles at key moments in the negotiations, and while European Union (EU) funding has been central to reconciliation efforts, the UK/Irish inter-governmental relationship has been the driving force of the peacebuilding efforts. BiH, on the other hand, has been the site of a much clearer 'international' peace intervention, whether through the presence of United Nations (UN) peacekeepers during the war, the North Atlantic Treaty Organisation (NATO) airstrikes during its closing stages, the monitoring role of the Organization for Security and Co-operation in Europe (OSCE) in early elections, or the presence of international administrative structures headed by the Office of the High Representative (OHR). While the OHR was strongly assertive in the early years of the post-conflict period, regularly stepping in to take key decisions when the politicians could not, BiH's status as an independent state means it is in a qualitatively different position to Northern Ireland. In the latter case, whenever the devolved political structures collapse, the UK government can step in to fill the legislative gap. The existence of this default fall-back position in Northern Ireland can be seen as a key factor in the stuttering nature of reconciliation efforts, and something that finds only a pale imitation in the activities of the OHR in BiH.

One interesting parallel, in terms of the conflicts, is how both can be seen as the 'dark side' of periods of upheaval and revolutionary change: the Northern Ireland conflict emerged from the civil rights movement, inspired by its counterpart in the US and the '1968' protests in Europe (McKittrick and McVea 2012, 46);[6] the Yugoslav wars, of which the BiH conflict was the longest and bloodiest chapter, came after the '1989' revolutions in eastern Europe (Woodward 1995, 1; Silber and Little 1996, 26). One common explanation for the two conflicts views them as resulting from attempts by conservative forces to retain control in the face of radical chance (Gagnon Jr. 2004, 7; McKittrick and McVea 2012, 45; Silber and Little 1996, 25). However, the development of such a comparative argument is not the key motivation of this book. Instead, I examine the two cases separately in the first four chapters, in order to demonstrate the utility of my Derridean approach for understanding the different ways in which the peace agreements have produced political systems in a process of deconstruction, while the final chapter examines the two cases together, in order to put forward a means of completing this deconstruction. I therefore do not provide detailed historical accounts of the conflicts in Northern Ireland and BiH,[7] beyond brief sketches in chapters 2 and 3 of the outbreak of the violence in both cases, and brief outlines in chapters 4 and 5 of the processes which led to the peace agreements being signed.

My separate analysis of the cases for most of the book allows for detailed engagement with the construction of understandings and ideas about the conflicts, and the correlations and inter-connections between academic discourse and the accounts of political actors engaging in and engaging with the conflicts (i.e. both belligerent parties and those attempting to mediate or intervene). In particular, I am interested in uncovering how this knowledge has been produced, how these understandings have shaped and structured attempts to end the conflicts, and the continuing impacts of these on the post-conflict political situations. Chapters 2 and 3 therefore critically examine both the academic literature on the conflicts and peace agreements, and the memoires of key actors involved, in order to uncover how certain understandings of the violence crystallise in these dominant accounts, and to trace the impact of these understandings on attempts at ending the conflicts. Chapters 4 and 5 then provide comprehensive readings of the peace agreements themselves, as well as in-depth analyses of the post-conflict politics of both places. The exhaustive engagement with the details of these peace processes are the necessary foundations on which I build my new, deconstructive approach to peace and conflict studies.

It will never be truly possible to understand why the first shots were fired in the conflicts in Northern Ireland and BiH, or what motivated the actors involved to escalate the violence to the levels it reached, or even what convinced some of those same actors to sue for peace when they did. The answers to these questions are time-locked, existing only in the contingent moments of decision that have since passed; even the individuals involved are unlikely to be able to recall precisely or accurately what drove them to act in the way they did. As has been commented upon in certain areas of the literature,[8] the pursuit of such detailed understanding and full explanation is inherently problematic. What *is* open to productive investigation, in my view, are the ways in which such actions and motivations have *themselves* been

understood by academics and practitioners alike, and what *can* be traced is
the *consequences* of such understandings for the peace settlements. It is this
form of investigation that this book undertakes: an analysis of the academic,
journalistic, practitioner and popular accounts of the two conflicts; a tracing
of how certain understandings of the conflicts have been embedded in the
peace agreements in both cases; and a consideration of the consequences of
this for the post-conflict politics of both places. By showing how the endemic
dysfunction and instability of the political institutions in Northern Ireland
and BiH is rooted in the dominant understandings of the conflicts that have
informed the peace agreements, I am then able to suggest a means of overcoming these impasses, through a new orientation towards the legacies of the
conflicts, that can be enacted through the political work of a deconstructive
conclusion undertaken in the contemporary period. Before I begin advancing
this argument, however, I must mark out more clearly my Derridean approach
to peacebuilding, by outlining the key aspects of Derridean thought that I
utilise in the book.

## DERRIDA AND DECONSTRUCTION

A key part of Derrida's philosophical oeuvre is the unsettling of the systems
by which Western metaphysics generates meaning through presence. Derrida
argues that the drive to enact systems of classification and ordering depend
upon acts of division which generate a false sense of wholeness and presence
by excluding from systems of thought that which cannot be classified, ordered,
or defined. This is the source, for Derrida, of the binary oppositions, such as
masculine/feminine, reason/passion and civilised/barbarian, that he sees as
structuring Western thought through a 'metaphysics of presence'. Rather than
viewing these binaries as simple opposites, Derrida (2005a, 38–39) contends
that the first term is in fact privileged over the second, meaning they are not
neutral dichotomies but violent hierarchies. The inauguration of these oppositions between an interior and knowable presence and an exterior unknowable
absence is, for Derrida, a fiction, something that cannot be sustained as the
absence pushed outside constantly reappears on the interior, unsettling the
claims to proximity and wholeness upon which Western metaphysics relies.

Such hierarchical oppositions are the target of Derridean deconstruction,
operating through a 'double movement', which Simon Critchley (2005) inter-
prets as a 'double reading' of a text. The first reading, analysing a text in its
historical context, seeks to make an 'incision . . . according to lines of force
and forces of rupture that are localizable in the discourse to be deconstructed'
(Derrida 2005a, 68). This first reading can, according to Critchley, provide
an authoritative reconstruction of the text, showing awareness of its original

context and the manner in which it was received. In other words, this reading deals with a text in its own terms. The second reading then highlights 'the privilege granted to the self-contradictions or the performative contradiction of a discourse', and deploys these as 'a strategic lever . . . in order to dislocate and destabilize the autointerpretive author of a major canonical text' (Derrida 2001a, 19). This second reading targets the defective cornerstones within a text, 'that which, from the outset, threatens the coherence and the internal order of the construction', even while being 'required by the architecture which it nevertheless, in advance, deconstructs from within' (Derrida 1989, 73). It is important to stress here that this weak spot must come from within the text, and not be imposed from outside, as it is crucial that the text be seen to *deconstruct itself*, rather than being deconstructed by an exterior agent. As Derrida (1989, 73, emphasis in original) has written, 'deconstruction is not an operation that supervenes *afterwards*, from the outside, one fine day; it is always already at work in the work'.

A deconstructive double reading thus aims to first invert the violent hierarchy present in the text, before 'marking the interval' between the over-turning and the creation of a new 'concept' that cannot be included in the binary system. These new 'concepts'[9] are the 'undecidables' that a deconstructive reading seeks to uncover within a text, that 'can no longer be included within philosophical (binary) opposition, but which, however, inhabit philosophical opposition, resisting and disorganising it, *without ever* constituting a third term', being captured by the logic '[n]either/nor, that is, *simultaneously* either *or*' (Derrida 2005a, 40, emphasis in original). The productive reading of deconstruction must reveal this undecidability within a text, to highlight the 'moment that genuinely threatens to collapse that system' (Spivak 2016, xcviii). It is therefore important to demonstrate how this *works*, rather than just describing it in an abstract sense. I therefore now demonstrate the Derridean deconstructive ethos, in a manner which also allows me to place my Derridean approach to peacebuilding within a wider context of the contemporary critical literature, through a deconstructive double reading of Roger Mac Ginty's 2011 work *International Peacebuilding and Local Resistance: Hybrid Forms of Peace*. This text has been selected as it represents Mac Ginty's first attempt to codify and elaborate on his understanding of the 'hybrid peace'. It also contains case study chapters on Northern Ireland and BiH, allowing me to situate Mac Ginty's understanding in relation to the two post-conflict polities I am analysing. This is undertaken in the manner of what Derrida (2001a, 19) has called a 'close reading'. Edkins and Zehfuss (2005, 456) describe such a reading as providing 'a very meticulous reading . . . of one author and one work rather than a more wide-ranging discussion' of a series of scholars. Undertaking a 'close reading' of Mac Ginty's text therefore serves as an introduction to the deconstructive approach of the book.

This is not to say that deconstruction is the 'methodology' that will be employed in my analysis, however. Indeed, Derrida always resisted the idea of deconstruction as 'method'. Instead of developing a 'practical theory' that is employed by 'deconstructionists', a 'quasi-doctrine that is teachable, institutionalizable and reproducible', Derrida (1995, 17, emphasis in original) views deconstruction as *'what happens or comes to pass'*. Derrida (1994, 36) is also keen to stress that deconstruction should be seen as akin to 'an ethical and political imperative . . . not a taste for the void or for destruction'.[10] I therefore see the deconstructive readings in this book as positive and affirmative engagements with the politics of Northern Ireland and BiH: as explaining how the post-conflict situations have 'come to pass', and as demonstrating how their conditions of possibility can be changed by affirmative critique targeted at pushing further the contradictions contained within the peace settlements. I now demonstrate this approach through my double reading of Mac Ginty.

## Reconstructing the Hybrid Peace (First Reading)

One strand of the critical peacebuilding literature that has achieved particular prominence in recent years is that provided by the 'hybrid peace' approach. This agenda developed out of a critique of the 'liberal peace', seen as the attempt to impose top-down, technocratic and institutional 'solutions' to conflict situations, building on 'liberal values' such as the primacy of the individual, the belief in the reformability of people and institutions, pluralism and toleration, the rule of law, and the protection of property (Mac Ginty 2010, 393). For Mac Ginty, described by Hameiri and Jones (2017, 59) as 'arguably hybridity's most sophisticated proponent', peace processes such as those in Northern Ireland and BiH have essentialised exclusive and opposed political positions, and constrained attempts at reconciliation, through their failures to take into account a plurality of bottom-up perspectives (Mac Ginty 2008, 145; 2009, 700; 2011, 147–49; 2016). In rejecting simplistic accounts of monolithic post-conflict interventions, and in focusing attention on how local actors resist, subvert and reshape peacebuilding endeavours, this literature seeks to generate 'a better understanding of the multiple and often critical agencies involved in peace formation' (Richmond and Pogodda 2016, 2). It has thus played a major role in the literature's 'local turn' to 'everyday' practices of peacebuilding, by providing an impetus for researching, analysing and understanding the agency of local actors in peacebuilding contexts, and moving beyond the study of local-international dynamics to engage with local-local relations (Kappler and Richmond 2011; Mac Ginty and Richmond 2013; Richmond 2010; 2012; Richmond and Mitchell 2012).

Mac Ginty's *International Peacebuilding and Local Resistance* defines hybridity as the 'composite forms of social thinking and practice that emerge as the result of the interaction of different groups, practices, and worldviews' (Mac Ginty 2011, 8). Mac Ginty (2011, 8, 51, 72) makes two further points about hybridity that are often reiterated in the text: that hybridisation is *not* the grafting together of two separate entities to create a third entity, but that all norms, practices, categories and identities are to be seen as the results of 'prior hybridisations'; and that hybridisation is to be seen as an everyday process, not just an 'exotic' one. Hybridisation is therefore regarded by Mac Ginty (2011, 51) 'as a dynamic and complex process in which prior-hybridised entities coalesce, conflict, and re-coalesce with other prior-hybridised entities to produce a context of constant mixing and interchange'. This means that he begins his argument by stating that 'liberal peace policies and their advocates are themselves the product of prior hybridisation', with their prescriptions representing an 'attempt to influence already hybridised environments that have experienced civil war or authoritarianism'. Peace interventions therefore generate further hybridisation 'as (the already hybrid) local and international interact, conflict, and cooperate' (Mac Ginty 2011, 10). In this two-way process between (already hybrid) international actors and (already hybrid) local actors, a 'hybrid peace' emerges that is neither a top-down technical imposition nor a bottom-up organic development. Mac Ginty (2011, 2, 6, 68–69) therefore argues that the concept of hybridity allows for the development of sophisticated critiques of the liberal peace that move 'beyond the level of caricature', while, at the same time, avoid any romanticising of the local level, by seeing categories such as 'local' and 'indigenous' (as well as the 'international') as subject to prior-hybridisations.

While recognising that social processes 'of such complexity and longevity [are] extremely difficult to capture' (Mac Ginty 2011, 77), Mac Ginty (2011, 8–9) proposes a 'four-part model' to assist understandings of hybridisation, in which the hybrid peace is seen to be a result of the interplay between: the ability of liberal peace agents to enforce compliance; the incentivising powers of liberal peace agents; the ability of local actors to resist, ignore or adapt the liberal peace; and the ability of local actors to present and maintain alternatives to the liberal peace. While this model is seen as 'an abstraction' and thus 'unable to capture the full extent and dynamism of a complex social process', he does contend that it can assist in conceptualising and visualising 'the main axes along which hybridisation may be projected or resisted in contexts experiencing liberal peace formations', as well as focusing attention on 'the full range of actors involved in liberal peace transitions' (Mac Ginty 2011, 77). This model can therefore be seen as part of the wider project of noting the 'explanatory and analytical potential' of hybridity, and highlighting its value 'in describing contextual situations, and explaining the dynamic nature of

peace and conflict' (Mac Ginty and Richmond 2016, 221–23). Viewing this
sketch of Mac Ginty's argument as a reconstructive 'first reading', I will now
undertake a deconstructive 'second reading', to highlight the cracks in Mac
Ginty's argument where the undecidability of hybridity can be traced and his
text can be shown to deconstruct under its own inconsistencies.

## Deconstructing the Hybrid Peace (Second Reading)

As recognised by Mac Ginty (2011, 71), the modern usage of the term hybridity in cultural and social criticism 'is most prominently associated with the
work of Homi Bhabha'. Developed through his readings of postcolonial texts
(in both their literary and governmental forms), hybridity for Bhabha represents the spaces and moments when new cultural forms are produced through
the encounter between colonial authority and its subjects. Rather than viewing this as a one-way process, either of imperial domination and subjugation,
or of resistance through the affirmation of indigenous identity, Bhabha argues
that colonial practices produce new identities which operate as markers of
rule while *simultaneously* creating the grounds for resistance. Bhabha (1994,
159) thus argues that hybridity 'is the sign of the productivity of colonial
power, its shifting forces and fixities'. This is perhaps more clearly stated by
Robert J. C. Young (1995, 21) when he writes that, for Bhabha, 'hybridity
becomes the moment in which the discourse of colonial authority loses its
univocal grip on meaning', in a movement that 'reverses the structures of
domination in the colonial situation'. Through producing hybridity, therefore,
colonialism creates the grounds for its own subversion at the very point of
the application of colonial power. Bhabha and other cultural critics utilise
this idea in their readings of postcolonial texts to trace the unsettling of
colonial authority and the creation of identities outside the control of imperial power. While Mac Ginty recognises that this theoretical approach can be
productively applied to peacebuilding situations, he does not hide his disdain
for much of the work which employs the term. 'A review of the literature on
hybridity needs to begin with a health warning' he contends, as it is 'dense
and inaccessible', specialising in 'circular arguments' and 'a single-mined
determination to avoid relevance to the "real world"' (Mac Ginty 2011, 70).
Thus while he wishes to retain something of the 'subversive potential' of the
concept as used by Bhabha, he is clear in his affirmation of the 'need to get
beyond the paralysing relativism that can attend discussions of hybridity and
hybridisation' (Mac Ginty 2011, 73).

Rather than follow Mac Ginty in his movement away from the theoretical
grounding of Bhabha's understanding of hybridity, I will instead follow the
threads of Bhabha's work even further, by highlighting the Derridean influences on Bhabha. In particular, Bhabha engages with the Derridean notion

of undecidability. This is evident at numerous points in Bhabha's writings, such as when he defines the hybrid as 'neither the one thing nor the other' (Bhabha 1994, 49), or when he writes about the 'ambivalence at the source of traditional discourses on [colonialist] authority' which 'enables a form of subversion, founded on the undecidability that turns the discursive conditions of dominance into the grounds of intervention' (Bhabha 1994, 160). For Bhabha (1994, 162), therefore, hybridity operates as an undecidable between the colonial and colonised culture, calling into question the authoritative ground on which these cultural distinctions are built. Greater fidelity to the usages of the term 'hybridity' in Bhabha's work therefore requires, by extension, closer affinity to the deconstructive ethos of Derridean thought, and in particular to the undecidability of the subjects of hybridisation.

Close reading of Mac Ginty's text reveals his failure to do this. While he is adamant that hybridity can help avoid conceiving of the international and local as separate and discrete entities, the manner in which he advances his argument leads to contradictions between this professed wish to avoid binaries and the re-assertion of division between the local and international, creating fault lines in the text open to deconstruction. A key conceptual point that Mac Ginty (2011, 73) highlights when outlining his view of hybridity, as mentioned above, is the 'need to get beyond the paralysing relativism that can attend discussions of hybridity and hybridisation'. He continues: 'If we accept that everything and everyone is a hybrid, then concepts such as endogenous and exogenous, indigenous and international risk losing their currency. The stance adopted in this book is to recognise the shortcomings of concepts and language but to move on.' Mac Ginty (2011, 45–46) seemingly wishes to both accept the messy and complex hybrid nature of social concepts and retain the conceptual clarity provided by neat divisions between binaries such as endogenous/exogenous and indigenous/international. Such a tendency is apparent in the following passage:

> While I do not wish to perpetuate another binary, it does seem that many international peace-support actors are more comfortable thinking about and exercising material forms of power (for example, the ability to project military force or humanitarian supplies), while local communities in some settings tend to think about power in terms of legitimacy and moral standing.

A shift from the affirmation that local and international are not discrete or homogenous terms, to an implicit reconstitution of an essential and determining distinction, is identifiable here. As Heathershaw (2013, 277) has argued, 'however much [Mac Ginty] is aware of these pitfalls he cannot quite escape them . . . [He] remains constrained by his analytical framework which relies on the bifurcation between ideal-types of local-indigenous and international-liberal'. Hameiri and Jones (2017, 56–59) also critique what they see as the 'inherently dichotomizing framework' of hybridity, which 'reifies local-traditional and international-liberal ideal-typical assemblages of institutions, actors and practices'. Despite Mac Ginty's repeated avowals that he does not view hybridity as the grafting together of two separate entities to form a third, 'it is not clear what else [hybridity] can be if one builds a model based on the existence of two oppositional and apparently dialectically related forces' (Heathershaw 2013, 277).

This tendency to revert back to the very binaries and simplifications that Mac Ginty seeks to avoid comes to the fore through the 'four-part model' of the hybrid peace discussed previously. The division between 'international' and 'local' is evident in the phrasing of this model. The first two dimensions, on compliance and incentivising powers, refer to 'liberal peace agents, networks and structures', while the second two dimensions, on resistance and alternatives, refer to 'local actors, networks and structures' (Mac Ginty 2011, 8–9). Furthermore, despite his attempt to maintain fidelity to the complexity of hybrid processes and the discrete and non-fixed nature of prior-hybridised international and local actors, Mac Ginty's language slips to a conceptual certainty when discussing this model. At first, Mac Ginty (2011, 77) states that it is 'an abstraction' useful for highlighting the main axes of formation of a hybrid peace and focusing attention on the full range of actors involved, but one that is 'unable to capture the full extent and dynamism of a complex social process' of hybridisation; later on in the text, however, he is arguing that '[c]aveats aside, the four-part formulation is designed as an aid to understanding or a *way of capturing* dynamics within a society subject to a liberal peace intervention' (Mac Ginty 2011, 89, emphasis added). Mac Ginty has therefore been seduced by the promise of schematisation and systematisation to overcome the radical complexity that he himself identifies in the social world. The main issue for Mac Ginty is the ability 'to discuss conflicts in ways that are comprehensible', which means that the work in question 'has to move beyond caveats and get to the point'. It is the exaltation of this aim of clarity and rigour that results in the conceptual simplifications that allow binaries and dichotomies to seep back into Mac Ginty's work, resulting in analyses of peacebuilding endeavours that fall prey to the very dichotomising and simplifying operations that Mac Ginty seeks to avoid.

The reconstitution of this binary is apparent at certain points of the empirical studies offered in the book, where Mac Ginty applies the model to cases such as the post-conflict situations in Northern Ireland and BiH. The chapter on Northern Ireland explores how '[l]iberal peace actors, in the form of the British and Irish governments, were able to deploy their incentivising and coercive powers to shape the environment in which civil society operated' while, at the same time, 'local civil society actors . . . were able to resist, subvert, and exploit elements of the liberal peace agenda' (Mac Ginty 2011, 184). The implication here is that international actors (in this case the UK and Irish governments) are able to create an environment in which local actors operate. The specific local actor examined in this chapter – the Orange Order – is also examined in such a way that suggests the 'careful caveats' of 'prior hybridization' have been abandoned. This organisation is presented very much as a 'local actor', as an example of 'grassroots social activism', with only passing references made to the presence of Orange Lodges 'further afield' (Mac Ginty 2011, 198). Mac Ginty only names the Republic of Ireland[11] as hosting the Orange Order outside Northern Ireland, when there are in fact lodges in mainland Britain and in ex-British colonies in North America, West Africa and Australasia, implicating it in certain transnational, diasporic and (post)colonial networks, alongside its rootedness in local communities (The Orange Order 2018). Furthermore, the main focus of the chapter is the opposition between the Orange Order's illiberal, sectarian orientation and the liberal peace agenda of the UK and Irish governments. What this fails to account for is the tension *within* the Orange Order's sectarianism (in that it bars Roman Catholics from being members) and its avowed aim, to quote Mac Ginty (2011, 197) of preserving 'religious (Protestant) liberty'. The formation of such an aim in the context of the development within Britain, in the years following the Glorious Revolution of 1688, of a liberal politics for Protestants alongside an entrenched anti-Catholicism, is not considered. The production of the Orange Order through 'prior hybridisation' in a wider context of British state development since the seventeenth century is therefore glossed over by Mac Ginty's construction of a binary opposition between the 'liberal' peace proponents of the UK government and the 'illiberal' Orange Order. This tendency to re-constitute the very dichotomies that the hybrid approach seeks to avoid is also apparent when Mac Ginty considers the inter-actions between 'international' and 'local' agency in BiH. When discussing the incentivising powers of liberal peace agents, Mac Ginty (2011, 155) argues that '[l]ocal political actors were drawn into a post-Dayton political architecture and issue agenda that was, in significant ways, the creation of international actors'. By identifying here an ability of international actors to generate a political environment which local actors are forced to contend with, Mac Ginty re-draws the dividing lines between these two levels.

This deconstructive double reading of Mac Ginty's text itself serves a double function. First, it demonstrates the shortcomings of this dominant critical approach to peacebuilding, and how it cannot maintain fidelity to its stated aims of unsettling and resisting the false distinctions between 'local' and 'international' in peace interventions. Further engagement with the approach, or arguments for an improved reading of the interactions between international and local actors in peacebuilding efforts, will therefore fail to escape these shortcomings. Second, it illustrates the close reading of texts that will be employed in the rest of the book. Subsequent chapters will engage in similar readings of the key political 'texts' of the peace processes in Northern Ireland and BiH, namely the peace agreements (and the political institutions bequeathed by these agreements), and wider texts provided by artistic, cultural, judicial and protest movements. This book, following Derrida (1989, 124), therefore extends deconstructive readings 'beyond so-called literary texts', and show how deconstruction is 'at work in history, culture, literature, philosophy': in everything with a meaning that is dependent upon context, and not just written material (Derrida 1988, 136–37, 148).[12] These close readings will uncover the undecidables within these 'texts' that reveal the post-conflict political structures of Northern Ireland and BiH to be already in a process of deconstruction. The final substantive task of this introduction is to outline two of the 'undecidables' that Derrida employs in his writings, and the temporal implications of these, that will be central to the deconstructive readings of subsequent chapters.

## UNDECIDABILITY AND THE TEMPORALITY
## OF DECONSTRUCTION

### Signification and Supplementation

One of the key ways in which Derrida seeks to enact a disruption of the 'metaphysics of presence' is through his unsettling of Ferdinand de Saussure's structuralist linguistics. Contra the Saussurean view of signification as the play of differences between signs within a closed system, in which meaning is attached to a sign through differentiation from what that sign *does not* refer to, Derrida argues that the play of difference between signs is an infinite and open process, with meaning constantly delayed and deferred due to the lack of any 'transcendental signifier' capable of fixing meaning, of attaching the floating signifier to the presence of the sign (Derrida 2016, 19–22). This introduces a conception of language as an open system in which meaning is constantly delayed and deferred, in which the proximity of the signified to the signifier is replaced by an endless chain of signifiers which can only be fixed by violent acts of closure.

In developing this challenge to the centrality of presence in Western metaphysics, Derrida also seeks to unsettle the binary opposition of speech and writing that he traces from Plato to Saussure. For the thinkers identified, speech is granted a privileged position due to its assumed proximity to the origin of language in conscious thought. Writing is considered an invention needed to transmit meaning in the absence of speech, and thus seen as a debased version of speech, something further from the full presence of thought, and lacking its authority. Furthermore, writing is seen as something that originates from outside language in the form of 'notation', the written mark that corrupts and contaminates language (Derrida 2016, 37). Yet at the same time, Derrida notes a pernicious ethnocentrism in which phonetic or alphabetic writing is seen by thinkers such as Jean-Jacques Rousseau as superior to other forms of writing, as a mark of a more advanced civilisation than those who use symbolic or hieroglyphic systems of representation, and certainly superior to those cultures which lack writing (Derrida 2016, 3, 118–19). In focusing in on the 'strange unity' (Derrida 2016, 156) of Rousseau's simultaneous valorisation and disqualification of writing, Derrida introduces a term that will be key to the analysis put forward in this book: that of the supplement.

Rousseau views writing as a supplement to speech, as something unnatural added to natural speech in order to extend its meaning beyond its immediate proximity, something which makes 'the immediate presence of thought to speech divert into representation and the imagination' (Derrida 2016, 57). For Derrida, the term 'supplement' implies such an addition, an 'extra' or 'extended' presence added to the presence of speech: but it also means something more. According to Derrida (2016, 157 emphasis in original):

> the supplement supplements. It adds only to replace. It intervenes or insinuates itself *in-the-place-of*; if it fills to brim [*comble*], it is as if one fills [*comble*] a void . . . . Supplementing and vicarious, the supplement is an adjunct, a subaltern instance which *takes-(the)-place* [*tient-lieu*]. As substitute, it does not simply add itself to the positivity of a presence, it produces no relief, its place is assigned in the structure by the mark of an emptiness . . . The sign is always the supplement of the thing itself.

These two meanings of 'supplement' are inseparable for Derrida. The addition at the same time replaces, simultaneously gives extra presence to that which is supplemented while revealing the absence that requires filling by the additional element. It is in this sense that the supplement is an 'undecidable': it is an *addition* that at the same time *replaces*, enacting both these operations simultaneously. The supplement is therefore one of the indeterminate undecidables that inhabit and overturn the settled concepts of Western thought maintained through the 'metaphysics of presence'.

While the metaphysical system of which Rousseau is a part attempts to maintain the full presence of thought and speech by viewing writing as something exterior that is added 'as pure addition or pure absence' (as it is added to something that is already 'full'), for Derrida (2016, 181) the necessity of supplementation indicates that the immediacy of presence is always a 'mirage', as if it was 'full presence' it would not require supplementation. This recognition therefore opens up meaning to a 'chain of supplements' (Derrida 2016, 170–71), an endless play of substitution and addition. The search for an original or full presence is thus rendered futile, as the concept of 'origin' is itself open to the play of supplementation. This process of disrupting presence through supplementation therefore has an inherently *temporal* dimension. I consider this further by turning to another key Derridean term employed in this book: that of *différance*.

## Origin and *Différance*

In the same way that Derrida views the metaphysics of presence as seeking to produce speech as interior fullness by excluding the exteriority of writing, the presence of the *present* is seen as produced by this metaphysics through dividing it from an absent past and future, attempting to create the present as the ground from which thought and speech can be enacted in the wholeness of presence. While Derrida uses the supplement to disrupt this, he also uses the undecidable of *différance* to denote both the state of being different and a delay or detour in meaning, to underline the temporal ramifications of his approach.

Derrida uses the term *différance*, which is identical to the French word 'différence' in its pronunciation and spelling save for the substitution of the second 'e' for an 'a', to subvert the phonetic conception of alphabetic languages, by making a non-audible alteration that can only be comprehended when the term is written down (or when the spelling is explained in speech: '*différance* with an "a"'), making it a word that 'is read, or it is written, but it cannot be heard' (Derrida 1982, 3–5). *Différance* thus reveals how there is no 'true' phonetic writing, as phonetic alphabets can only be utilised in legible writing with the addition of non-phonetic marks such as punctuation, and the silent 'spacing' between words and letters that allow the differences between phonemes to be comprehended. More than this, Derrida uses *différance* to unsettle the classical opposition between speech and writing, whereby speech is the privileged term, as *différance* is a word that conveys more meaning when written than when spoken. This is thus one way in which *différance* can be considered an undecidable, in that it disrupts the binary opposition of speech/writing.

Yet, *différance* is an undecidable in another way: one which highlights its temporal dimensions. This arises from the double meaning of the word 'différence' in French, which *différance* plays upon. This word can mean both 'difference', in the sense of being different, and 'deferral', in the sense of being delayed. Derrida uses the interplay between these two meanings to insert *différance* into Saussurean linguistics. Derrida argues that the signification of language is only possible by giving form to the presence of each element of language in a present moment of time. We can see this in the way sentences are constructed by placing words in a linear order, in which their meaning unfolds through time (Derrida 2016, 71). However, Derrida (1982, 13) argues that the presence of each element of language, each specific part of the linear sentence, can only be constructed by dividing it from what came before and what will come after. Thus 'each element appearing on the scene of presence is related to something other than itself, thereby keeping within itself the mark of the past elements, and already letting itself be vitiated by the mark of its relation to the future elements'. In other words, the 'present' can only be marked out by dividing the present from what it is not (the past and future). For Derrida, what is divided from the present cannot be kept outside, but re-appears within the presence of the present, dividing the present and 'thereby also dividing, along with the present, everything that is thought on the basis of the present'. The interval that divides the present is what Derrida calls '*spacing*, the becoming-space of time or the becoming-time of space (*temporization*)'. *Différance*, as simultaneously a (spatial) difference and a (temporal) delay, therefore marks the undecidability between spacing and temporisation: it '(is) (simultaneously) spacing (and) temporization'.

This understanding of *différance* as the undecidability of speech and writing, and as the undecidability between spacing and temporisation, is not intended to invert these dichotomies by placing the non-privileged term at the origin. Rather, '*différance* is the displacement of this oppositional logic' (Derrida 1992, 8), something which unsettles *all ideas* of a prior-ness or origin. By connecting the production of meaning to the operation of *différance*, Derrida (1982, 17) seeks 'to reconsider all the pairs of opposites on which philosophy is constructed', such as speech/writing and past/future,

> not in order to see opposition erase itself but to see what indicated that each of the terms must appear as the *différance* of the other, as the other different and deferred in the economy of the same (the intelligible as differing-deferring the sensible, as the sensible different and differed; the concept as different and deferred, differing-deferring intuition; culture as nature different and differed, differing-deferring . . .).

The concept (such as speech or temporisation) and its differed or deferred other (such as writing or spacing) are therefore not totally divided and separated opposites, but are related through their very alterity. As Derrida (2005b, 38) has written, 'what is also and at the same time at stake – and marked by the same word in *différance*', is the 'experience of the alterity of the other, of heterogeneity, of the singular, the not-same, the different, the dissymmetric, the heteronomous'. *Différance* thus connects the real and sensible to its 'irreducible and nonappropriable . . . other' (Derrida 2005b, 84), marking out the manner in which binary oppositions are simultaneously different and the same, and produced together through the play of difference and deferral, rather than one proceeding the other on a linear temporal schema.

It is in the same manner that the supplement must not be seen as 'prior' or 'after' that which it supplements: rather the two must be seen as enacted in a single temporal moment that stretches simultaneously backwards and forwards along the chain of supplementation. In this way, *différance* operates to 'put into question . . . the quest for a rightful beginning, an absolute point of departure, a principle responsibility', at the same time as it questions the authority of presence (Derrida 1982, 6–10). There is no authoritative origin on which to ground meaning for Derrida: instead, there is nothing more than the play of *différance*, the chain of supplementation in which the 'supplement is always the supplement of a supplement' (Derrida 2016, 330). Putting these undecidables to use in my readings of the post-conflict politics of Northern Ireland and BiH thus requires deeper engagement with the central themes of Derrida's thinking on temporality.

## Deconstruction and 'the hinge'

Derrida uses the term 'trace'[13] to further unsettle the temporality of the metaphysics of presence. For Derrida (2016, 72, emphasis in original), the trace is 'that which does not let itself be summed up in the simplicity of a present', that which challenges the 'concepts of *present, past* and *future*, everything in the concepts of time and history which implies classical evidence for them—the metaphysical concept of time in general'. In engaging with the need to go 'beyond simple *reversals* of a metaphysics of presence', Derrida (2016, 74–75, emphasis in original) introduces the notion of the 'hinge [*brisure*] of language' that can lead us to the renunciation of 'all distinctions between writing and the spoken word', of phonologism itself; the hinge that 'marks the impossibility that a sign, the unity of a signifier and a signified, be produced within the plenitude of a present and an absolute presence'. Derrida returns to the image of the hinge at numerous points in his writings, as a symbol of dislocation, disadjustment and discontinuity (Derrida 1982, xxv; 1994, 20–27, 96, 139; 1996, 68–69). Derrida (1995, 14–15, emphasis in original) goes as far as comparing deconstruction itself (while simultaneously disassociating himself from what he designates as a 'nickname') to 'a door on its hinges', that can turn and fold 'back on itself . . . *bend to* and obey itself, without the least certainty'. He writes that deconstruction 'has never been at peace with its hinges—which is perhaps its way of tirelessly reminding us of disjointment itself, the possibility of any disjunction'. This leads him to two important reflections on the relationships between deconstruction and the experience of temporality, which will inform my later analyses of the post-conflict situations in Northern Ireland and BiH.

Firstly, Derrida considers whether deconstruction might precisely be a movement aimed at revealing the 'untimeliness' of things through 'dislocating, displacing, disarticulating, disjoining, putting "out of joint" the authority of the "is"'. Deconstruction, Derrida (1995, 24–25) continues, may consist in 'measuring itself against the historical experience… of that which in the "is", in time or in the present time of the "is", remains precisely "out of joint"'. In other words, deconstruction is presented here as that which reveals the inability of things to ever be truly contemporary with themselves, as they are always haunted by traces of the past and looking forward to their fulfilment in some future time. Secondly, Derrida (1995, 30–31) takes this dislocating movement of deconstruction, and applies it to linear concepts of temporality, by suggesting that

> the teleological schema (birth, growth, old age, sickness, end or death) can be applied to everything, and to everything about deconstruction, except, in all certitude and in the mode of a determinant knowledge, to that which in it begins by questioning, displacing, and dislocating the machine of this teleology, and thus this opposition between health and sickness, normality and anomaly, life and death.

For me, this statement is a provocation to oppose systems of thought or action which derive legitimacy from a conception of a beginning, by *beginning* with a *questioning of this beginning*, beginning with a question of any conception of 'the beginning' as such. Critique which responds to this provocation must refuse and displace attempts to derive legitimacy or authority from a conception of beginning. Such critique must argue not for thought or action that is groundless, but which recognises that it creates its own ground in the moment of thinking, of uttering or of acting. It would not seek to displace its authority to a remote past or stake it on the redemption of some future epoch, where it cannot be challenged, but seek authority on its own merit, on its ability to make decisive interventions, to re-articulate and re-animate settled patterns of thought and allow new formulations to develop and emerge, that can capture the 'moments that are characterized by their urgency in the present' (Dauphine 2007, 84). Such critique may be called, following Derrida, a 'deconstructive conclusion'. The critique of a deconstructive conclusion must recognise that to identify a process of supplementation is to recognise that one cannot 'go back *from the supplement to the source*' as 'there is *a supplement at the source*' (Derrida 2016, 330, emphasis in original). Such critique must also recognise that to identify a relationship of *différance* is to 'erase the myth of a present origin' and think 'outside any teleological or eschatological horizon' (Derrida 1978, 255), and to put into question 'precisely the quest for a rightful beginning' (Derrida 1982, 6).

The guiding task of this book is to think through what such critique means for the peace settlements in Northern Ireland and BiH. The supplement and *différance*, alongside my wider engagement with Derrida's writings on temporality, are used throughout the book to deconstruct the peace settlements in Northern Ireland and BiH. I demonstrate how understandings of the conflicts in both cases operate as supplements within the peace agreement, in a manner that allows the settlements to operate as the basis of political systems, but ones that are in persistent states of dysfunction. This supplementation is also shown to tie the 'post-conflict' period to the time of the 'conflict', producing one 'as the *différance* of the other' (Derrida 1982, 17). By this, I mean that the 'post-conflict' is not the simple 'opposite' of the 'conflict', in the sense of the conflict being ended or annulled: rather, the two are tied together through the difference and delay of the peace agreements. Furthermore, the 'post-conflict' period is not to be seen as following the 'conflict' as on a continuous, linear temporal schema: rather, both are seen as constituted in the same temporal moment, through the peace settlements, which produce a qualitative difference in the politics of the two periods, but in a way which produces the 'post-conflict' as the *differed* and *deferred* other of the 'conflict'. This is how I deconstruct the peace settlements: not as a destructive act designed to undo the peacebuilding measures undertaken in Northern Ireland and BiH, but through the constructive act of a deconstructive conclusion aimed at breaking the chains binding the current political settlements to narrow understandings of the conflicts and allowing the post-conflict politics to be more than the conflict differed and deferred.

## MAPPING A DECONSTRUCTIVE READING OF POST-CONFLICT NORTHERN IRELAND AND BOSNIA AND HERZEGOVINA

The book is divided into two parts, which deal separately with the two cases before and after the signing of the peace agreements, and a final chapter, which engages with the two cases together. By focusing on just one case per chapter in the first parts of the book, I ensure there is enough space to provide the extensive and detailed readings required by a poststructural analysis (Hansen 2006, 11). Therefore, while the book is intended to be read from start to finish, those interested solely in the Northern Ireland case study can read chapter 1, 2, 4 and 6, while those interested only in BiH can read chapters 1, 3, 5 and 6.

The first part of the book, 'Supplementing Conflict', details the dominant understandings of the two conflicts within academic and political discourse, and traces the impact of these understandings on attempts to negotiate an end to the violence. Chapter 2 focuses on the 'ethno-national' account of 'the troubles' in Northern Ireland, tracing its academic development and its importance to political engagements with the conflict. The chapter critically examines the details of the ethno-national account, specifically interrogating the relationship between the 'ethno' and the 'national' aspects, to highlight when they are in tension, and the slippage that often occurs between them. This tension and slippage between the 'ethno' and 'national' aspects, I argue, is sidestepped through reference to the 'two communities' thesis, which is identified as a supplement to the ethno-national account. This supplement is seen as producing an undecidable 'two communities' analysis of the conflict, which allows both the more rigid emphasis on 'ethnic' identity, and the more fluid focus on 'national' identification, to co-exist together. The impact of this 'two communities' supplement is then traced in the failed peace attempts up to the mid-1990s. This supplementation is therefore seen as replicating the undecidability of the 'two communities' analysis into the contemporary period. Chapter 3 turns to the case of BiH, to explore two dominant framings of the war, which I call the 'ethnic war' and 'international aggression' discourses. These presented contradictory understandings of the conflict, and incompatible arguments for resolving it. The chapter argues that these contradictory framings are made to work together through reference to the wider 'Balkans' context of the conflict, which is identified as a supplement to the two discourses. This supplement is seen as producing an undecidable 'Balkans' account, which allows the 'ethnic war' understanding of BiH as a Balkans space where ethnicity drives politics, to co-exist with an explanation of the manipulative political culture behind the 'international aggression' discourse, based on the idea of the Balkans as a place where political leaders are particularly willing to resort to the use of force, and to mobilise ethnicity as a means to do so. I argue that the presence of this 'Balkans' supplement allowed the two framings to operate together in the final stages of the conflict, particularly during the US-led efforts to generate a lasting peace settlement, which resulted in the signing of the DPA in November 1995.

The second part of the book, 'Deferring conflict', explores how the processes of supplementation discussed in part one transmit the undecidable understandings of the conflicts into the post-conflict periods, rendering the post-conflict period not as conflict over or annulled, but as conflict *differed* and *deferred*. Chapter 4 examines how the 'two communities' supplement became embedded in the GFA, with the institutional safeguards and community designations required for power-sharing government between the 'two communities' generating a 'communal politics' that allows for a (re) enactment of a 'two communities' struggle. The performance of communal politics in the present is also seen as giving strength to the analysis of the conflict as a 'two communities' clash, introducing a temporal dimension to the undecidability. However, by locating the production of this communal politics in processes of supplementation and *différance*, I argue that it is already in a process of deconstruction. I identify this deconstruction in two areas of political contestation: first, through the electoral performance of parties who reject community designations; and, second, through artistic and cultural endeavours which demonstrate fluidity and exchange between the 'two communities'. Chapter 5 explores how the 'Balkans' supplement became embedded in the DPA, with the internal territorial and institutional divisions put in place generating an 'ethnic politics' that allows for a (re) enactment of a 'Balkans' struggle. I argue that the political performance of a 'Balkans' struggle in the present gives strength to understandings of the conflict as a 'Balkans' war, introducing a temporal element to the undecidability. However, this contemporary politics is seen as already in a process of deconstruction, which is demonstrated through two areas of political contestation: first, through legal challenges to the ethnic logics of the political system; and, second, through protest movements that reject the ethnic basis of politics in BiH.

The final chapter argues that the artistic, cultural, judicial and protest movements, discussed in chapters 4 and 5 as examples of 'deconstruction in action', cannot provide sustained challenges to the divisive and dysfunctional nature of post-conflict politics in Northern Ireland and BiH, as they fail to deconstruct the supplement of the historic understandings of the conflicts which operate as the legitimising foundation for the current political orders. The chapter demonstrates how a deconstructive conclusion, developed from my reading of Derrida's writings on temporality, can allow for an overcoming of the divisive logics embedded in the post-conflict political systems, by challenging these while *simultaneously* challenging the narratives of the conflicts that they are based upon. In other words, this deconstructive conclusion engages with the supplements identified in chapters 2 and 3 *at the same time* as engaging with the temporal effects of these supplements traced in chapters 4 and 5. By arguing for a deconstructive conclusion to the conflicts which would *also* be a deconstructive conclusion of the *peace agreements*, as that which produces the 'conflict' and 'post-conflict' as the *différance* of each other, this final chapter provides the basis for political acts which, unlike those considered in chapters 4 and 5, can provide effective challenges to the divisive politics inaugurated through the peace processes in Northern Ireland and BiH, and bring about a 'conclusion' to the conflicts and the dysfunctional post-conflict political structures created through the peace agreements.

*Part I*

# SUPPLEMENTING CONFLICT

# Chapter 2

# Ethno-National Policy Learning

## The 'Two Communities' Supplement and 'the Troubles' in Northern Ireland

Northern Ireland came into being as a political entity in 1921, under the terms of the 1920 Government of Ireland Act. This Act finally granted Home Rule to Ireland, after a decades-long campaign by Irish Nationalists (those who aspire to a unified and sovereign Irish state); but, due to the opposition and threats of resistance from Ulster Unionists (those who seek to maintain the political links between their part of Ireland and Britain), Ireland was partitioned between two Home Rule Parliaments. Events in 'Southern Ireland' overtook this Westminster solution to the 'Ireland question', however, with the violent actions of Irish Republicans (a term I use to refer to the proponents of Irish Nationalism who are more willing to use, or legitimise the use, of violence) forcing the UK government into negotiating the Anglo-Irish Treaty in December 1921. This created the 'Irish Free State' in the twenty-six counties that would have made up 'Southern Ireland', and in effect confirmed partition by leaving the Northern six counties in the UK, but with substantial autonomy (Tonge 2002, 14). The creation of Northern Ireland was itself marked by bloody violence, with over 400 deaths occurring there between June 1920 and June 1922 (McKittrick and McVea 2012, 4). The two polities in Ireland then began to look inwards, with the Free State undertaking a journey through civil war to full republic status outside the British Commonwealth by 1949, while the Ulster Unionist Party (UUP) set about consolidating their grip on the machineries of state in Northern Ireland. This was achieved through what is now widely recognised as a programme of political, economic and social discrimination against Catholics and Nationalists in Northern Ireland (McKittrick and McVea 2012, 8–26).

Groups such as the Northern Ireland Civil Rights Association and the People's Democracy, inspired by the civil rights movement in the US, began campaigning in the late 1960s for an end to this discrimination. Their marches and protests, while generating some concessions from the Unionist government, often ended in violent clashes with the police or gangs of Loyalists (a term I use to refer to the proponents of Ulster Unionism who are more willing to use, or legitimise the use, of violence). Opposition to the piecemeal reforms offered by the Northern Ireland PM Terrence O'Neill came both from those who opposed all change and those who wanted change to come at a more radical pace, creating a tense and polarised political environment. The activities of paramilitary groups was also a major factor in the rising tension: a new iteration of the Ulster Volunteer Force was formed in 1966 (the original group was founded in 1912 to provide opposition to Home Rule), which committed three murders that year, and a bombing campaign against electricity and water supplies in early 1969; and a split in the Republican movement in late 1969 resulted in the Marxist-oriented 'Official' Irish Republican Army competing with the more violent and militaristic 'Provisional' Irish Republican Army (PIRA). Violence in the cities of Londonderry[1] and Belfast in the summer of 1969 saw the local security services pushed to breaking point, leading to the Northern Ireland government requesting the deployment of the British Army. The initial successes of these troops in easing tensions was quickly forgotten as the PIRA stepped up its violent campaign against the police and army, provoking a strong security response, including: the internment without trial of thousands of Catholics; allegations of torture and mistreatment of prisoners; the proroguing of the Stormont-based Northern Ireland Parliament and the imposition of Direct Rule from Westminster; and the killings in Derry of thirteen unarmed civilians during a civil rights march in January 1972, in what became known as 'Bloody Sunday'. The year 1972 saw nearly 500 deaths, further atrocities such as 'Bloody Friday', when the PIRA exploded 20 bombs in just over an hour in Belfast city centre, killing 9, and the setting of a pattern of violence committed by Republican and Loyalist paramilitaries and state security forces, known euphemistically as 'the troubles', that was to last until the 1990s (McKittrick and McVea 2012, 46–100).

I have begun this chapter with this brief sketch of the outbreak of 'the troubles' for two reasons. The first is a common-place, even mundane one: I am aware that some readers may be unfamiliar with the key dates and events in relation to the Northern Ireland conflict, and will thus be happy to receive some historical orientation (which chapter 1 did not provide) before I begin my argument. Second, I provide this sketch as an example of conventional approaches to 'understanding conflict', which seek to determine causes, and consequently delineate solutions, through reference to the historical origins of violence. As David Campbell (1998, 34–44) argues, when discussing the work of Haydn White and before engaging in an analysis of competing understandings of the war in BiH, historical meaning is generated through the 'emplotment' of events in a narrative, which presents outcomes as immanent in the beginnings of historical processes.

The central claim advanced in this chapter is that peacebuilding requires the construction of an understanding of the conflict to be resolved, in a manner which shapes attempts to negotiate an end to political violence. I develop this argument by focusing on one key narrative of the Northern Ireland conflict: the 'ethno-national' account, associated with academics such as John McGarry and Brendan O'Leary, which views 'the troubles' as the most recent iteration of historical conflict over the constitutional status of Ireland, the relationship between Britain and Ireland, and the competing national aspirations of people identifying as 'British' and 'Irish' in Ireland. The first section outlines how proponents of this account describe its argument, focusing on the historical narratives this builds upon. I then examine the evidence which suggests that actors within the UK and Irish governments did indeed accept many of these arguments, in order to trace the impact of the account on failed attempts to achieve a political settlement to the conflict. The second section critically examines the details of the ethno-national account, specifically interrogating the tensions that often exist between the 'ethno' and the 'national' aspects. In the third section I turn to Derridean thought, to argue that the tensions and slippages between the 'ethno' and 'national' aspects are often side-stepped through reference to the 'two communities' thesis, which operates as a *supplement* to the ethno-national account, producing an undecidable 'two communities' analysis of the conflict which allows the more rigid focus on 'ethnic' identity to co-exist with more fluid emphases on 'national' identification. The impact of this 'two communities' supplement is then traced in the failed peace attempts up to the mid-1990s. The ethno-national account, and its 'two communities' supplement, will thus be seen as crucial to the peace process and post-conflict politics discussed in chapter 4, due to its central role in generating an idea of the conflict as something that can be resolved through conflict management strategies.

## THE ETHNO-NATIONAL ACCOUNT OF THE NORTHERN IRELAND CONFLICT

Many analyses of 'the troubles' look to historical events in order to explain and understand the conflict. The most common historical reference point is the occupation of land formerly under the control of Ulster Gaels by Scottish and English settlers in the sixteenth and seventeenth centuries: a long and complex process often simplified under the label of the 'Plantation of Ulster'. Tonge (2002, 4), for instance, argues that the 'origins of the current political problems of Northern Ireland lie in historical conflicts between Planter and Gael', while McKittrick and McVea (2012, 290) state that it 'is obvious ['the troubles'] had their roots centuries earlier, stretching back at least to the plantations and the patterns established then', with settlers 'bound to develop a siege mentality' while the natives were 'naturally resentful' of the new ascendant class. For Clayton (1998, 50), this 'settler mentality has proved extremely durable'.

While sectarian accounts of 'the troubles' point to the confessional division introduced through the plantation, with Protestant Scottish and English settlers displacing the Catholic natives, proponents of the ethno-national account stress the wider political differences produced through this movement of people. The presence of two distinct communities of 'Planter and Gael' in the north of Ireland over the last 400 years is thus seen to have given rise to the current existence of two distinct ethno-national identity groups in Northern Ireland: one community, largely Protestant, which identifies as British and seeks to maintain the constitutional link with the UK; and another community, largely Catholic, which aspires to a united Ireland. In their work, Ruane and Todd (1996, 12; 1998, 56–64; 1999, 4) provide a complex version of this argument, referring to the 'deep historical and structural roots' of 'the troubles', suggesting that the conflict arose from the 'structure of dominance, dependence and inequality in the mode of Ireland's integration into the English/British state in the sixteenth and seventeenth centuries', which produced 'two distinct communities in Ireland divided by religion, ethnic origin, settler-native status, cultural stereotype and (later) national identity and allegiance'. This 'conflictual legacy' is posited as a constant that later developments, such as the emergence of Unionism and Nationalism as political ideologies in the nineteenth century, partition in the early twentieth century, or the dissolution of the Stormont government in 1972, served to reproduce, exacerbate or aggravate.

The term 'ethno-national' is thus often employed to capture the manner in which a dispute over nationality maps onto 'ethnic' issues of religion, language and culture. According to Hayes and McAllister (1999, 32), the 1980s and 1990s saw 'an emerging academic consensus' that understood the conflict in Northern Ireland as 'essentially ethnonationalist in origin': an interpretation which 'found favour with the British and Irish governments' and underpinned the 'concept of identity' given 'political expression' in the GFA. Numerous academics share in this assessment, both in terms of ethnonational competition being the main cause of the conflict, and in terms of its influence on the GFA. For Rolston, this coincided with the end of the Cold War, and the diagnosis of 'ethnic conflict' in various parts of the world, leading to the ethno-national account supplanting colonial analyses of Northern Ireland (Rolston 1998, 260–1). O'Leary and McGarry (1996, 3), perhaps the most prolific and high-profile proponents of this view, argue that the Northern

Ireland conflict is 'fundamentally national', being sustained by the long-term 'conflictual external relations between the British and Irish nations', and the specific political evolution of the UK and Irish states. While arguing for an account informed by both endogenous and exogenous factors, McGarry and O'Leary (1995, 356) locate the roots of competitive ethno-nationalism in 'the colonial settlement of historic Ulster', with this transforming into conflict over competing nationalisms since the nineteenth century. Elsewhere, McGarry and O'Leary (1995, 354–55) are even more emphatic in making the case that 'the conflict in Northern Ireland is ethno-national, a systematic quarrel between the political organizations of two communities who want their state to be ruled by their nation'. I engage with the contradictions involved in hyphenating the 'ethno' with the 'national' in the next section. The remainder of this section examines the wider impact of the ethno-national account beyond the pages of academic texts, by exploring how it influenced the failed peace negotiations throughout the years of 'the troubles'.

## The 'Consociational Narrative'

In O'Leary's view, UK policy-makers underwent a process of 'ethno-national policy learning' throughout 'the troubles'. O'Leary (1997, 669–75) argues that inter-governmental strategies, spearheaded by the co-operative actions of the UK and Irish governments, became the favoured 'management method' from 1980 onwards, developing alongside a recognition that the conflict was 'ethno-national, and bi-governmental, as well as bi-national, in nature'. This idea is also strongly stated by O'Duffy (2004, 422), who argues that 'the British-Irish intergovernmental relationship is causally prior to the "solution" of ethnonational conflict between Catholic/nationalists and Protestant/unionists in Northern Ireland'. By this he means that the possibility of stronger inter-governmentalism, with a posited end point of joint British-Irish sovereignty over Northern Ireland, operates as an incentive to both Unionist and Nationalist politicians to make the compromises needed to sustain power-sharing, so as to avoid giving more authority to an 'alien' government (that based in Dublin for Unionists, and that based in London for Nationalists). O'Duffy (2004, 410) posits the GFA as the pinnacle of this conflict management approach, in that it recognises the conflict as driven by 'conflicting questions of national self-determination', which it attempts to resolve through the British and Irish governments' acknowledgement of the symmetry of their rival claims to sovereignty over Northern Ireland.

The various failed attempts to create a power-sharing government to oversee the re-installation of devolved government after 1972 (that I will discuss below) are therefore viewed by proponents of the ethno-national account as arising from the UK government's inadequate analysis of the conflict. It was only when 'the troubles' was understood as driven by rival nationalisms, rather than by sectarian difference or socio-economic factors, that it became possible to manage the conflict through inter-governmental regulation that could accommodate the opposed ethno-national communities through appropriate institutions. Cillian McGrattan (2010a, 123) labels this as the 'consociational narrative': an imagined teleological process through which 'Britain and Ireland eventually learned to manage the two warring ethnic communities and gradually convinced those belligerents of the benefits of consociational logic'. McGrattan (2010b) is highly critical of this literature's identification of a linear progression towards better conflict management, and the self-reproducing logic of this account, whereby it selectively highlights evidence from the historical record of failed conflict regulation that supports the understanding of the conflict as ethno-national in character. While noting that historians have criticised the teleological nature of this approach, McGrattan (2010a, 123) recognises that this account has become the 'dominant narrative of the peace process'. Therefore, while rejecting the neat teleology produced by this account, I recognise its importance as the 'orthodoxy' (Tonge 2002, 199) in current explanations of 'the troubles', and as something that has shaped attempts at resolving the conflict.

The memoires of key UK and international figures involved in Northern Ireland demonstrates the influence of this thinking on the peace process. Two common understandings are evident in the writings of the main contributors to the final stages of the negotiations: the historical impact of British-Irish relations on inter-community dynamics, and the entrenching of division over time. Major (1999, 435), who was UK PM during the first PIRA ceasefire and the initial stages of all-party talks, expresses this latter point when writing that '[a]ncient feuds and fears had locked the political parties into entrenched and rigid reflexes'. Tony Blair (2011, 152–54), who came to power in June 1997 and oversaw the signing of the GFA, approaches the ideas of the ethno-national account when writing that 'there has been centuries of hatred in which religion and disputed territory were mixed in an evil chemistry'. He echoes his predecessor when suggesting that the 'hatred had become entrenched and horribly vicious over the centuries', and recounts how, in his experience, Unionists and Nationalists have 'a different way of speaking, a different attitude, a different nature', suggesting that the divisions caused by religious and territorial dispute had coalesced around distinct identities. Jonathan Powell (2008, 57–58), Blair's chief of staff and a key aide in the talks, mirrors the views of his former employer when providing separate outlines of 'the two different traditions, two different identities and two different histories Tony [Blair] and I needed to comprehend' in order to lead effective negotiations.

Blair's first Secretary of State for Northern Ireland, Mo Mowlam (2002, 31, 299), recognises that 'the Brits' were part of the problem, through historical actions like the partition of Ireland, but combines this with a view that the conflict has been driven by disputes 'over land and power . . . a large dose of religion, bigotry and intolerance and an even larger dose of mismanagement and incompetence by generations of rulers and politicians'. Former US senator George Mitchell (1999, 13, 28), appointed by President Clinton as Special Envoy to Northern Ireland and a key mediator and chair of the talks process, writes in his account of his time in Northern Ireland that 'the troubles' 'can be understood only in the context of the long history of British domination of Ireland', something which produced a divided political environment in which leaders such as Gerry Adams and Ian Paisley were able to articulate two 'completely different views of the same society'. Mowlam and Mitchell are therefore perhaps the participants who come closest to the academic ethnonational account of the competing national aspirations of different groups in Ireland, driven by conflictual British-Irish relations, generating a divided society prone to violent conflict. Further evidence can be found for the influence of the ethno-national account by examining the detailed unfolding of 'ethno-national policy learning' throughout the years of 'the troubles'.

## The Unfolding of 'Ethno-National Policy Learning'

According to Dixon (2008, 101, 282), the UK government's initial attempts at resolving the emerging Northern Ireland conflict in the years 1968–1971 were aimed at bringing the polity up to 'British standards' of democracy and good governance, with a 'normal', two-party, first-past-the-post political system and consensual policing. Disillusionment quickly set-in, argues Dixon, when the UK government realised their reformist efforts were 'ill-equipped to deal with communal conflict'. There were then two attempts to re-instigate devolved government in Northern Ireland in the decade following the 1972 suspension of the Stormont Parliament. Tonge (2002, 124) argues that both these efforts failed for the same, if inverted, reason: the provision of an all-Ireland dimension, or the lack of such a dimension. The first attempt at creating a power-sharing government came through the Northern Ireland Assembly Act, passed in May 1973. Elections to this new Assembly held in June 1973 produced a solid majority for parties in favour of power-sharing, and an executive was duly formed, constituting members of the UUP, the Social Democratic and Labour Party (SDLP) and the Alliance Party. What brought down the Assembly, however, was the negotiations held at Sunningdale in December 1973 between the new Executive and representatives from the UK and Irish governments, over the formation of a 'Council of Ireland'. It was agreed that this Council would be formed by a 'Council of Ministers', with seven delegates from both the UK and Irish governments empowered to discuss 'matters of substantial mutual interest', and a 'Consultative Assembly', comprising thirty members elected from both the Irish Parliament (Dáil Éireann) and the Northern Ireland Assembly. This can be seen as early recognition by the UK government that national aspirations were driving the conflict, with the all-Ireland dimensions of the Sunningdale Agreement intended to placate Nationalists, by demonstrating progress towards their goal of a united Ireland, and encourage them to support the status quo of Northern Ireland's position in the UK. However, enough Unionists and Loyalists were alarmed by this aspect to bring the Assembly down. An ill-timed UK general election called by Conservative PM Edward Heath in February 1974 provided anti-Sunningdale Unionists with an opportunity to gain electoral support, using slogans such as 'Dublin is just a Sunningdale away' to link the agreement and Assembly to the prospect of a united Ireland. The Loyalist-organised Ulster Workers' Council (UWC) strike of May 1974 then paralysed the country, leading to the resignation of the Unionist members of the Executive, and the demise of the Assembly (Tonge 2002, 115–20).

The next attempt at restoring Stormont-based government came with the 1982 Northern Ireland Act, which created another elected Assembly. This time there was no formal power-sharing arrangements, and no all-Ireland dimension, but a policy of 'rolling devolution' whereby legislative powers would be delegated from Westminster on an area-by-area basis, once 70% of members approved. This high threshold of approval implied cross-community consensus, and until such consent was given the Assembly would have scrutinising authority only. The elections for the Assembly were notable for marking the entry of Sinn Féin, the political wing of the PIRA, into the electoral politics of Northern Ireland, with the party winning 10% of the vote in the aftermath of the election of hunger striker Bobby Sands to the House of Commons the previous year (O'Leary 1997, 665). However, the practical workings of the measure were never tested, as both Sinn Féin and the SDLP contested the elections only after giving notice of their intentions to abstain from the Assembly (Tonge 2002, 124–25). This still-born attempt at devolution was therefore 'the death knell for attempts at purely internal solutions to the problem of Northern Ireland' (Tonge 2002, 124). The abject failure of 'rolling devolution' plays a key role in the narrative of 'ethno-national policy learning' towards conflict management in Northern Ireland, by demonstrating the unsuitability of any proposals lacking an all-Ireland and/or British-Irish dimension.

The first instance of a shift from 'internal solutions' towards 'inter-governmentalism' came in December 1980, when UK PM Margaret Thatcher and Irish PM (or Taoiseach) Charles Haughey set up 'joint Anglo-Irish studies on matters of common concern' (Tonge 2002, 123). This tentative step towards inter-governmentalism was superseded five years later with the signing of the Anglo-Irish Agreement (AIA) at Hillsborough Castle (Tonge

2002, 127–30). This was the high-water mark of pure inter-governmentalism, with the UK and Irish governments agreeing an international treaty on the future of Northern Ireland. One key provision was the re-affirmation of the transfer of the veto over Irish unity from Stormont, where it was lodged in the 1949 Ireland Act, to the people of Northern Ireland, which was first enacted by the Northern Ireland Constitution Act of 1973 (HM Government 1973a), through the determination that a change in the constitutional status of Northern Ireland would only come about with the consent of a majority of its people. This 'principle of consent' has been central to all subsequent agreements, including the GFA. The AIA also established an Intergovernmental Conference, with a secretariat based at Maryfield, outside Belfast, to discuss political, security, legal and cross-border issues. The scope of this Conference was linked to the devolution of powers to a future Northern Ireland Assembly, with matters under the authority of any devolved administration being removed from the remit of the Conference. This therefore represents an example of O'Duffy's (2004) causal relationship between inter-governmentalism and agreement between Unionists and Nationalists in Northern Ireland, as power-sharing is made more attractive as a means of limiting the potential development of 'joint sovereignty'. The strongest instances of this came in the articles on the Intergovernmental Conference, which state that it can, if sustainable agreement on devolution is not forthcoming, operate as 'a framework within which the Irish Government may, where the interests of the minority [i.e. Nationalist] community are significantly or especially affected, put forward views on proposals for major legislation and on major policy issues', and for 'the promotion of co-operation between the two parts of Ireland concerning cross border aspects of economic, social and cultural matters' (HM Government and Government of Ireland 1985). For Tonge (2002, 129), this was specifically about pressuring Unionists to agree to a devolved assembly for Northern Ireland as the only mechanism for limiting the role of the Irish government in Northern Irish affairs. Such stipulations provoked strong Unionist and Loyalist opposition, including mass rallies, electoral machinations, and an attempt to re-run the UWC strike, but with no local target in the form of a functioning Assembly, this had little visible success (Tonge 2002, 132–34).

The AIA can therefore be seen as driven by a recognition of the need for an Irish dimension in any comprehensive political settlement (Thompson 2003, 61), and as representing 'a shift *towards* parity of status of the two opposing sovereigns as patrons of the rights to self-determination of the two ethno-national communities in Northern Ireland' (O'Duffy 2004, 404, emphasis in original). This drive to engage with the 'totality of relationships' between Britain and Ireland was further formalised in the talks spearheaded by Secretary of State for Northern Ireland Peter Brooke in 1991, which first introduced the division of negotiations into 'three strands': one on Northern Ireland's internal political arrangements; one on cross-border, all-Ireland issues; and one on British-Irish relations (Powell 2008, 63–64; Tonge 2002, 146). This division of labour was to characterise all subsequent discussions and is reflected in the three strands of the GFA (on Democratic Institutions in Northern Ireland, the North/South Ministerial Council, and the British-Irish Council and British-Irish Intergovernmental Conference, respectively).

The next centrepiece of inter-governmentalism, meanwhile, was the December 1993 Joint Declaration on Peace, more commonly known as the 'Downing Street Declaration', given by the sitting Taoiseach and PM, Albert Reynolds and John Major. For Ruane and Todd (1999, 6–7) this marked 'a decisive shift in the analysis of the conflict and in the approach to it', by locating 'the roots of the conflict in a historical process on the island of Ireland which primarily affected the people of Ireland, North and South'. Of particular importance to proponents of the 'consociational narrative' is the manner in which this diagnosis chimed with the analyses put forward by Nationalist politicians at this time. According to McKittrick and McVea (2012, 157), SDLP leader John Hume was now arguing 'that the heart of the Irish question was not the British but the Protestants, that the problem was the divisions between Unionist and nationalist . . . The mission of nationalism, he contended, was not to drive out the British but to convince Unionism that its concerns could be accommodated in an agreed Ireland'. Simultaneously, Sinn Féin were moving away from calling on unilateral British withdrawal and Unionist acceptance of a united Ireland, towards arguing for the UK government to act as persuaders to the Unionist community of the benefits of unity (Tonge 2002, 145). These modifications allowed the leaders of the two Nationalist parties to issue joint 'Hume-Adams' statements in 1993 and 1994, which recognised the need to bring about 'agreement among our divided people' through institutions that command the 'allegiance of the different traditions on this island by accommodating diversity and providing for national reconciliation' (Hume and Adams 1993; 1994). According to McGrattan (2010a, 128), these statements demonstrated a 'common understanding of the Northern Ireland problem and a similar preference for its solution', in that the leaders 'stressed the primordial nature of the Northern Ireland conflict', which they viewed as 'inevitable given the deep ethnic divisions within the North'. A growing confluence of opinion between the British and Irish governments and both strands of Irish Nationalism is therefore seen in this account as the necessary precursor to a comprehensive settlement.

The Downing Street Declaration is seen by proponents of the ethnonational account as another attempt by the two governments to take the lead in producing a framework within which future peace talks could be advanced (Aughey 2005, 55). The UK government reiterated that they had 'no selfish strategic or economic interest in Northern Ireland' (Reynolds and Major 1993), something first signalled in the mid-1970s by the Secretary of State Merlyn Rees (McKittrick and McVea 2012, 128),[2] while the Irish government gave notice of intent to amend the claim of sovereignty over Northern Ireland contained in the state's constitution. Both governments pledged to respect the current constitutional status and to enact the necessary legislation to give effect to such change as freely and democratically expressed by the people of Northern Ireland. These affirmations helped create the environment for the multiparty talks that took place during the PIRA ceasefires of 1994–1996 and after 1997, and found their way into the text of the GFA. The 'principle of consent' in both jurisdictions of Ireland was a key part of that agreement, as was the Irish government's determination to revoke the constitutional claim on the North. As O'Duffy (2004, 400, 420) notes, the GFA was distinct from earlier attempts at resolving the conflict in that it was both an international treaty between the Irish and UK governments, and something entrenched in UK and Irish law, meaning that, for him, it 'represents the pinnacle of bi-national intergovernmental conflict regulation'.

## INTERROGATING THE ETHNO-NATIONAL ACCOUNT: ETHNIC IDENTITY OR NATIONAL IDENTIFICATION?

The narrative I have just presented suggests that the GFA was the culmination of decades of policy learning by the UK and Irish governments, in which they came to recognise their ability to dampen the violence of 'the troubles' by mitigating the ethno-national demands of the conflicting parties. I do not subscribe to this narrative, neither in terms of its simplistic account of the violence, nor in the neat teleology it imposes onto the irregularities of the peace process. I view the success of the negotiations as an inherently contingent event: it is what 'happened', but this was not pre-ordained or bound to occur. It is only after the event that teleological narratives are enacted to explain the success. Many of the memoires of those involved in the final stages of the peace negotiations (Ahern 2009; Blair 2011; Mowlam 2002; Powell 2008) are useful in demonstrating this. They share a common evocation of the fraught nature of the process: the claustrophobic confines of Castle Buildings on the Stormont Estate; the many false dawns; and the occasions when all seemed lost. While no doubt heightening the tension for dramatic purposes, these accounts show that the final agreement was as much the product of chance encounters as pre-planned meetings, and dependent upon individual decisions made under immense pressure (Little 2004, 28), in a manner which strongly challenges the idea that the GFA represents the culmination of a long process of 'policy-learning' building on ever-more accurate understandings of the conflict. However, this does not change the fact that the ethno-national account has become the hegemonic understanding of 'the troubles', in academic and policy circles. Before I can explore the impact of this on the GFA and the post-conflict politics of Northern Ireland (see chapter 4), I must therefore interrogate more closely the substance of the ethno-national account.

McGarry and O'Leary, the two authors most associated with this analysis, see competitive ethno-nationalism as the key endogenous cause of the conflict, which they argue must be viewed alongside exogenous factors such as UK and Irish 'state-building and nation-building failures' since 1920, and global developments such as European self-determination in the post–First World War period, post–Second World War global decolonisation, the civil rights movement in the US and the peace movements in South Africa and Israel/Palestine in the early 1990s (McGarry and O'Leary 1995, 360–63). At times they place their emphasis on competing nationalisms, and the debate over the 'national question' in Ireland – that is, which 'nation' (Britain or Ireland) do the inhabitants of Ireland belong to, and which 'nation' (Britain or Ireland) has the right to exercise sovereignty over Ireland? Historically, this was a question for the whole of Ireland: since partition in 1921 it has been resolved for the twenty-six counties that left the UK, but not for the six counties which remained. This is therefore an account that locates the origins of the conflict in inherently *political* questions, of sovereignty and national identity, and one that recognises how the competing answers to these political questions are shaped by changing historical currents and external events. At their strongest on these points, McGarry and O'Leary (1995, 357) rail against what they see as the 'common intellectual failing' of converting the '"markers" which distinguish the two groups with distinct national identities [i.e. religion, language and culture] into factors that are claimed to have crucial explanatory content in their own right'. In such passages, the emphasis is very much on the 'national' as an explanatory factor, with 'ethno' seemingly relegated to shorthand for the groups who articulate 'competing national aspirations'. However, even within this quote, there is evidence of the slippage from a more political account based on *national identification,* to a more fixed account of *ethnic identity.* This is because McGarry and O'Leary are implying here that there are indeed 'two groups' in (Northern) Ireland and that they possess 'distinct national identities'. They are at pains to avoid conflating these 'distinct national identities' with religious, linguistic or cultural 'markers', but in doing so they translate national identification *itself* into a distinct category of identity. Thus 'national' merges with 'ethno' to create an *ethnic* identity that is based on *national* aspiration.

Such a tendency is more strongly evident elsewhere in their work, particularly in *The Politics of Antagonism.* They argue in the introduction (O'Leary and McGarry 1996, 3–4) to that book that the conflict in Northern Ireland is 'fundamentally national', in that 'different nations' are engaged in competition 'over the composition of their nation(s), and their national territories'. In the next paragraph, they go on to define 'ethnic communities', as 'culturally bounded and self-consciously differentiated from other such communities', which are 'mostly endogamous descent-groups'. While arguing these should not be confused with races (which they do not define) or religious communities, they accept that ethnic communities may be based upon religious lines. They then assert that the conflict in Northern Ireland must 'not be seen just as an endogenous ethnic conflict', but the 'equally important exogenous dimensions' must be recognised. By this, they seek to focus attention on how 'the two ethnic communities in Northern Ireland have been partially mobilized into the Irish and British "nations"'. This suggests some sense of a contingent and constructed element to ethnic identity, viewing it as something shaped by larger political forces: but it still implies that there were 'two ethnic communities' present in Ireland who could then be 'mobilized' by British and Irish state actors. They then go on to categorise the two communities: one as 'Irish nationalists. . . a sub-set of a wider ethnic community, the "native" Irish of Ireland, whose ancestors once spoke Gaelic', who are 'usually but not invariably Roman Catholic'; and the Ulster Protestants, 'usually religiously labelled even though by no means all its members are religious', made up of 'the descendants of Scottish and English settlers in Ireland' who 'now regard themselves as British'.

Within the space of two paragraphs, McGarry and O'Leary have therefore gone from a straightforward characterisation of the Northern Ireland conflict as one based on competing national aspirations, to a complicated and confused mixture of ethnic and national elements. Even their definitions of the 'two communities' mixes these elements, shifting from political markers ('Irish nationalists') to linguistic ('once spoke Gaelic') and religious ('Roman Catholic') ones, and from religious markers ('Ulster Protestants') to national ('descendants of Scottish and English settlers') and political ('regard themselves as British') ones. Such fuzziness is also evident in the first chapter of *The Politics of Antagonism* (O'Leary and McGarry 1996, 8–53) which, the introduction claims, 'demonstrates that Northern Ireland is the site of an ethnic war' (O'Leary and McGarry 1996, 4). The chapter provides a detailed account of the scale of the violence, in terms of killings, injuries, and economic, social and political costs, while also placing this in a global context. This may arguably demonstrate that Northern Ireland has been the site of a 'war' (though this is a contentious point, not least because of the political concerns that terrorist violence may be legitimised if labelled as 'acts of war'), but it does not demonstrate the 'ethnic' character of that 'war'. Indeed, the chapter stresses the national and political objectives of the parties to the conflict, with Republican paramilitaries described as 'revolutionaries' engaged in a war of 'national liberation', and Loyalists as 'counter-revolutionaries' seeking to prevent this. There is also extensive cataloguing of violence occurring *within* 'communities', be that through bloody paramilitary schisms, or the disciplining of communities through 'punishment beatings' and shootings. The chapter does describe some of the more general sectarianism that is prevalent in Northern Ireland, whether embodied in the parading culture, the flying of flags or bunting to mark territory, or displaying of emblems and posters in a manner designed to intimidate or exclude others. This is unpalatable behaviour often carried out by bigoted groups or individuals, but it has no necessary relation to paramilitary violence, and certainly does not constitute an 'ethnic war'. It is therefore unclear what the purpose of this 'ethnic' label is, and what it adds to the characterisation of the conflict as driven by national competition. As McGrattan (2010c, 186) notes, '[r]ather than defining what is meant by ethnicity or saying why identities become fixed, ethnic conflict theorists instead claim that the conflict was simply about rival national aspirations'.

Such a tendency for slippage between 'national' and 'ethnic' is also evident in the work of other proponents of the ethno-national approach. Hayes and McAllister (1999, 33–36), for instance, begin by highlighting the dynamic relationship between ethnic and national identity, arguing that ethno-nationalism 'does not cause conflict or instability in and of itself', but that it is 'when ethnic and national identity are out of alignment' that the potential for conflict exists. However, they characterise this conflict as 'ethnic conflict' and stress the 'clash of identity' as the root cause. Tonge (2002, 1–2) highlights how the primary political problem of who should govern Northern Ireland is 'deepened by the religious, cultural and social divide which often coincides with the political divide', while also characterising the 'ethnic division' in Northern Ireland as one 'based upon nationality and religion'. Oberschall and Palmer (2005, 77, 90) provide a textbook example of this slippage: after framing the conflict as one between 'Irish nationalists and British unionists in Northern Ireland' (i.e. in the terms of 'competing national aspirations'), they move immediately to a discussion of 'sectarian violence between these two communities'. This movement from the 'national' to the 'ethnic' is backed up through an endnote, which states: 'Although relations are complex, most Irish nationalists are Catholic, whereas most British unionists are Protestant. Accordingly, the terms "Catholic" and "Protestant" are often used as ethnic markers in Northern Ireland.' Hennessey (2000, 218), finally, conflates the two sides of 'ethno-national' by describing the conflict as 'not, primarily, a conflict between the British Government and the Irish people', but as 'an ethnic conflict between two national communities'. This review of proponents of the ethno-national account illustrates the tendency of such authors to slip from 'competing national aspirations' to 'ethnic conflict' in their analyses. I will now argue that this slippery and at times contradictory understanding is able to operate as the basis of the peace settlement due to the presence of what I call the 'two communities' supplement.

## THE 'TWO COMMUNITIES' SUPPLEMENT

The understanding of the Northern Ireland conflict as driven by the incompatible positions of 'two communities' is a central theme in analyses of 'the troubles'. When surveying academic understandings of the violence up to 1990, Whyte (1990, 202–204) recognises the dominance of what he calls the 'internal-conflict' model, in which the violence is seen as a consequence of the clash between two communities within Northern Ireland, while Ruane and Todd (1999, 4) chart the historical forces which, in their view, produce 'Protestants and Catholics as communities with sharply opposed interests, identities and strategic options'. The prevalence of these types of analyses has been recognised by many scholars critical of the reifying effects of such a characterisation of identity in Northern Ireland. Little (2003, 374–75), for instance, argues that 'most interpretations of Northern Ireland have been sucked into the understanding of the problem as one of a single division (e.g. of religion, nationality, etc.) or set of divisions (i.e. a fusion of cultural, religious, political issues)', meaning that the political developments of the peace process era have defined 'difference only in terms of the "two traditions"', with the wider diversity of identities in Northern Ireland 'neglected'. Rolston makes a similar point, and reaches a similar conclusion as Little: the 'ultimate irony' of the focus on what he terms the 'two traditions' means that discussions of the conflict, and attempts at addressing its causes, 'involves always, and only, two players', with the effect of overlooking 'the real diversity and conflict within each "tradition"' (Rolston 1998, 270). Rolston (1998, 254–61) is also one of the many scholars (McEvoy, McEvoy, and McConnachie 2006; McVeigh 2002; McVeigh and Rolston 2006) who have argued that explaining the conflict through reference to struggle between the 'two communities' serves to mask structural inequalities between Catholics and Protestants in Northern Ireland, as well as absolving the UK state from culpability in producing and maintaining these inequalities. 'Community relations' endeavours are a particular target for these academics, as they are seen as nullifying criticism of the state by placing blame on the 'two communities' themselves. While Little (2004, 377–78) accepts the importance of community designators for self-identification, he is adamant that the 'two communities' in Northern Ireland 'are not divided in a straightforward way, on cultural or religious lines'. For McGrattan (2010c), in failing 'to interrogate the "two-communities" justifications of elite politicians, ethnic conflict theorists reproduce dominant narratives, bolster the status quo and marginalise the experiences of those individuals who refused to buy into strict nationalistic logic'. In McGrattan's opinion, therefore, theorists such as McGarry and O'Leary are guilty of strengthening the self-expressed motivations of violent actors in Northern Ireland, conflating their contingent and shifting political goals with the necessity of inevitable inter-communal competition.

A plethora of authors writing in Zalewski and Barry's edited volume on Northern Ireland take a similar position, with many suggesting that the 'two communities' thesis represents a simplification of the causes of the conflict, with wider consequences for how it is understood and engaged with. Many of the contributors point to different aspects of the reifying effects of reliance on the 'two communities' thesis, whether that is through: combining the language of 'two communities' with that of 'two traditions' in order to inform the notion of 'parity of esteem' that is central to the GFA[3] (Conrad 2008, 117); informing 'cross-community peacebuilding' measures which excise the UK (and Irish) government of culpability for the violence (Bryan 2008, 126); or putting forward an internal view of the conflict which ignores exogenous factors such as the decision to partition Ireland (O'Callaghan 2008, 144). These critical scholars therefore all recognise the limitations of the 'two communities' thesis, and the distorting impact it has on understandings of identity and belonging in Northern Ireland, by simplifying the complex web of relations that exists there into a two-way divide between monolithic community blocs. The impact this has had on attempts to find solutions to the conflict is also noted. However, by emphasising the reifications and simplifications inherent in the 'two communities' thesis, what these scholars *do not* recognise is the *productive function* that the 'two communities' thesis plays as a *supplement* to the dominant ethno-national account. Beginning with a closer look at Vaughan-Williams's chapter in Zalewski and Barry's edited volume, I will now argue that the 'two communities' supplement generates an undecidable 'two communities' understanding of 'the troubles', which allows a politically contingent conception of 'competing national aspirations' to operate *together* with an ethnically determined vision of identity in Northern Ireland, producing an analysis of the conflict that operates as the basis for the peace process.

## The Productive Supplement

Vaughan-Williams (2008, 39–40) argues that there is a simplification behind many analyses of 'the troubles', which serves to replicate and transmit the 'problem' of Northern Ireland as the inevitable clash of 'two communities' who cannot live together peacefully. Vaughan-Williams (2008, 35–36) writes that the GFA 'reflects faith' in the logic that 'ready-made solutions' can be found 'for already-given problems between two indefatigably opposed communities', and suggests the Irish border as a site where this simplification can be complicated, and where the possibility of different identities, and different political constellations, can be recognised in the contingency of the border itself (Vaughan-Williams 2008, 45). While this analysis may be accurate when it comes to academic accounts that reproduce a 'two communities' narrative, it cannot be straightforwardly applied to the *impact* that such academic discourse has had on the unfolding of the peace process. For one thing, this misses how the GFA, operating in the three-stranded framework institutionalised since the early 1990s, contains North/South (all-Ireland) and East/West (UK-Irish) dimensions, as well as prescriptions for the internal governance of Northern Ireland. It is therefore not a pure reflection of a 'two-communities' thesis which, according to Vaughan-Williams (2008, 40), eschews complex understandings of identity 'in favour of conceptual simplicity', creating a 'fantasy of coherence' which 'simplifies dynamic matrices of diversity and . . . delimits the range of possible ways of dealing or coping with conflict'. Instead, it deals with the consequences of 'ethnic' division *within* Northern Ireland (in Strand One) *at the same time* as engaging with the 'competing national aspirations' of those identifying as British and Irish *across* these islands (in Strands Two and Three).

Rather than embodying a simplified view of the Northern Ireland problem, therefore, I suggest that the GFA enacts a *complication* of the conflict, a *recognition* that it has been driven by competing, and contradictory, understandings of identity and national belonging in Ireland. It cannot be said that the GFA reproduces a simplified view of politics in Northern Ireland when its inter-locking geometry allows for multiple expressions of identity, such as that generated by explicit acceptance of the right of persons born in Northern Ireland to claim and possess both Irish and British passports, and to enact an Irish identity, or a British identity, or both[4] (O'Duffy 2004, 422; Ó Caoindealbháin 2006, 14). Furthermore, Vaughan-Williams's analysis fails to recognise that the border *is* seen by the GFA as a factor in the conflict, and in the solutions it proposed (through instruments such as the North/South dimensions, which can be claimed by Nationalists as a weakening of the border, existing alongside the entrenchment of the principle of consent, which Unionists can claim as solidifying the border). The GFA does not treat the border as a 'container' for the conflict, which can then be problematised: one could even argue that the GFA *itself* problematises the border. Indeed, no one following debates over the future of the Irish border (and of the GFA more generally) in the context of the UK's attempts to negotiate an exit from the EU would characterise anything about this issue as 'simple'. The complexities of the citizenship clauses are also highlighted by the legal case brought by Emma de Souza against the

UK government, over her right to treatment as an Irish, rather than British, citizen (Bowcott 2019).

The 'two communities' understanding of the conflict therefore has a productive function, rather than enacting a simplification. It operates as a supplement to the ethno-national account, allowing its contradictory elements to hang together through an undecidable 'two communities' understanding of the conflict. This supplementation allows peace interventions to be mobilised on the basis of an apparently settled understanding of the conflict as a 'two communities' struggle, which can then be managed through political structures designed to contain the two entrenched and antagonistic groups, while *at the same time* presenting these identities as contingent and capable of transformation. This 'two communities' understanding therefore remains an undecidable, operating through supplementation, rather than a reification that fixes and freezes identities in place. Tracing the operation of this undecidable 'two communities' account into the post-conflict politics of Northern Ireland will be the task of chapter 4. The final step of this chapter, however, is to identify the influence of this 'two communities' thesis on the pre-GFA attempts at ending the violence.

## Bringing Peace to the 'Two Communities'

As stated above, the first attempt at a political solution to 'the troubles' came in 1973, with the creation of a power-sharing Assembly. The legislation creating this did not make any specific references to power-sharing between 'two communities', as would be the case with the GFA. Instead, much fuzzier language is employed in the section of the Constitution Act on 'Devolution orders', which states that the Secretary of State may begin the Parliamentary process of transferring powers to a Northern Ireland Executive if they believe this has the support both of the Assembly and the electorate, so that it is 'likely to be widely accepted throughout the community' and capable of providing 'a reasonable basis for the establishment in Northern Ireland of government by consent' (HM Government 1973b). This was therefore a model of 'voluntary coalition' rather than enforced cross-community power-sharing. A more explicit reference to the 'two communities' came in the 1982 Government White Paper on 'rolling devolution', which justifies its exceptional measures for governing part of the UK through reference to Northern Ireland's 'divided community, its geography and the history of its politics' (Tonge 2002, 125). The AIA then institutionalises this recognition of 'two communities' in intergovernmental views of the conflict (Wilson 2010, 122). As such, it demands closer attention.

The AIA not only recognises the centrality of Irish-British relations to the conflict (as discussed above), but through it the two governments pledge to 'recognise and accommodate the rights and identities of the two traditions in Northern Ireland' (HM Government and Government of Ireland 1985). The AIA first defines these 'two traditions' in terms of political aspiration, stating that the two governments accept

> the need for continuing efforts to reconcile and to acknowledge the rights of the two major traditions that exist in Ireland, represented on the one hand by those who wish for no change in the present status of Northern Ireland and on the other hand by those who aspire to a sovereign united Ireland achieved by peaceful means and through agreement.

This then shifts to the language of 'two communities', expressed more in terms of identities that need to be protected, when the governments affirm their recognition and respect for 'the identities of the two communities in Northern Ireland, and the right of each to pursue its aspirations by peaceful and constitutional means'. An eagerness to locate the causes of the conflict within clashing identity groups is therefore evident even within this high-water mark of inter-governmentalism. For Thompson (2003, 61), the AIA was a consequence of the 'change of philosophy by the British government' around this period, when they accepted the need to recognise the 'two traditions' in order to gain legitimacy for future political institutions in Northern Ireland.

The bi-national inter-governmentalism that the likes of McGarry, O'Leary and O'Duffy view as essential to the eventual success of the GFA must therefore be seen as operating alongside a recognition that the conflict was the result of the clash between 'two communities' in Northern Ireland. Central to this was the growing convergence of Sinn Féin and SDLP opinion on the causes of the conflict, and the most optimal solutions to it (as discussed above). This Nationalist alignment proved compatible with the next major statement of inter-governmentalism, the Downing Street Declaration. In this statement, both governments recognise that 'the ending of divisions can come about only through the agreement and co-operation of the people, North and South, representing both traditions in Ireland', while the Taoiseach states that the lessons of Irish history demonstrate 'that stability and well-being will not be found under any political system which is refused allegiance or rejected on grounds of identity by a significant minority of those governed by it' (Reynolds and Major 1993). The cross-pollination between the language of the Hume-Adams statements and the Downing Street Declaration are easily identifiable, complicating O'Duffy's view that the inter-governmentalism represented in the latter was causally prior to the solution of ethno-national conflict in Northern Ireland.

The need to bring about consensus amongst the 'two communities', defined in terms of majority support of the Unionist and Nationalist communities, was then a key element in the final stages of the peace process. The elections to the Northern Ireland Forum in May 1996, which determined who could send delegates to the all-party talks (Tonge 2002, 172–3), was also used as a measure of 'sufficient consensus' between the 'two communities' in the final round of negotiations from September 1997. When the Democratic Unionist Party (DUP) and United Kingdom Unionist Party (UKUP) immediately walked out, due to the inclusion of Sinn Féin after the second PIRA ceasefire but without prior acts of decommissioning, the fact that the share of the vote won by the remaining Unionist parties (the UUP, Progressive Unionist Party (PUP) and Ulster Democratic Party) equalled 56% of the 'Unionist'[5] vote was seen as fulfilling 'the requirements for cross-community participation' needed to make the talks possible. This gave legitimacy to these final stages, despite the absence of two Unionist parties who together won nearly 43% of the 'Unionist' vote in the Forum elections (Ruane and Todd 1999, 7–10). According to Wilson (2010, 132), 'as the ethnonationalist parties came to dominate the political stage during the "peace process", London and Dublin came to favour greater and greater institutionalism of ethnicity'. The idea of the need to recognise and give legitimacy to 'both traditions' was then given form in numerous aspects of the GFA, from the detailed institutional mechanisms to be used in the Assembly, to the more amorphous idea of 'parity of esteem'. The manners in which the GFA embodies different aspects of the ethno-national account of the conflict, and the role of the 'two communities' supplement in allowing these to operate together, will be discussed in detail in chapter 4.

## CONCLUSION

This chapter has examined the dominant ethno-national account of the Northern Ireland conflict and identified the presence of a 'two communities' supplement which allows the contradictions between the 'ethno' and 'national' aspects to work together through an undecidable 'two communities' analysis of 'the troubles'. The construction of this understanding was traced through various attempts at ending the violence, in order to demonstrate how peace interventions generate understandings of the conflicts they seek to resolve. It is important to recognise what is left out of this 'two communities' account, whether that is the activities of campaign movements such as the 'Peace People',[6] or the attempts of certain political parties[7] to operate across or beyond the community divide, which provide evidence that politics was not uniformly or universally reduced to ethno-national competition at this time (as well as being the precursors to the 'non-communal' politics I will discuss in chapter 4). Furthermore, as this 'two communities' understanding is an unstable undecidable, operating through supplementation not reification, the 'successful' peace interventions based on this analysis carry this instability and contingency into the post-conflict period.

Chapter 4 will trace this process, by exploring how the 'two communities' supplement became embedded in the GFA, replicating at key moments in the document an understanding of the conflict as driven by the clash of two historic traditions within Ireland, and placing their accommodation at the heart of the political institutions it inaugurated, while simultaneously embodying, at other key points, an understanding of identity as capable of transformation. The impact of this supplementation will then be traced into the post-conflict politics of Northern Ireland. In doing so, I will move from my first key Derridean term (the supplement) to my second: that of *différance*. This term will be used to examine how the process of supplementation generates the post-conflict environment in Northern Ireland not as the 'two communities' conflict over or annulled, but as the 'two communities' conflict *differed* and *deferred*. Certain aspects of the post-conflict politics of Northern Ireland, namely devolution and the electoral process, allow a (re)enactment of a 'two communities' struggle, while other aspects of politics (in both the formal and informal spheres) contest this 'two communities' binary. Therefore, by locating processes of supplementation and *différance* at the centre of the peace agreement and post-conflict institutions of Northern Ireland, I argue that this politics is already in a process of deconstruction. Chapter 3 will, however, examine the attempts at bringing peace to BiH.

# Chapter 3

# Contradictory Conflict Frames

## *The 'Balkans' Supplement and the War in Bosnia and Herzegovina*

BiH was one of the six republics of the SFRY, and as such had substantial autonomy under the 1974 constitution. When the socialist regimes in Eastern Europe began to collapse in late 1989, SFRY was seen by many as best suited to make the transition to a liberal market economy, as its break with the Soviet sphere in 1948 had allowed for numerous connections to be formed with Western states and international organisations (Woodward 1995, 1; Silber and Little 1996, 26). However, this openness meant SFRY was exposed to the 'structural adjustment' policies of the International Monetary Fund (IMF) earlier than the Eastern bloc. For Susan Woodward (1995, 15, 47–81), these interventions weakened the economy to such an extent that it expatiated a 'disintegration of governmental authority and the breakdown of a political and civil order'. This political vacuum was filled, to a large extent, by nationalist politics (Mulaj 2005, 3–5).

The war in BiH was intrinsically linked to the breakup of SFRY, brought about by the confluence of Slovenian and Croatian nationalists seeking independence for their national republics, and Serbian nationalists seeking to turn SFRY from a federal, decentralised state into one dominated from Belgrade.[1] This latter tendency is often linked to the political career of Slobodan Milošević, who gained control over the Serb and Montenegrin republics between 1987 and 1989, in a context of disputes over the autonomous region of Kosovo. This process gave Milošević de facto control over four of the eight votes in the Yugoslav presidency, triggering Slovenian and Croatian nationalist calls for greater autonomy. By May 1990 nationalists had won multiparty elections in Slovenia and Croatia, setting the polities on the road to independence. Referenda in the two republics ratified the nationalist positions, with independence declared by both on 25 June 1991. While Slovenia exited SFRY with very limited violence between their new armed forces and the Yugoslav People's Army (JNA), this was not the case for Croatia. The departure of these two republics gave added impetus to rising Serbian nationalism, with the Serb Democratic Party (SDS) being formed in Croatia in February 1990, and declaring autonomy for what they viewed as the 'Serb' parts of Croatia. This set a pattern that was to be repeated in BiH: Croat and Serb nationalist parties declaring what they viewed as 'their' areas to be autonomous from the republic, and seeking union with their 'homeland'. With violence breaking out between the 'Krajina Serbs' and the new Croat National Guard, the JNA was soon seen to be acting on behalf of the Serbs. There was major violence in the cities of Vukovor and Dubrovnik, as well as massacres and 'ethnic cleansing' in smaller towns and villages. The European Community (EC) and UN mobilised a mediation effort, leading to the deployment of a 12,000 strong UN Protection Force (UNPROFOR) in March 1992, with its headquarters in Sarajevo.

By this stage, however, BiH was on the verge of its own outbreak of violence. The Croat nationalist Croatian Democratic Union (HDZ) party had declared an independent 'Herceg-Bosnia' region in November 1991, while the SDS branch in BiH followed suit, declaring their self-proclaimed 'Serbian Republic' (RS) as an independent region in January 1992. Concurrently, the BiH president and leader of the Muslim or 'Bosniac' nationalist Party for Democratic Action (SDA), Alija Izetbegović, sought popular approval for the independence of the Bosnian republic in its entirety. A referendum, boycotted by many in RS, approved this in March 1992, and the independence of BiH was recognised by the EC and US in April 1992. War began almost immediately, with Izetbegović's government forces fighting to prevent the disintegration of BiH in the face of secessionist violence from the leaders of RS and Herceg-Bosnia. Like in Croatia, the conflict was characterised by assaults and sieges of major cities (such as Sarajevo and Mostar), virulent practices of ethnic cleansing and massacres in the towns and villages, and the mobilisation of EC and UN humanitarian and peacekeeping efforts. Unlike Croatia, however, these outside interventions did not succeed in 'freezing' the frontlines, but instead operated while the bloodshed continued. By December 1995, when a NATO bombing campaign precipitated successful peace talks in Dayton, Ohio, over 100,000 people were dead and over two million people had fled their homes.

This brief sketch of the war in BiH began with the economic restructuring of SFRY, but quickly moved to a focus on nationalist politics and the violent practices of ethnic cleansing. Like the opening paragraphs of chapter 2, these details are provided both for the benefit of those unfamiliar with the outbreak and course of the violence, and to provide an indicative example of approaches to conflict which seek to understand the reasons for the violence through interrogating the historical record. The analysis undertaken in this chapter differs from that of the previous one, however, in that I do not focus on one key narrative of the conflict, but on two contradictory conflict framings that shaped and influenced the international response to the violence. These are what I call the 'ethnic war' discourse, and the 'international aggression' discourse. The recognition of (at least) two competing narratives of the war in BiH, and the differential impacts they had on understandings of, and approaches, to the region, has been widely noted in the literature. According to Woodward (1995, 3, 7–15) 'conventional wisdom' viewed the wars as a result of either 'peculiarly Balkan hatreds or Serbian aggression'. Hansen (2006, 13), meanwhile, identifies two discursive clusters generating Western policy. These are labelled as 'the Balkan discourse', which viewed the war as 'the product of ancient Balkan hatred and hence a conflict that the West could and should not solve'; and 'the Genocide discourse', which saw the war as 'a genocide committed by Serbian military and political leaders', with the West having 'an ethical obligation to come to Bosnia's rescue'.

My argument in this chapter differs not in the substance of the competing discourses I identify, nor in the recognition of the multifaceted or fluid nature of these accounts. Instead, the originality in my analysis arises from my focus on the *contradictory* nature of these discourses, and from my account of how these contradictions were made to work together in the post-war settlement. In a similar manner to my identification of the 'two communities' thesis as a productive supplement to the ethno-national account of the Northern Ireland conflict, this chapter argues that repeated reference to the wider 'Balkans' context of the war in BiH side-steps the contradictions between the 'ethnic war' and 'international aggression' discourses through the addition of a 'Balkans' supplement, allowing the competing discourses to operate together in an undecidable 'Balkans' understanding of the conflict. This is seen as particularly apparent in the final stages of the war, when a renewed US-led mediation effort brought the conflict to an end through the DPA, but in a manner which strengthens the 'ethnic war' discourse by presenting BiH as a Balkan space where ethnic identity drives politics, while also explaining the manipulative politics of the 'international aggression' discourse through reference to the Balkans as a place where political leaders are particularly willing to resort to the use of force, and to mobilise ethnicity as a means to do so.

The first section of the chapter discusses the 'ethnic war' discourse, detailing its key characteristics and mapping its impact on the international interventions and peacebuilding efforts during the war. I then turn to the 'international aggression' discourse in the second section, highlighting how it differed from the 'ethnic war' framing, and tracing its role in the more active efforts of mediation and conflict resolution. The third section argues that these seemingly contradictory framings were able to work together, both in academic analysis and in governmental practice, through reference to the wider 'Balkans' context, producing an idea of the conflict as something that can be resolved through conflict management strategies. This allows the conclusion to point towards the argument of chapter 5, which will trace the presence of this 'Balkans' supplement within the DPA, and the post-war political landscape it created.

## THE 'ETHNIC WAR' DISCOURSE

Many commentators employed ethnic tropes to understand the war in BiH, viewing it as a conflict between three divergent and opposed ethnic groups – Muslim Bosniacs, Catholic Croats and Orthodox Christian Serbs – with its causes located in the deep past of the region. It is not hard to find the deployment of such views on the war in BiH, both in academic texts and in the memoires of those involved in attempts to negotiate a peaceful resolution to the conflict. Brendan Simms (2002, 25–26), for instance, discusses how key members of the UK government viewed the conflict as a civil war, with the different 'parties' or 'factions' to the conflict sharing the blame for the outbreak of violence and, consequently, being responsible for finding peace themselves. Simms (2002, 140–42) also argues that the EC mediator from 1992 to 1995, David (Lord) Owen, quickly accepted this analysis. The UN Secretary-General at the time, Boutros Boutros-Ghali (1999, 37, 42), while recognising that the multi-ethnicity of BiH has produced 'periods both of mutual amity and of hate-spawned violence', still writes that he agreed with the first EC peace envoy Peter (Lord) Carrington that 'no party in Bosnia was free of at least some of the blame for the cruel conflict'. In Owen's (1995, 1–2) own account of his failed attempts to generate a meaningful peace process, the language of historical and ethnic determinism dominates. 'Nothing is simple in the Balkans', he writes in the opening pages. 'History pervades everything'. While accepting that '[m]any of the people with whom I have had to deal in the former Yugoslavia were literally strangers to the truth', he argues that it 'is not sufficient to explain away the frequently broken promises, the unobserved ceasefires merely as the actions of lying individuals'. Instead, he suggests that these characteristics 'were also the product of South Slavic history, particularly its most recent phase of exposure to Communism'. While the Communist phase is seen as adding a new tendency towards dissimulation and deviancy, Owen (1995, 3) sees the deeper currents of historical events as producing a predisposition towards violence in the peoples of the Yugoslav region. The UK PM for the duration of the war, John Major (1999, 532), echoes such a sentiment when writing that the conflict was 'as near impossible to deal with as any political problem could be. Its roots were bewildering, and the motives of the participants often far adrift from those expressed in public'.

This discourse therefore viewed all parties to the conflict as equally to blame, on account of their innate ethnic animosity.

In terms of academic accounts that reproduce such an understanding, Burg and Shoup are exemplary in their reductive analysis of ethnic agency in BiH. They place the Bosnian war within a 'history of ethnic conflict and controversy over the national question', and define the 'essence of ethnic conflict' as 'the struggle between mobilized identity groups for greater power' (Burg and Shoup 2000, 4). Despite warning of the 'dangers' of a narrowly ethnic definition of the conflict, which may 'exclude economic, political, and especially moral issues from the analysis', they resort to some shocking primordialist language, no more so than when writing that BiH's 'difficult history was rooted in the most fundamental characteristics of Bosnian geography and the distribution of ethnic communities' which 'bred a culture and society of "mountain men"' (Burg and Shoup 2000, 18). Like Owen, they suggest that the physical environment and historical record have combined in the Yugoslav region to produce certain characteristics within the population, which they then look to in order to understand and explain the war. As well as transmitting an ethnic logic into the attempts at negotiating a peace agreement (as I discuss below), this understanding of the conflict serves to absolve the international community of any responsibility for the outbreak or conduct of the war. Commentators such as Mulaj (2005, 3–5), Silber and Little (1996, 199–201) and Woodward (1995, 200–201) challenge this by viewing actions such as the IMF's imposition of state-weakening economic reforms, and the EC's recognition of Slovenia and Croatia, as evidence of international culpability for the descent to war in BiH.

A further key aspect of the 'ethnic war' discourse that must be examined, and the apparent source of its analytical strength, is the idea that the communist regime of Josip Broz Tito somehow operated to 'repress' ethnic rivalries. The death of Tito in 1980 is often seen as the starting point for the most recent conflagration, in that the tight grip of this leader on the innate ethnic characteristics of the population was loosened, setting Yugoslavia on the road to inter-communal strife. This viewpoint is summarised by Woodward (1995, 7–8) as the argument

> that communist regimes had kept their populations in a deep freeze for forty years, repressing their ethnic identities and freedoms. Freedom throughout the region had restored to countries their national histories of the precommunist era . . . which included . . . enduring and venomous animosities between ethnic groups that had exploded to new cycles of revenge when the repression lifted.

Again, it is not hard to find such an understanding in accounts of the conflict. Burg and Shoup (2000, 4) argue that the collapse of communism meant that 'older, historical identities – religion, ethnicity, national identity, and even region – reemerged as bases of political mobilization and claims to statehood'. The EU peace envoy who replaced Owen, Carl Bildt (1998, 8–9), states that Tito 'had put the lid on' the ethnic hatred unleased by the massacres committed by Croatian and Muslim collaborators during the Nazi occupation, but that 'what was repressed in public life moved on in individuals and families', only to escalate and explode into warfare after 1992. Owen (1995, 11) himself notes the suppression of nationalisms by Tito, while US President Bill Clinton (2005, 502) describes Yugoslavia in his memoires as 'a cauldron of diverse ethnic provinces, which had been held together by the iron will of Marshall Tito'. The portrayal of the communist period as somehow 'freezing' identity in the former Yugoslavia suggests that the 'normal', default mode for the region is one of deep-rooted ethnic rivalry. Only the quasi-totalitarian nature of Tito's communist regime was able to repress this, through the promotion of 'brotherhood and unity', and the subordination of any notion of ethnic belonging through the promotion of a pan-national Yugoslav identity. With the collapse of the communist regime, the suppression was lifted, and the various Yugoslav peoples reverted back to their natural characteristics – characteristics which had not changed for thousands of years.

This idea of 'Tito's repression' is also important in terms of understanding how this discourse produced the international actors as capable of intervening in the conflict, in order to drag the Bosnian people beyond the constraints of their history. This is because it puts forward an understanding of time as malleable, as something that can be manipulated by political power. The communist government of SFRY is credited with interrupting the usual temporality of the region, and halting the cycles of violence, retribution and revenge that were seen to constitute Yugoslav history. The implication here is that Western liberalism can achieve a similar temporal adjustment, and drag the backward region into the modern world. Through the prevalence of this understanding of 'Tito's repression', international actors in BiH replicated what Hutchings (2008, 160, emphasis in original) describes as 'the temptation of thinking that politics is conditioned by the possibility of *making* or *controlling* time'. As Bildt (1998, 118–19) writes, [i]f you do not understand the origins of war, you can scarcely hope to stop it recurring, apart from temporary, short-term solutions'. We thus see the first contradiction *within* the 'ethnic war' discourse: while ethnic actors in BiH are doomed to repeat the same patterns of internecine conflict, intervention by those capable of standing 'outside' this history is seen as capable of pushing the ethnic groups beyond these cycles of violence. Thus the 'ethnic war' discourse was mobilised both by those who called for no or very limited intervention, *and* by those who called for some form of intervention designed to keep the warring parties apart. This variation in the effects of the 'ethnic war' discourse is mapped out in the following sub-section, which discusses the impact of the discourse on international interventions during the war.

## 'Ethnic War' and War-Time Interventions

For those who saw the conflict in BiH as a civil war, with blame on all sides, there was little that could be done to halt the atavistic bloodletting. This was a view prevalent on both sides of the Atlantic. The UK Foreign Minister Douglas Hurd (1992) downplayed the possibility of successful intervention when he stated at the August 1992 meeting of the International Conference on the former Yugoslavia that '[a]ncient hatreds are not easily soothed by outsiders', while President George H. W. Bush (1992) simply affirmed that '[b]lood feuds are very difficult to resolve'. The prevalence of such ideas amongst international actors and commentators had profound, if variable, consequences for the type of response enacted.[2]

In its most pessimistic formulation, the argument that the conflict was driven by unchanging 'ancient hatreds' led to a 'nothing can be done' attitude, at least in terms of finding practical or immediate solutions to the bloodshed. The only meaningful interventions that could be undertaken, according to this view, were those of a humanitarian character (Hansen 2006, 123–32). Major (1999, 533–35) expresses such a sentiment in his autobiography. After providing an explanation of the violence as motivated by 'memories from Yugoslavia's crypt of ethnic murder', and revealing that his military chiefs advised in August 1992 that 400,000 troops would be needed to keep the 'three warring factions' apart, Major laments that all that could be done was to 'save as many lives as we could while the slaughter continued', and attempt to find ways to 'limit the conflict'. For Simms (2002, 6–26), this perspective was endemic in UK foreign policy at the time due to the 'conservative philosophical realism of its practitioners', including Major, Hurd and Defence Secretary Malcolm Rifkind. This perspective, according to Simms, cast doubt on the ability of an interventionist 'international community' to solve human-made crises, particularly those, such as the war in BiH, for which the blame resides on 'all sides'. While Major seemed to possess this view from the start of the conflict, Warren Christopher (1998, 347), the Secretary of State during Clinton's first term as president, recounts how the executive office's initial enthusiasm for a policy of 'lift and strike' (which I will discuss in more detail below) waned throughout 1993, due to a combination of Clinton's reading of books such as Robert Kaplan's *Balkan Ghosts*, which 'presented a grim picture of prospects for reconciliation' in BiH, and the military's aversion to getting drawn into another Vietnam-style 'quagmire'.

As the quotes from Major and Christopher above indicate, two active policies did follow from this pessimistic reading of the war. Firstly, an emphasis was placed on providing a *humanitarian* response, in order to limit the number of deaths that would result from the playing-out of the conflict. When surveying UN Security Council resolutions referencing the area in the years 1991–1995,[3] it is apparent that time and time again the UN viewed events through a humanitarian lens. As early as December 1991, Resolution 724 was passed (United Nations 1991), in which the Secretary-General was urged to 'pursue his humanitarian efforts in Yugoslavia', to liaise with international humanitarian organisations and take 'urgent practical steps to tackle the critical needs' of those affected by the conflict. The situation was thus framed from the beginning in humanitarian terms. The phrase 'ethnic cleansing', meanwhile, first entered the lexicon of the Security Council in August 1992, through Resolution 771 (United Nations 1992c). A sense of greater apprehension as the conflict develops is also evident, with every new instance of atrocity being received with a fresh round of condemnation. Resolution 776, passed on 14 September 1992, extended the mandate of UNPROFOR to BiH, with the explicit direction to provide protection to humanitarian convoys organized by the United Nations High Commissioner for Refugees (UNHCR) (United Nations 1992d). December 1992, meanwhile, sees the first mention of the systematic and organised rape of women in BiH, which is then duly denounced (United Nations 1992e). The targeting of humanitarian convoys designed to alleviate suffering caused by the conflict is also censured (United Nations 1993a). The issue of the 'eastern enclaves', namely Srebrenica, Goražde and Žepa, becomes a major issue throughout the spring and summer of 1993. These Muslim-majority towns, surrounded by Serb forces and cut-off from their Bosnian-government allies, are declared 'safe areas' through Security Council Resolutions 819, 824 and 836, which also apply the label to the cities of Sarajevo, Tuzla and Bihać (United Nations 1993a; 1993b; 1993c). By September 1995, the Security Council is describing the situation in BiH as a 'humanitarian crisis of significant proportions' (United Nations 1995). The assault of cities, the targeting of civilians, mass rape – all the litany of human rights abuses that came to be known under the term 'ethnic cleansing' – are thus reiterated throughout the texts of Security Council resolutions directed at the war in BiH.

This focus on engaging with the war only through its humanitarian consequences has been viewed by many as a deeply *depoliticising* manoeuvre. Simms (2002, 22), for instance, argues that the UK support for UNPROFOR was conditional on it being a force tasked only with the delivery of aid, rather than more muscular intervention, as 'part of a strategy to relativize and depoliticize the conflict and turn it into a purely humanitarian problem'. This analysis chimes with the argument of Jenny Edkins (2003a, 255–6) and Jasmina Husanović (2004, 212), who both argue that the humanitarian desire to save 'victims', who are often coded in gendered and racialised terms, renders a break with politics, through a narrow focus on the consequences of violence, which serves to obscure the political situation that lead to the outbreaks in the first instance.[4] Hansen (2006, 45, 189–92) emphasises the role of gender in this, with 'Balkan women' being seen as the victims of a sexually violent 'Balkan masculinity', and thus in need of Western protection.

The separation between a humanitarian and a political response to the conflict was evident in the one-day conference held in Geneva in the summer of 1992, where the member states of the EC discussed the refugee crisis emanating from BiH. Led by the UK Minister of Overseas Development, Lynda (Baroness) Chalker, the EC decided that the refugees should not be taken in by their member states, but accommodated as close as possible to their homes, so that they could be returned as soon as the fighting stopped (anyone familiar with the recent 'refugee crisis' caused by the Syrian conflict will note the profound similarities between the UK government's position in 1992 and in 2015). What they failed or refused to take into account was that the fighting was designed to ensure this could not easily happen. In other words, the context of the rescue operation was ignored, in favour of a focus solely on the act of rescue itself, with the refugee crisis seen as a humanitarian issue, not a political one – a side effect of the war, if you will, rather than one of the key aims of the belligerent parties. Chalker was unable to conceive of refugees as an intended consequence of a premeditated military and political strategy. This was not merely people fleeing a conflict, people trying to get out of harm's way, but the *forced expulsion* of persons from their homes, as an *objective* of military action. The text of Security Council Resolution 758 also belies such a reliance on this conceptual separation, when it deplores the continuation of the fighting in BiH due to the negative effect it is having on the distribution of assistance to Sarajevo and its environs (United Nations 1992b). It is easy to detect here an understanding of the conflict as *getting in the way* of the humanitarian effort, as an *obstacle* to it, rather than being directly responsible for the humanitarian crisis – as if the war is merely making it more difficult to deliver humanitarian aid, rather than being the factor that has drawn humanitarian groups to the region. As Silber and Little (1996, 256) state, international agencies 'dealt with the war as though it were a flood or an earthquake, enthusiastically addressing the symptoms of the conflict, without making any real effort to challenge its causes'.

The second policy to follow from the pessimistic vision of the war as driven by 'ancient hatreds', with 'blame on all sides', was that which sought to *contain* the conflict within BiH, and to prevent it spreading beyond the borders of the former Yugoslavia (Christopher 1998, 347; Daalder 2000, 7–36; Silber and Little 1996, 287–88). While accepting that the violence in BiH would have to play-out to its bloody denouement, international actors were taking on some responsibility through this policy of containment to ensure that other countries were not dragged into the vortex. There were two concrete manifestations of this policy: the general arms embargo enforced by the UN Security Council against SFRY from 25 September 1991, which was in force for the duration of the war; and the economic sanctions imposed by the EC from November 1991, initially against all of SFRY, but then lifted for successor states apart from Serbia and Montenegro, and those imposed by the UN against the rump Yugoslavia constituting the Serbian and Montenegrin republics and known as the Federal Republic of Yugoslavia (FRY), which were in force from May 1992 until the end of the war (Owen 1995, 368; Silber and Little 1996, 196–8, 258–59). Silber and Little (1996, 288–89) also characterise the 'Joint Action Plan' announced by the US, Russia, France, UK and Spain in May 1993 as aiming to 'seal' BiH to prevent incursion or military support from Serbia and Croatia, as well as creating six Muslim 'safe areas'.

The prevalence of understandings of the Bosnian conflict as an 'ethnic war' did not only provoke policies of humanitarianism and containment, however: it also had a concrete impact on attempts to negotiate a political solution to the conflict. Above all, the view that this was a civil war with 'blame on all sides' informed the attempts to generate peace through some form of ethnic *partition* of BiH. As Campbell (1998) argues, the nexus between territory and identity was treated as an ontological fact, in a manner which coloured all attempts at negotiating a settlement. Such an ethnicising logic can be seen as far back as the Brioni Agreement of 7 July 1991, which enforced a moratorium on Slovenia and Croatia's declarations of independence, and allowed for the withdrawal of JNA forces from Slovenia. The first of the five principles in the agreement stated that it 'is up to the Yugoslav peoples to decide their future': phrasing which gives decisive power to collective, national or ethnic groups in SFRY, not to individual Yugoslav citizens (Woodward 1995, 169). This logic was then transferred from SFRY as whole to BiH in particular. As Campbell observes, partition was first prescribed for BiH in March 1992, *before* war had reached BiH, when the 'Statement of Principles' agreed in Lisbon proposed a BiH divided into three constituent parts as the only peaceful way forward. For Campbell (1998, 128–9), the meaning of this is clear: 'the first peace proposal for [BiH] embodied, prior to the outbreak of open conflict, the very nexus between identity and territory on which the major protagonists also relied',[5] driven by the conceptualisation amongst international mediators that the war in BiH was being fought between three homogenous ethnic groups competing for an ethnically homogenous territory. For Campbell (1998, 130), such ideas contributed to the 'ethnicization of Bosnia by the international community, in tandem with the parties to the conflict', until BiH was enshrined in the political imaginary 'as a place where political identity is fixed in terms of ethnic exclusivity' (Campbell 1998, 157). The creation of an ethnically divided BiH was thus installed as the surest solution from the earliest stage possible.

The next agreement to suggest a de facto partition was the Vance Owen Peace Plan, announced in Geneva in January 1993, which called for the division of BiH into ten provinces, overseen by a weak central government. While this differed from the Lisbon Agreement in that none of these provinces were given an explicit 'ethnic' designation, the ethnic character was implicit in the details of the plan, especially in the provision for Serb and Croat forces to be stationed in particular provinces (Owen 1995, 95; Silber and Little 1996, 276). Owen (1995, 124), the EC mediator who co-authored the plan, also betrays its ethnic logic when writing that the changes made to the accompanying map in February 1993 around Tuzla and Brčko were 'ethnically totally justified' due to the pre-1992 Muslim majority in those areas, suggesting that ethnic calculations were also behind the original boundary lines. This was seen by some critics as fuelling the violence of Croat forces in particular, who sought to gain control of the cantons 'granted' to them by the plan. Some authors recall the anecdote that members of the Herceg-Bosnia armed forces, the Croat Council of Defence, joked that their initials HVO meant 'Hvala Vance Owen', or 'thank you Vance Owen' (Silber and Little 1996, 276–77; Simms 2002, 142–43). The Owen-Stoltenberg Plan, announced in July 1993, moved back to the initial three-way ethnic partition through a 'Union of three republics', made up of a contiguous Serb republic on 53% of the territory, a two-part Croat republic on 17%, and the rest left to a Muslim republic. Both these partition plans faced the criticism of rewarding ethnic cleansing (as would the DPA), while failing to attract the unified support of the parties to the conflict and the interested outside actors (Daalder 2000, 10–11; Silber and Little 1996, 288–306).

By the end of 1993, a formula for the de facto partition of BiH was to emerge that continues to influence the political structure of BiH today: the idea of a two-way partition between a Croat-Muslim Federation (which was being negotiated with US support from August 1993) and RS, with a 51–49 territorial split between the two areas (Owen 1995, 256). With the Federation coming into being through the Washington Agreement, signed in March 1994 (Silber and Little 1996, 319), this two-way partition became the basis for all future peace talks. It was central to the Contact Group Plan of July 1994 (Bildt 1998, 18), and many have argued that the acceptance of the validity of such a division drove the tacit support given by the US and NATO to the Croatian Army (HV)[6] offensive against the Krajina Serbs in August 1995, and the overrunning of RS territory in eastern BiH by the HV and the Army of the Republic of Bosnia and Herzegovina (ARBiH)[7] that this allowed, as it moved the frontlines on the ground closer to an approximation of the 51–49 split (Bildt 1998, 112; Chollett 2005, 94; Owen 1995, 364). The ratio was then included in the 'Agreed Basic Principles' which, when accepted by the foreign ministers of BiH, FRY and Croatia in September 1995 (Owen 1995, 359), created the basis for the final peace negotiations at Dayton. With the help of the US's 'PowerScene' mapping technology, a final map was agreed at Dayton which divided BiH into the two 'entities' of the Federation of Bosnia and Herzegovina (FBiH) and RS according to these proportions.[8]

The 'ethnic war' discourse therefore informed not only the more pessimistic hand-wringing of certain outside actors, but also played a crucial role in the various peace plans that eventually informed the DPA negotiated in November 1995. However, what was even more important in motivating the muscular, US-led intervention in the autumn of 1995, which precipitated the final mediation efforts, was the competing conflict framing, which I call the 'international aggression' discourse. It is to this discursive cluster that I will now turn.

## THE 'INTERNATIONAL AGGRESSION' DISCOURSE

The 'international aggression' conceptualisation puts forward an understanding of the BiH conflict that seemingly contradicts that embodied in the 'ethnic war' discourse discussed above. This is the idea that the war was caused by Serb and Croat aggression, inspired by the violent and conservative nationalism of Serbian President Milošević and Croatian President Franjo Tuđman, and mainly directed against innocent Bosnian Muslims. This discourse chimes with a constructivist conceptualisation of ethnic conflict, with instrumental elites seen as 'ethnic entrepreneurs' who mobilise differences along previously existing ethnic cleavages in order to achieve specific political goals (Gagnon Jr. 1994/95; Hansen 2006, 113–14). Rather than viewing ethnic resentment as the products of innate forces residing within fixed ethnic identities, proponents of this discourse are more likely to see animosity as a *consequence* of the hardening of ethnic identities through extreme violence (Kaufmann 1996). Silber and Little (2016, 244–45) express this view when they describe how ethnic cleansing was implemented in such a way as to instil hatred and fear that would ensure Serbs and Muslims could not live together again, while Woodward (1995, 264–67) discusses the radicalising of populations through acts of violence.

The discourse is also evident in the writings of two key figures in the US's mediation effort: Secretary of State Christopher and Richard Holbrooke, who was Assistant Secretary of State for European and Canadian Affairs from September 1994, and the lead negotiator for the US in BiH from August 1995. In his annotated collection of foreign policy speeches, Christopher (1998, 343–44) writes that the primary cause of the violent break-up of

Yugoslavia 'was nationalism, stoked more by cynical, power-hungry leaders than by ancient ethnic hatreds', and that the 'primary aggressors were the Serbs'. In his account of the peace negotiations, Holbrooke (1999, 22–23) is very critical of the 'ancient hatreds' thesis, which he puts down to the 'bad history' which gave people 'the sense that nothing could be done by outsiders' and 'trivialized and oversimplified the forces that tore Yugoslavia apart'. Violence was therefore 'not foreordained', according to Holbrooke, but 'the product of bad, even criminal, political leaders who encouraged ethnic confrontation for personal, political, and financial gain'. This view is also expressed in some journalistic and academic accounts of the conflict. Both Silber and Little (1996, 25–26) and Simms (2002, xv) place the blame on nationalist leaders, with Tuđman and, to an even greater extent, Milošević singled out for condemnation. The strength of the 'international aggression' discourse was such that even those who on other occasions put forward a more primordialist account of the causes of the conflict at times expressed themselves in its terms. Burg and Shoup (2000, 62–127), for instance, singled out above for their essentialist understanding of ethnic identity in BiH, also provide a detailed account of how the decisions of nationalist leaders throughout SFRY, in concert with the decisions of external actors, led to war.

A common theme amongst many interpretations within the 'international aggression' discourse is the stress placed on *Serb* culpability for the conflict. This is therefore very far from the 'ethnic war' understandings that saw an equivalence between actors, with blame on all sides. In its most extreme form, this emphasis on Serb violence reduced the complexities of the conflict to a binary of aggressive Serb perpetrators/innocent Muslim victims (Hansen 2006, 96), effectively erasing the Croat role in the violence. As Nik Gowing (1996, 87–90) notes, this manifested itself in the disproportionate focus on the siege of Sarajevo, which was prosecuted by Serbs, at the expense of the Croat siege of Mostar, which was comparably destructive and bloody. Elizabeth Dauphinee (2007, 95) points out that identifying Serbs as mostly responsible for the war served to downplay and trivialise violence perpetrated against them, such as the forced expulsion of the Serbian residents of Krajina by the HV in the summer of 1995. As we will see below, that offensive was a key point through which the 'ethnic war' and 'international aggression' discourses merged. Woodward (1995, 146–47, 183, 200–201), meanwhile, argues that the German government's successful campaign within the EC to recognise Croatian and Slovenian independence was driven by their view that the war was caused by Serb aggression: a decision that, she argues, gave impetus to the violent unravelling of Yugoslavia. I will now consider the impact of this discourse on international efforts to resolve the conflict in BiH.

## 'International Aggression' and War-Time Interventions

The idea that international, or possibly only Serb, aggression was the driving force behind the conflict produced two clusters of policy responses to the war. First, it informs the arguments that were made at various times for some form of military intervention, to turn the tide of the conflict and generate leverage for the enforcement of a political settlement. When assuming the US presidency in January 1993, Clinton was in favour of the so-called 'lift and strike' option, which would have involved lifting the arms embargo against the Bosnian government, and undertaking airstrikes against the Bosnian Serb forces, in order to create a more 'level-playing' field (the logic being that, while the Serbs had access to the weaponry of the JNA, the Bosnian government were being denied the opportunity to defend themselves against their superiorly-armed opponents).[9] Major (1999, 540) writes about the tension this created when juxtaposed with European leaders' 'neutral' humanitarian aid policy. However, as noted above, Clinton's reading of Kaplan's *Balkan Ghosts* seemingly dissuaded him from pursuing this option in 1993. A variation of this policy was also championed by the EC mediator Owen (1995, 302–12), which he labelled 'leave, lift and strike'. This mirrored the US policy but with an initial stage of UN withdrawal, as Owen recognised the dangers that the UNPROFOR troops would face from Serb retaliation during an air campaign.

While neither variant of the 'lift and strike' policy was enacted, the 'international aggression' discourse found concrete expression through NATO airstrikes against Bosnian Serb forces. The growing sense of outrage regarding the violence of the siege of Sarajevo, particularly incidents such as the February 1994 market shelling, which killed over sixty people,[10] and the assaults on the eastern enclaves of Srebrenica, Žepa and Goražde, encouraged US and European leaders to re-assess their military options as war continued. So-called 'pin-prick' strikes were launched in April 1994, after the RS armed forces ignored the NATO ultimatum regarding their assault on Goražde (Silber and Little 1996, 327–29), and by the end of 1994 the US government had committed to sending in ground troops as part of any NATO mission to replace UN forces (a key moment in the shift from a 'neutral' humanitarian response to one targeted against the Serbs). France and the Netherlands also pledged troops to a 'Rapid Reaction Force' from May 1995, capable of undertaking armed aggression, unencumbered by the restrictive peacekeeping mandate of UNPROFOR (Biltd 1998, 19–21). By the summer of 1995, with reports emerging about a large-scale massacre at Srebrenica, the move away from neutrality was completed. A new ultimatum was issued over Goražde, and the so-called dual key, by which both the UN and NATO leadership had to authorise airstrikes, was abandoned under the 'London rules' agreed in July 1995, with authority granted to NATO alone to decide on the use of airpower if Goražde was attacked. This was then extended to include attacks on Sarajevo, and when another mortar hit a Sarajevo market on 28 August, this time killing over thirty people,[11] the decision was made to launch a military response (Daalder 2000, 75–79; Holbrooke 1999, 72–102). A two-week bombing campaign, codenamed 'Operation Deliberate Force', duly began in the early hours of 30 August. According to Daalder (2000, 131), by the time 'the operation ended on September 14, a total of 3,515 aircraft sorties had been flown, delivering 1,026 high explosive ammunitions against 336 aim points on 58 Bosnian Serb targets'. Silber and Little (1996, 366) describe the consequences as follows: 'Ammunitions stores, anti-aircraft batteries, radar installations, communications facilities, warehouses, artillery units, command bunkers and bridges were destroyed. The result was to cripple Bosnian Serb communications and temporarily incapacitate their ability to respond and reinforce.' These airstrikes played a key role in altering the military balance and encouraging the parties to the conflict to agree to a peace deal at Dayton.

Secondly and concurrently with the arguments for a militarised response to the war, the 'international aggression' discourse also influenced attempts to negotiate a settlement to the conflict. While the DPA's de facto partition of BiH can be linked to the 'ethnic war' discourse, the maintenance of BiH within its SFRY-era borders, and the wider regional or post-Yugoslav focus of the DPA, was influenced by the 'international aggression' discourse. The DPA was not just a 'Bosnian' peace deal, but one negotiated and signed by Milošević and Tuđman, the Presidents of FRY and Croatia respectively, as well as by Izetbegović, the President of BiH. It also produced an interim agreement on the eastern Slavonia region of Croatia, demonstrating its focus beyond BiH. By signing the DPA, the three 'parties' (i.e. the Republic of Bosnia and Herzegovina, the Republic of Croatia and the FRY) pledge to fully respect each other's sovereign equality, territorial integrity and political independence, while Annex 1B deals with the regional and arms control issues seen as 'essential to creating a stable peace in the region'.[12]

What this demonstrates is that the mediators of the DPA accepted that the war was an international conflict, requiring a solution that involved the three 'states' involved in the violence. Such a Yugoslav-wide framework for peace was evident as far back as September 1991, in the Carrington Plan, which envisioned a comprehensive settlement allowing the different components of SFRY to seek different levels of integration or separation, and with strong guarantees for minorities (Silber and Little 1996, 199–201). With international recognition of Slovenian and Croatian independence in December 1991, such a Yugoslav-wide option was off the table, and peace efforts turned to focus on BiH alone: despite the admission after the event by Owen (1995, 54) that he and Vance 'never shifted from the view that peace in the former

Yugoslavia depended, above all else, on a Belgrade-Zagreb rapprochement'. The DPA also maintained BiH's borders as those of the former Yugoslav republic. This idea had a much stronger genealogy in previous peace agreements, being central to plans such as those agreed at Lisbon and London in 1992, that put forward by the Contact Group in 1994, and that promoted by US National Security Advisor Anthony Lake in August 1995 (Silber and Little 1996, 219–20, 261, 335–37, 361).

These are some of the ways in which the 'international aggression' discourse found its way into the DPA. However, this was not at the expense of the 'ethnic war' account: rather, as the next section shows, these contradictory framings were made to work together through the presence of what I call the 'Balkans' supplement, which allowed both the 'ethnic war' and the 'international aggression' discourses to operate together in the DPA through an undecidable 'Balkans' understanding of the conflict. Similar to my identification of the 'two communities' thesis as a 'productive supplement' in chapter 2, I argue that the 'Balkans' supplement is a productive operation that allows the contradictory conflict framings to operate together, while tracing its role in the final mediation efforts during the war in BiH.


## THE 'BALKANS' SUPPLEMENT

In her detailed and astute study *Imagining the Balkans*, Maria Todorova charts the cultural origins and political effects of the designator 'Balkans'. Beginning with its usage as a purely geographical moniker from the fifteenth century, for the mountain range that still bears the name, she traces the spatial and connotational expansion of the word. She notes how 'Balkans' became a Romantic term, favoured by poets and travel writers, to describe the wider geographic region of 'South-Eastern Europe'. It was in this literary context that the word first became synonymous with notions of antiquity and of the past (Todorova 1997, 22). This idea of the 'Balkans' as 'ancient lands' seeped in history was linked in with Enlightenment ideals of progress and teleology to feed into the dichotomous thinking regarding 'East-and-West', whereby those in Western Europe see themselves as more politically and culturally advanced than their backward Eastern neighbours (Hansen 2006, 102–104). As Todorova (1997, 7) puts it, Western characterisations of the 'Balkans' as a geographic and cultural entity were bound-up in 'a discourse utilizing the construct as a powerful symbol conveniently located outside historical time'. The Balkans was thus seen as a land left behind by the onward march of history that had carried the West into modernity.

In the early twentieth century, ideas of Balkan backwardness were overlaid with notions of the region as a centre of conflict and violence. The Balkan

Wars of 1912–1913 displayed the belligerence of these nations to the world, and with the assassination of Archduke Franz Ferdinand in Sarajevo in June 1914, and the subsequent slide to global war, the term 'Balkans' was tied yet further to ideas of negativity, danger and menace. Todorova (1997, 33–34) notes how the term 'Balkanisation' was first used after the First World War to designate disintegration, conflict and internecine strife. Over the next eighty years, 'Balkans' and 'Balkanisation' became international stereotypes (Hansen 2006, 104–106; Todorova 1997, 122), bywords for anarchy and violence. The conceptual anchoring to the geographical region 'the Balkans' was loosened and, by the end of the Cold War, 'Balkanisation' was used to describe a variety of social and political ills in the US, Europe and the world (Campbell 1998, 166–68; Todorova 1997, 35–36). Such use of the term often strayed into the realm of pure hyperbole. In 1993, for example, the author of an article in the journal *Commentary* gave the title 'The Age of Balkanisation' to a piece bemoaning the rise of separatism and fragmentation that accompanied the demise of the Cold War system – whether this took the form of political collapse in Czechoslovakia and Yugoslavia, the resurgence of racism in Europe, or the rise of identity politics in America. The threat posed by divisive political and cultural movements is perceived to be so great that the author states that 'the multiculturalist doctrine that is fragmenting [US] universities as well as our intellectual life, and the "ethnic cleansing" of the Serbs, belong to the same troubling cultural and historic moment' (Glynn 1993, 24). 'Balkanisation' is used here as the embodiment of all the post-modern evils chipping away at the empire of reason.

As well as being a region placed far behind Western Europe on the imagined teleological schema of political advancement, the Balkans has been represented as spatially distinct, as a region incongruent with Europe. The region was geographically other-ed from Europe in large part due to its historical incorporation into the Ottoman Empire, a situation which persevered in parts of the region until the early twentieth century. The communist nature of Tito's post–Second World War regime also separated Yugoslavia from capitalist Western Europe. Dichotomies of West–East were thus over-laid with those of European–Ottoman, capitalist–communist, and democracy–dictatorship to create a 'symbolic geography of eastern inferiority' (Bakić-Hayden and Hayden 1992, 3–4), with the Balkans relegated to the 'other' of Europe 'proper' (Coles 2007a, 258–59). The Balkans has thus long occupied a curious position within the Western political imaginary – in Europe but not of Europe, touched by civilisation but not civilised. Even when under communism the status of the area remained ambiguous, as Tito broke from Stalin's Soviet sphere to play a leading role in the Non-Aligned Movement.

When conflict broke out in the former Yugoslavia in 1991, therefore, the 'Balkans' discourse was invoked and revitalised as a grid of intelligibility through which the international community could make sense of the events, without having to grapple with the complexities of the conflict or the concrete political causes and objectives. As Todorova (1997, 136) states, 'the persistent use of "Balkan" for the Yugoslav war . . . rekindled old stereotypes and licensed indiscriminate generalizations about the region'. I now examine how references to the 'Balkans' operate as a supplement which allowed the 'ethnic war' and 'international aggression' accounts of the conflict to bleed together during the final stages of the international engagements with the war in BiH.

## The Productive Operation of the 'Balkans' Supplement

When references are made to the 'Balkans' in accounts associated above with the 'ethnic war' discourse, the 'Balkans' supplement operates to give additional strength to these ethnically-based analyses of the violence. For instance, and as quoted above, Owen (1995, 1) starts his text with the assertion: 'Nothing is simple in the Balkans. History pervades everything, and the complexities confound even the most careful study'. Two marks can be made here on a 'Balkans bingo' card: a region steeped in history, and one in which the historical intricacies create a labyrinth of meaning inaccessible to outsiders. Owen (1995, 3) continues a couple of pages later:

> History points to a tradition in the Balkans of a readiness to solve disputes by the taking up of arms and acceptance of the forceful or even negotiated movements of people as the consequence of war. It points to a culture of violence within a crossroad of civilization where three religions . . . have divided communities and on occasion become the marks of identification in a dark and virulent nationalism.

Three pages in, and we almost have the full house: the Balkans 'tradition' is described as one in which resorting to violence is always close to hand, and where religion and nationalism combine to create a 'culture of violence' where war is used as an instrument of population exchange. Such a sentiment runs throughout the book, with Owen (1995, 387, 401) concluding that a 'Balkan solution had been imposed on the battlefield' through the HV and ARBiH offensives in the summer of 1995, and warning that 'they do not forget in the Balkans', implying that the population shifts of that summer will have repercussions. It is hard to escape an impression that Owen believes such violence is somehow uniquely prevalent in the Balkans: at the very least, he is rearticulating such a stereotypical view through his choice of language. In this text, therefore, the 'Balkans' supplement is operating to give additional weight and strength to the argument that primordial chains of belonging drove actors towards violent conflict in BiH.

What is more interesting, however, is the references made to an apparent 'Balkans temperament' in texts associated above with the 'international aggression' discourse. In these instances, the 'Balkans' supplement is operating to explain the predilection of Balkan leaders to resort to violence, their willingness to mobilise ethnic differences to do so, and their inability to engage in rational politics without outside assistance. Holbrooke, for example, who I associated above with the 'international aggression' discourse, resorts to the stereotypical language of the 'Balkans' framing in his account of the final stages of the peace negotiations. The Bosnian Serbs are singled out for this treatment when Holbrooke (1999, 152) writes that the 'Western mistake over the previous four years had been to treat the [Bosnian] Serbs as rational people with whom one could argue, negotiate, compromise, and agree. In fact, they respected only force or an unambiguous and credible threat to use it'. Again, a 'Balkan mentality' of the willingness to use, or respond to the use, of force is evident here. Holbrooke (1999, 166) then invokes the idea of the Balkans as a land of feuds and retaliatory killings, when writing that while '[r]evenge might be a central part of the ethos of the Balkans . . . American policy could not be party to it'. We have here not only the rearticulation of a 'Balkans' stereotype, but its insertion into a dichotomy by which rational 'American policy' is raised above the violent 'Balkan ethos', in a manner which erases the common utilisation of 'revenge' motifs in US foreign policy and military action, from wars against Native Americans to Pearl Harbor, September 11 and beyond (Cox and Wood 2017; Liberman 2014). Holbrooke (1999, 165) also expresses another aspect of the 'Balkans' discourse when describing a meeting between Tuđman and Izetbegović. With the exchange going very badly, the Bosnian Foreign Finister Muhamed Sacirbey asks Holbrooke to intervene, and once Holbrooke requests permission to comment on the discussion 'both Presidents abruptly turned toward me. It was suddenly clear that they wanted the United States to tell them what to do – a strange moment, which we often recalled later. An aspect of the Balkan character was revealed anew: once engaged, these leaders needed outside supervision to stop themselves from self-destruction'. The description of this encounter reconstructs an idea of Balkan political juvenility, a quasi-imperialist discourse of their unsuitability for self-government, their tendency to descend into violent conflict if left unsupervised, and their need for benevolent assistance if they are to resolve their problems peacefully. The 'Balkans' supplement is therefore working here to give additional strength to the idea that outside actors (in this case, the US) are capable of standing outside the streams of history that force the ethnic groups of BiH into conflict, and thus able to intervene into this temporal vortex in order drag the belligerents into peaceful modernity.

Some commentators, while not affirming their belief in the reality of a 'Balkans temperament', seem to accept that parties to the conflict *themselves*

believe that the Balkans is a place of violent animosities and historical grav-
ity. Bildt (1998, 46), for instance, expresses such a sentiment when discussing two key figures in the conflict, Tuđman and Bosnian Serb military leader
Ratko Mladić. He views Tuđman as the leader who most clearly expressed his
politics as managing the conflict between national groups, and believing that
'the clash of civilizations is at the core of the conflicts in this part of Europe',
meaning that 'cultural and ethnic separation is the only possible long-term
solution'. He then recounts his first meeting with Mladić, stating that, 'just
as I expected', he gave 'a long and bitter review of all the alleged injustices
throughout Serb history'. 'He seemed both unwilling and unable', Bildt
(1998, 53–54) continues, 'to extricate himself from this burden of history',
acting as if he was engaged in 'an everlasting struggle against the injustices
to which history and the rest of the world had subjected the Serb people'. It
therefore seems that Biltd *believed* that these *leaders believed* in the determining hand of history in the Balkans.

This is therefore an example of the 'Balkans' supplement operating as
an undecidable which allows the 'ethnic war' and 'international aggression' discourses to function together. In cases such as this, an outside actor
dismisses the reality of the idea that 'history pervades everything' in the
Balkans, while still stating that the actors *within BiH believe* that 'history
pervades everything'. While such an observer might think the conflict was
driven by political motivations and maintained by the violent mobilisation of
constructed ethnic identities, if they *simultaneously* believe that actors on the
ground accept these constructed ethnic identities as 'real', then this 'reality'
of ethnic conflict (from the perspective of the warring parties) will be seen
as a factor driving the violence, and thus something that must be grappled
with in attempts to resolve the conflict. The 'Balkans' supplement thus operates here, enacting the slippage between the 'ethnic war' and 'international
aggression' discourses, making the two contradictory understandings work
together productively. It also operates here as another means of instigating
a hierarchy between the interveners and the actors on the ground, with those
outside BiH asserting their ability to see the political machinations behind
calls to ethnic mobilisation, while those in BiH are seen as imprisoned in their
primordial fantasies.

The presence of the 'Balkans' supplement can also be identified within
the 'international aggression' discourse, when the international or interstate
conflict is coded in *ethnic* terms. This is an observation made by Woodward
(1995, 14), who argues that those who saw the conflict in BiH as 'external
aggression were drawn increasingly toward the same conclusion' as those
who saw it as a civil war and accepted the need for an 'ethnically defined
solution', as 'they defined that aggression and its victims ethnically – Serbs
against Bosnian Muslims or Croats'. What could have been seen only as a

conflict based on strategic control of land, and the desire to carve-out viable territories containing as many resources as possible,[13] was analysed through the 'Balkans' supplement as also a contest for historically and emotionally meaningful land (Chollet 2005, 173; Holbrooke 1999, 286), and one driven by the inability to accommodate ethnic groups within national territory. The 'international aggression' discourse therefore becomes conflated with the 'ethnic war' discourse through the productive operation of the 'Balkans' supplement.

This is important to note, not just because of the intellectual slippages it generates in academic accounts of the violence in BiH, but because it had concrete effects on the course of the conflict, through its role in the international engagements with the closing stages of the war. As noted in many discussions of the HV and ARBiH offensives in the summer and autumn of 1995, the strategic use of NATO airstrikes was deployed in order to tip the balance of the war in favour of the Croats and Bosnians, but without going so far as to precipitate total Bosnian Serb collapse. In other words, while recognising the *international* dimension to the conflict through the support given to the HV in expelling the Krajina Serb population from the territory of Croatia (Silber and Little 1996, 360–61), the *ethnically* determined 51–49 territorial split of BiH (as discussed above) was still the guiding aim. Any military gains on the Croat or Bosnian government side that jeopardised this aspiration was to be avoided. Burg and Shoup (2000, 352–53), for instance, argue that the NATO airstrikes were undertaken in order to compel Bosnian Serb forces to pull back from Sarajevo while not altering the wider territorial balance. Chollet (2005, 94) also makes references to the need to maintain the 51–49 split and not let the Croat-Bosnian offensive gain too much territory, while Bildt (1998, 112) refers to 'all the horrors of the summer and early autumn months as the "cleaning of the map" in preparation for the final battle over territory at the peace talks themselves', suggesting a conterminous logic between the war and the peace negotiations.[14]

Owen (1995, 364), however, provides the strongest evidence of the undecidability between the 'international aggression' and 'ethnic war' discourse in this period, by suggesting that NATO did not enforce the no-fly zone over BiH in order to *allow* Bosnian Serb airpower to be used to defend Banja Luka. This shows that even when the NATO powers had seemingly accepted the international, and specifically Serb, culpability for the war, and were actively engaged in bombing raids against Serb military forces, they were simultaneously acting *against* the 'international aggression' discourse, by allowing the Serb 'aggressors' to defend themselves: and all to ensure the territorial balance that could allow for a negotiated de facto ethnic partition of BiH would not be destroyed. This chimes with what Holbrooke (1999, 160) claims to have told Tuđman that summer: 'I urge you to go as far as you can, but not to take Banja Luka'. Simms (2002, 336), meanwhile, laments that by this stage of the war the Clinton administration had accepted 'the partition-ist, ethnically exclusive, and "realistic" paradigms which had characterized all previous European – particularly British – solutions', with their refusal to push the Croat-Bosnian military advantage towards the creation of a unitary BiH.

Through these practical and highly impactful decisions, the 'international aggression' discourse was folded back into the 'ethnic war' discourse, by reference to the wider 'Balkans' context in which the war was understood to take place. With ethnic rivalry seen as the norm in the 'Balkans' space of BiH, either due to its determining effect on identity, or due to the mobilisation of ethnic difference by manipulative political leaders, a solution providing some degree of parity between competing ethnic groups was exalted as the only option for success. The 'defeat' or routing of the Bosnian Serbs in the summer of 1995 could not be countenanced by such an understanding, as this would be seen as simply laying the groundwork for later iterations of ethnic bloodletting, either when resurgent Serbs seek their revenge due to innate eth-nic hatreds, or by providing material for Serbian politicians to utilise in their mobilisation of ethnic hatreds. The 'Balkans' supplement therefore operates at this key moment in the war to merge the two contradictory conflict fram-ings into an understanding that can function as the basis for the peace settle-ment that the Clinton administration was ready to impose: one that accepted Serb (and Croatian) culpability for the violence by maintaining BiH within its Yugoslav-era borders, but simultaneously viewed the conflict as ethnically-motivated by enshrining the 51–49 territorial split.

## CONCLUSION

This chapter has argued that the contradictory conflict framings that moti-vated the various attempts to negotiate a peaceful settlement to the conflict in BiH were able to work together due to a process of supplementation, which allowed the 'ethnic war' and 'international aggression' discourses to operate through an undecidable 'Balkans' understanding of the conflict. The practi-cal importance of this supplementation in the closing stages of the war was stressed, when I detailed how the 'Balkans' supplement allowed the war to be seen *simultaneously* as a consequence of the international aggression of the Serbs, *and* as an ethnic conflict requiring an ethno-territorial solution. This stage of the peace interventions thus generated an understanding of the conflict as inherently shaped by its 'Balkans' context: an understanding which then informed the peace settlement provided through the DPA. As with the ethno-national account of the Northern Ireland conflict, it is important to highlight what is left out of such an account, whether that is peace movements such as the anti-war demonstrations held in Sarajevo in April 1992,[15] or the maintenance of class-based politics in the city of Tuzla (Filic 2018), which indicate how politics was not uniformly or universally reduced to a typical 'Balkans' struggle during this time (as well as being the precursors to the 'non-ethnic' politics I will discuss in chapter 5). It is also crucial to stress the contingency of the process that led to the signing of the DPA: rather than being a case of outside actors finally discovering the 'secret key' to unlock the mediation efforts after a long process of policy learning, this was the stumbling upon a formula for a peace settlement that happened to be acceptable to the key parties at this specific moment in time, and backed up by sufficient political will and military force.

Chapter 5 will explore how the 'Balkans' supplement became embedded in the DPA, and the impact this has had on the post-conflict politics of BiH. In tracing the impact of the supplementation through the peace agreements, I will move from my first key Derridean term (the supplement) to my second: that of *différance*. This term will be used to examine how the process of supplementation generates the post-conflict environment in BiH not as conflict over or annulled, but as conflict *differed* and *deferred*. Certain aspects of the post-conflict politics of BiH, namely the consociational political and electoral system, allow a (re)enactment of a 'Balkans' struggle between ethnic groups, while other aspects of politics (seen most prominently through legal challenges and protest movements) seek to contest the mobilisation of ethnic identity by the typically 'Balkan' political leaders in BiH. Therefore, by identifying the presence of the 'Balkans' supplement within the DPA, I argue this agreement serves to *complicate*, rather than simplify, the post-conflict political landscape of BiH by producing a political system that replicates the contradictory accounts of the conflict discussed in this chapter, and thus one already in a process of deconstruction. Before making this argument, however, chapter 4 will turn to the post-conflict situation in Northern Ireland.

*Part II*

# DEFERRING CONFLICT

## Chapter 4

# Post-Conflict Northern Ireland

## Différance *and Devolution*

As discussed in the previous two chapters, the GFA and DPA brought peace to Northern Ireland and BiH in 1998 and 1995, respectively. In each case, the settlements bequeathed new political arrangements based on power-sharing principles designed to prevent a return to violent hostilities. The political systems of both societies are born out of these agreements designed as much to end a conflict as to provide for effective governance. Legacies of violence thus hang heavy in Northern Ireland and BiH. Beyond the imprint of conflict on their political structures, issues of post-conflict commemoration and justice feature regularly in political and social debate, whether this is around inquests into unsolved murders by both state and paramilitary actors in Northern Ireland (Lundy 2009; 2011), or on the contested issues of war crimes and genocide in BiH (Kent 2013; Orentlicher 2018). Northern Ireland and BiH are therefore commonly considered to be post-conflict societies.

This chapter interrogates what it means to be a post-conflict society, with specific reference to Northern Ireland. A similar analysis will be undertaken in relation to BiH in chapter 5. In its common-sense and everyday usage, the term 'post-conflict' implies a society which has moved on from a position of conflict to a relative (if potentially unstable) peace. A time of conflict has been and gone, replaced by a time of peace. The effects of the conflict may still be widely felt, whether through physical destruction, the existence of refugees, displaced persons or traumatised populations, the continuing existence of barriers and divisions erected during the conflict, or the long-term socio-economic impacts of the violence. In societies where the passage from conflict to post-conflict is brought about by negotiated settlements mediated by outside parties, these effects are usually the target of some form of peacebuilding or conflict-transformation measures.[1] The legacies of violence are therefore often recognised as something to be worked through in the

post-conflict period, but the qualitative change brought about by the transition
from a conflict to a post-conflict situation is seen as the necessary foundation
for this transitional process. A fundamental change in context is thus implied
by the passage across the threshold of conflict to post-conflict status.

By continuing to utilise the Derridean concept of the supplement, and by
drawing out its explicitly temporal dimensions through reference to the notion
of *différance*, this chapter unsettles the common-sense understanding of post-
conflict politics and society. Rather than viewing the 'post-conflict' period in
Northern Ireland as truly distinct from the time of the 'conflict', as something
marked by the passage from one specific temporal state to the other, I argue
(following Derrida) that one is the *différance* of the other. While recognising
that the period of the 'post-conflict' *is different* from the period of the 'conflict', this is not to say that we have moved on the linear temporal schema
from a time of 'conflict' to a time of 'post-conflict': instead, the 'conflict' and
'post-conflict', as they are understood from the perspective of contemporary
politics, are to be seen as the *différance* of each other, generated by *deferral*
and *delay* through the detour of the GFA. The GFA is thus seen as allowing
for the determination of what the 'conflict' was – the dates within which it
unfolded, the key actors, its nature and its causes – as well as allowing for
the identification of the time *after* the peace agreement as the 'post-conflict'
period. Labelling the relationship one of *différance* focuses attention on the
central role of the peace agreement in constituting the distinction between
conflict and post-conflict, allowing for the post-conflict to be understood, not
through a dichotomous or oppositional logic as the conflict ended or annulled,
but as conflict *differed* and *deferred*.

The central aim of this chapter is to examine how the GFA, and the political institutions it inaugurated, embody an undecidable 'two communities'
understanding of the conflict, viewing it as both driven by a fixed reality of
opposed groups who must be accommodated, and as driven by contingent
political grievances that can be transformed. By identifying the presence
of both the ethno-national account and the 'two communities' supplement
within the text of the GFA, I argue that the 'two communities' understanding
of the conflict is in a very real sense *constituted* through the text of the GFA,
and thus generated as something that is then read backwards into the historical record, rather than simply providing a 'prior' understanding of the conflict
that the GFA then reflects. The political environment that has been generated by the devolution of power from Westminster to the Northern Ireland
Assembly and Executive is to be seen as allowing what I call a *(re)enactment*
of a 'two communities' struggle. I use this term, with the 're' in parentheses,
to focus attention on two key aspects of how the post-conflict period is tied to
the conflict through a process of *différance*. First, it highlights how this post-
conflict politics is not a simple re-enactment of the conflict in its totality, as

'the troubles' was more than a simple clash of 'two communities', but something driven by a range of social, political, economic and military factors, and prosecuted by multiple actors with diverse motivations.[2] Thus, the post-conflict period *is different* from the period referred to as the 'conflict': particularly when we consider (as I do below) how the GFA empowers a politics which seek to move beyond this 'two communities' understanding. Secondly, it demonstrates how the performance of the 'two communities' struggle in the post-conflict period gives strength to historic understandings of the conflict as a clash between 'two communities', in a retroactive movement.

My argument in this chapter then has one further step. The presence of the 'two communities' supplement within the GFA is seen as transmitting the undecidability of this supplement into the present, generating institutions that are already in a process of deconstruction. I therefore move beyond simplistic arguments that contemporary politics in Northern Ireland is nothing more than a re-staging of the conflict 'by other means': instead, by focusing on the *contradictions* of the ethno-national account that requires supplementation by the 'two communities' understanding, I am alert to the currents of contemporary politics in Northern Ireland that view the 'two communities' as capable of transformation. A central focus of my argument is that *both* the divisive politics that replicates the conflict between the 'two communities', generating dysfunction and collapse, *and* the (potentially) transformative politics that exists in Northern Ireland, are rooted in the GFA: the former is not a symptom of the betrayal of the 'spirit' of the GFA, or a consequence of its mechanisms being twisted for the political ends of two parties (Sinn Féin and the DUP) who had little or nothing to do with the negotiations of the devolved institutions[3]; and the latter do not arise in spite of or in opposition to the political structures created by the GFA. Instead, *both* these contradictory currents arise from the *internal undecidability* of the GFA.

I am not the first to observe a contradiction in the GFA: Oberschall and Palmer (2005, 77) note this same inconsistency between the political institutions created by the GFA which entrench division and the sections on 'human rights, justice, policing and equality' which attempt 'to foster greater integration between the two communities'. In their view, this contradiction 'obstructs the emergence of a non-sectarian, centrist governing coalition' and 'works against the goals of peaceful coexistence and inter-communal reconciliation'. However, their approach is one of attempting to *resolve* this contradiction through reform of the GFA, specifically through changing its incentive structure to favour a 'winning coalition of the middle drawn from conciliatory unionist, nationalist, and centrist groups' that will work towards 'cross-community cooperation and inter-communal reconciliation'. I follow Graff-McRae (2010, 15) in employing a deconstructive approach which 'does not attempt to resolve contradictions'. This is not simply due to my theoretical attachments, but because of my scepticism of piecemeal reform of the GFA that does not challenge the 'two communities' supplement: indeed, Oberschall and Palmer's suggestions give strength to these tropes with their talk of 'greater integration between the two communities'.

My argument in this chapter therefore presents these contradictions as the outcome of processes of supplementation and *différance* that reveal the GFA to be already in a process of deconstruction. This is because the GFA generates a 'communal politics' through the institutional safeguards and community designations put in place as the basis for power-sharing government between the 'two communities', allowing for a (re)enactment of a 'two communities' struggle between 'communal parties' (a term I use to refer to those who choose to designate as one of the 'two communities' upon taking seats in the Assembly, that is, as either 'Unionist' or 'Nationalist'); while it *simultaneously* empowers others to try to move beyond the 'two communities' paradigm. It is the clash between these contradictory tendencies, both of which arise *from within* the GFA, which generates the endemic breakdowns in the political institutions. The GFA is thus already undergoing deconstruction, in a process arising from within that text, and not as the result of external forces brought to bear by those who would challenge or overturn it.

The first section of the chapter provides a close reading of the GFA, in order to locate within the text the contradictory strands of the ethno-national account, and the productive supplement of the 'two communities' thesis (as introduced in chapter 2). The second section then indicate how the post-conflict electoral politics of Northern Ireland can be read as (re)enacting a 'two communities' struggle, particularly as communal parties considered the more 'extreme'[4] proponents of Unionism and Nationalism have entrenched their electoral dominance, and as this has produced repeated deadlock over contentious identity issues such as parades, flags and language. Crucially, this is *not* to be seen as a simple re-staging of 'the troubles', as the conflict was *not* (only) a clash of 'two communities'. This point is important to underline, as it is central to my argument that the GFA plays a role in constituting an understanding of the conflict that is then read back into the historical record. The third section then outlines a different vision of post-conflict politics in Northern Ireland, by highlighting how, both in the formal sphere of electoral politics, and in informal spheres of art and culture, trends and currents can be identified which view the 'two communities' binary as capable of transformation. By exploring the (admittedly mixed) electoral record of 'non-communal parties' (a term I use to refer to those, such as the Alliance Party, the Green Party and People Before Profit (PBP), who designate as 'Other' in the Assembly), and the 'Temple' and Turas projects which contest fixed notions of identity and belonging, the section complicates the picture of post-conflict politics in Northern Ireland, and demonstrates how the GFA is already in a process of deconstruction.

## RECONSTRUCTING THE GOOD FRIDAY AGREEMENT

The GFA was negotiated between the governments of the UK and Ireland, a cross-spectrum of Northern Ireland political parties representing both Republican and Loyalist paramilitaries and the wider strands of Nationalism and Unionism, with outside mediation spearheaded by former-US senator George Mitchell (Hennessey 2000: 100–102). While ten local parties gained access to the peace talks through special elections held in May 1996, the exact number engaged fluctuated over time. Sinn Féin were only admitted after the renewal of the PIRA ceasefire in September 1997 (McGrattan 2010a, 158), while this triggered a walk-out by the DUP and UKUP (Wolff 2001, 168). According to the memoires of key figures involved in the final stages of the negotiations (Ahern 2009; Blair 2011; Mowlam 2002; Powell 2008), this was a fraught process, taking place in the claustrophobic confines of Castle Buildings on the Stormont Estate, with many false dawns and occasions when all seemed lost.

In this section, I focus on a close reading of the text of the GFA[5] itself, rather than engaging with the memoires of those involved, or the second-hand accounts from journalists and commentators. This reading is undertaken with the 'two communities' supplement in mind. I highlight the presence of this productive supplement in the GFA, revealing how it complicates the text, and how it allows contradictory understandings of the conflict – as something generated by the existence of the entrenched and opposed 'two communities', *and* as something arising from contingent political grievances that can be transformed and transcended – to exist and operate together within the GFA. This undecidability is to be seen as generating the contradictory political currents discussed later in the chapter (i.e. those which allow a (re)enactment of a 'two communities' struggle, and those which seek to move beyond the 'two communities' paradigm), thus indicating how the GFA contains the source of its own deconstruction.

### Commitments and Constitutional Issues

The GFA begins with a 'Declaration of Support', through which the participants commend the agreement to the people of Ireland. Central tenets of the peace process, such as commitments to reconciliation, tolerance and human rights, and the use of exclusively democratic and peaceful means, are re-affirmed. This section frames the conflict as one brought about by 'the substantial differences between our continuing, and equally legitimate, political aspirations', thus suggesting an analysis akin to the 'competing national aspirations' aspect of the ethno-national account. No explicit references are made to the 'two communities' thesis, beyond the vague language of 'partnership, equality and mutual respect'. The 'competing national aspirations' understanding of the conflict then takes centre-stage in the 'Constitutional Issues' section, where the two governments affirm their respect for the principle of consent, and pledge to put this into effect through legislative change in the UK, and constitutional change in Ireland. Both governments make a new commitment in this section to 'recognise the birthright of all the people of Northern Ireland to identify themselves and be accepted as Irish or British, or both, as they may so choose'. Previously, Irish legislation claimed all persons born on the island of Ireland as citizens (under the 1956 Citizenship and Nationality Act): this was now modified with a recognition of the right of persons born in Northern Ireland to choose if they wished to exercise their right to claim Irish citizenship (Ó Caoindealbháin 2006, 14). This section also made a pledge to retain this dual-citizenship right in the event of any 'future change in the status of Northern Ireland' – that is, in the event of a united Ireland. This was shaped by Sinn Féin's acceptance in 1994 of the right of people in a future united Ireland to retain a British passport (Tonge 2002, 149). Annex B of this section represents a substantial achievement of the GFA, in that it sets-out a process for replacing the territorial claim on the entire island of Ireland contained in Articles 2 and 3 of the Irish constitution, with a recognition of citizenship rights as discussed above, alongside an aspirational statement on Irish unity: but one that recognises that this will only come about through 'the consent of a majority of the people, democratically expressed, in both jurisdictions in the island'. As Aughey (2005, 93) perceptively notes, this ironically inserts another veto point into any process for achieving Irish unity – this new one held by the electorate of Ireland – after decades of armed struggle attempting to remove the British veto over Irish unity.

While this section is largely within the parameters of the 'competing national aspirations' account of the conflict, in recognising overlapping citizenship rights and the role of British and Irish territorial and sovereign claims in producing the overall framework of the conflict, there is one example here of the operation of the 'two communities' supplement. The section affirms that whichever government has sovereign jurisdiction over the current territory of Northern Ireland will exercise that authority

> with rigorous impartiality on behalf of all the people in the diversity of their
> identities and traditions and shall be founded on the principles of full respect
> for, and equality of, civil, political, social and cultural rights, of freedom from

discrimination for all citizens, and of parity of esteem and of just and equal treatment for the identity, ethos, and aspirations of both communities.

The implication here is that national aspirations are bounded within 'both communities' who must be treated fairly and equally. This is the first of many references in the GFA to 'parity of esteem', something which is 'articulated (though never defined) throughout' the document (Conrad 2008, 117). This is also the first instance when a clause which begins with universalising language of equality and rights ends with references to 'two communities' (in this case, framed as 'both communities'). I will return to the latter of these themes below.

However, this section is also important in highlighting the instability of the 'two communities' thesis, and its operation as an undecidable supplement which (as Derrida argues) does not provide full presence to that which it is added to. By providing persons in Northern Ireland with the right to hold both a British and an Irish passport, the GFA is recognising the overlapping nature of these identities: that persons may view themselves as *both* Irish and British, rather than seeing Irish and British identity as an either/or binary. This clause has also allowed many people to pragmatically claim an Irish passport in order to retain their EU citizenship despite the UK leaving the EU.[6] The mechanism by which the GFA allows for equal recognition of the 'two communities' (in the sense of those identifying as Irish and those identifying as British), thus *simultaneously* allows for the transcendence of that binary. Thompson makes a similar argument about the larger concept of 'parity of esteem', which he views as embodying an array of different, and even contradictory, logics. For Thompson (2003, 70), parity of esteem must be understood as part 'of a political project that seeks to shape each of the two traditions into forms which are acceptable to the other', presupposing an idea of cultural transformation. By providing space not only for the recognition of 'two communities', but for the 'transformation' of these identities into something new (i.e. a shared idea of 'British-Irish identity', or of 'Northern Irish' identity divorced from traditional Unionist or Nationalist aspirations), the parity of esteem agenda can be seen as challenging, as well as reinforcing, community identification. This tendency to simultaneously reinforce the 'two communities' binary, and allow for its transcendence, is a strong example of how the 'two communities' supplement replicates the contradictions of the ethno-national account, even while this supplement allows the GFA to function as the basis of the current political institutions.

## Cross-Community Power-Sharing

The GFA then turns to 'Strand One: Democratic Institutions in Northern Ireland'. This section provides for the creation of an Assembly, with

Members of the Legislative Assembly (MLAs) elected using the Single-Transferable Vote (STV) method, to oversee the devolution of various aspects of public policy from Westminster to Belfast. To insure against a return to the Unionist-majority and single-party rule that characterised the Northern Ireland Parliament in the years 1921–1972, a variety of 'safeguards' are instituted. Initially these measures are framed in terms of protecting 'the rights and interests of all sides of the community' and ensuring that 'all sections of the community can participate and work together successfully in the operation of these institutions'. This phrasing suggests that the safeguards are designed to protect minorities and groups outside the 'two community' binary, and is backed-up by the allocation of 'Committee Chairs, Ministers and Committee membership in proportion to party strengths', without reference to 'community' membership, through the 'd'Hondt method' (which I explain below), and by the references to human rights.

However, this soon slips to the language of 'cross-community' support and ensuring 'parity of esteem between the two main communities'. This is seen most clearly in the special arrangements which 'ensure key decisions are taken on a cross-community basis'. For important matters such as the election of the Speaker, approving budgets, and amending standing orders (i.e. the rules governing the functioning of the Assembly), two mechanisms for ensuring 'cross-community' support are listed: first, through 'parallel consent', whereby both an overall majority of MLAs and a majority of both Unionist and Nationalist members present and voting endorse a proposal; or, second, by 'weighted majority', whereby a measure receives support from 60% of all members present and voting, as well as the support of 40% of Unionist members and 40% of Nationalist members present and voting. A right to lodge a 'petition of concern' is also created, whereby thirty MLAs can ensure cross-community support is needed to pass a particular measure.[7] MLAs are required to register a 'designation of identity' as 'Unionist', 'Nationalist' or 'Other', in order to measure cross-community support. As McCrudden, McGarry, O'Leary and Schwartz (2016, 24) note, these rules 'are not based on ethnicity or religion, but on political opinion or national identification', and are thus an example of the focus on the 'national' in the ethno-national account. The 2006 St Andrews Agreement (SAA) made it possible to change community designation during an Assembly term only in the event of switching to another political party, which can be seen as tying group identity more firmly to party affiliation. While the ability to identify as an 'Other' is one way in which the GFA avoids reifying the binary account of Northern Ireland as home to 'two communities' only,[8] the cross-community measures give additional authority to those who designate as 'Unionist' or 'Nationalist'. For the consociational theorist Donald Horowitz (2002, 194–95), this places the GFA firmly in the category of the 'consociational practice' that provides 'groups in the conflict' with 'explicit recognition and [makes] their representatives the bearers of explicit group guarantees'. Thus while identities outside the 'two communities' are recognised and accepted in the Assembly, in practice they have less voting rights than those who identify with the two main community blocs.

As noted by Dixon (2008, 269), the argument that these cross-community measures operate to reify a fixed conception of identity, built around a division between 'two communities', has been made by numerous academics. For Wilford (2010, 139), this creates, in effect, 'two orders of Assembly members: in relation to key decisions there are those whose votes always "count" and those whose votes never do so'. For Conrad (2008, 111–16) the institutionalisation of the 'two communities' model through these mechanisms 'limits access to politics by legitimising only these identities', meaning that any challenges to this binary are either subsumed into communal politics or pushed outside the political process. Little (2004, 27), while accepting that community designation is 'strategically required by the power-sharing impetus which underpins the Agreement', argues in a similar vein that it 'reproduces and substantiates the belief that ethnic divisions in Northern Ireland are static and intransigent, and that rather than challenging these assumptions we should establish institutions which contain them'.

I accept the validity of these criticisms, but I do not think they get to the central issue here. It is not that these measures freeze in place the divisions that were mobilised in the conflict, but rather that they *constitute* a *very particular understanding* of identity that can then be *read back into the historical record*. 'The troubles' was not (only) the clash between 'two communities' in Northern Ireland, but was driven by a range of political actors from within and beyond Northern Ireland, with diverse motivations. By making these institutional arrangements central to the peace agreement, the GFA implies that the conflict was about the competing aspirations of the 'two communities'. The paragraphs of the GFA on the petition of concern and cross-community voting measures are therefore the parts of the text where the 'two communities' supplement is at its strongest, and the parts where its undecidability functions across temporal barriers, gaining strength from historic accounts of the 'two communities' conflict, while strengthening these historical accounts by allowing for the performance of 'communal politics', based on the community designations and other power-sharing arrangements set out in this strand of the GFA, in the present (which I chart in the next section).

In some key aspects, the functioning of the Assembly recognises the plurality of political opinion in Northern Ireland, such as through allowing access to the Executive on the basis of popular support alone, and by avoiding the very strongest manifestations of consociationalism, such as separate electoral rolls and quotas for different identity groups. However, when the requirement for cross-community support is triggered, the votes of MLAs who claim to speak on behalf of one of the 'two communities' become more important than the voice of those who reject such a designation. This process is therefore a concrete manifestation of the tendency evident in the GFA whereby the language of pluralism, equality and human rights becomes transformed into one of protecting group interest, framed in terms of the 'two communities' who must be accommodated and protected. Nowhere is this more apparent than in the paragraph which empowers the Assembly to 'appoint a special committee to examine and report on whether a measure or proposal for legislation is in conformity with equality requirements', such as those found in the European Convention on Human Rights (ECHR).[9] The ratification of any reports from this committee is then subject to cross-community support procedures. We therefore go here from a universal statement of rights and equality, to empowering MLAs designating as members of one of the 'two communities' to determine matters of rights and equality. This is therefore a mechanism for translating individual rights into group rights. The consequences of this slippage can be seen in the use of the petition of concern and cross-community voting to block equality issues such as the legalisation of gay marriage in Northern Ireland, despite simple majority support amongst MLAs for such legislation (Tonge and Evans 2015, 128).[10] While many[11] bemoan the use of an instrument designed to 'protect rights' being used to 'deny rights', this is in fact the correct functioning of the system, when you recognise that it is about protecting the rights of the 'two communities', not other minority group rights or individual rights.

In terms of the Executive, as mentioned above membership of this body is determined purely on the basis of party strength in the Assembly. This 'liberal' element is hardened by the procedure for appointing the joint office of the First Minister (FM) and Deputy First Minister (DFM), who lead the Executive. While the GFA provided for the joint election of the FM and DFM on a cross-community basis, this was amended by the SAA, which empowers the largest parties in each community designation to nominate their chosen candidates. As the Alliance Party (2006) noted at the time, this reform can be seen as a challenge to the 'joint' nature of the office, moving 'in the direction of power-division rather than power-sharing', as well as something which removes the collective authorisation of the FM and DFM by the Assembly. However, it does allow for the possibility of an 'Other'-designating member being elected to one of these offices, if the 'Others' supplant one of the community designations in terms of numbers of MLAs. The rest of the Executive positions are still filled as set out in the GFA, using the proportional d'Hondt method of appointment, which calculates a ranking based on Executive positions available and number of MLAs held by each party, and allows parties to pick ministries in order of this ranking. McGarry and O'Leary (2016,

501–502) strongly support this 'sequential and proportional process' for Executive formation, as it allows parties to select ministries based purely on number of MLAs, and not on any sort of ethno-national logic, in a manner which side-steps the sort of lengthy post-election negotiations that are required in places like BiH before a government can be formed. They note how '[h]ardline parties have incentives to enter government because failure to do so results in their ministerial entitlements going to rival parties, and not in an immediate failure to form the executive', while they are 'able to share power with rivals without having expressly to consent to the correctness of any of their rivals' convictions, or policies'.

Before 2016 this led to what was often referred to as 'mandatory coalitions' of four or five parties though, as McGarry and O'Leary (2016, 509) point out, parties were always free not to take up their ministerial picks, even if strongly encouraged to do so by the selection process. A bill passed in March 2016[12] changed this incentive structure, however, by allowing parties entitled to Executive seats to form an 'Opposition' instead, with attendant rights in terms of posing questions to ministers and time for debating Opposition Business in the Assembly. The UUP and SDLP took up this opportunity, serving as an Opposition from May 2016 until the Assembly's suspension in January 2017 (Tonge 2016). All eligible parties joined the Executive upon the restoration of devolution in January 2020 (which I discuss below). While the d'Hondt method ensures that the Executive is broadly representative of party strengths in the Assembly, it makes it very difficult to generate any sort of 'collective responsibility' (Aughey 2005, 88), and encourages ministers, 'sequestered in their departmental silos, to go on solo policy runs' or 'act unilaterally', resulting in an Executive that lacks 'cohesion, direction and a collectivist style' (Wilford 2010, 144). McEvoy (2015, 80) labels the decisions of the first Sinn Féin ministers, Bairbre de Brún and Martin McGuinness, on maternity services and the abolition of post-primary academic selection, respectively, as early 'instances of ministers operating their "ministerial fiefdoms"'. More recently, the scandal over the gross mismanagement by DUP ministers of the Renewable Heat Incentive (RHI), which brought down the Executive in January 2017, can be seen as a consequence of a lack of 'joined up' government or Executive-wide responsibility, as the financial issues stored up by the botched scheme were not placed under the widespread scrutiny that may be expected in a 'cabinet'-style government, where collective responsibility operates (Meagher 2017).

## Relationships, Rights and Reviews

In the following sections of the GFA, on 'Strand Two: North/South Ministerial Council' and 'Strand Three: British-Irish Council', the 'competing national aspirations' understanding of the conflict is most identifiable, dealing as they do with the 'totality of relationships' between Britain and Ireland, and attempting to find a political formula that can accommodate both the aspiration towards a united Ireland and the determination to retain Northern Ireland's place in the UK. One key aspect of the North/South bodies is that they are 'mutually inter-dependent' with the Assembly, meaning that one cannot function without the other. Described in Blair and Powell's memories as akin to the Cold War 'mutually assured destruction' doctrine, this was designed to prevent Nationalists sabotaging the Assembly then using the North/South bodies as a proxy for a united Ireland, and to prevent Unionists sabotaging the North/South bodies and using the Assembly to entrench Northern Ireland's position in the union. Strand Three also contains details on new inter-governmental instruments to supersede those of the AIA: a sop to placate Unionists by allowing them to claim the destruction of the hated Maryfield secretariat and other AIA institutions.[13]

The GFA then goes on to engage with wider aspects of the peace process, starting with a section on 'Rights, Safeguards and Equality of Opportunity'. The presence of the 'two communities' supplement can be identified at the very beginning of this section, when a substantive list of civil liberties is placed in a context of 'the recent history of communal conflict'. This is then made explicit in the paragraph on the 'new Northern Ireland Human Rights Commission', which is 'invited to consult and to advise on the scope for defining, in Westminster legislation, rights supplementary to those in the [ECHR], to reflect the particular circumstances of Northern Ireland'. These 'additional rights', the paragraph continues, may 'reflect the principles of mutual respect for the identity and ethos of both communities and parity of esteem'. The language of universal human rights is therefore being (literally, in this case) supplemented with that of the group rights of the 'two communities'. This is also institutionalised in the composition of the Human Rights Commission, which is to reflect the 'community balance' of Northern Ireland. Human rights are therefore transformed in this section into group rights, through the supplement of the 'two communities' thesis. In the subsection on 'Economic, Social and Cultural Issues', the discussion of linguistic diversity moves to a more pluralist conception of identity, referencing not only Irish and Ulster-Scots (the languages commonly associated with the Nationalist and Unionist communities, respectively), but also 'the languages of the various ethnic communities, all of which are part of the cultural wealth of the island of Ireland'. The section on 'Policing and Justice', meanwhile, makes various references to 'the community', challenging the bifurcation of the 'two communities' thesis. These examples highlight the undecidability within the GFA, and how it can be seen to simultaneously reify *and* challenge the 'two communities' understanding of identity in Northern Ireland.

The GFA then ends with a re-assertion of inter-governmentalism, detailing the steps that the two governments will take to entrench the terms of the agreement in their domestic, and in international, law. This final section on 'Validation, Implementation and Review' also stretches beyond inter-governmentalism by determining the process by which the GFA will be put to referenda in both jurisdictions in Ireland. While this text may have been the product, as per consociational theory, of elite negotiations – 'an example of elite intervention designed to resolve ethnonationalist conflict', according to Hayes and McAllister (1999, 31) – it was ratified by the electorate of Ireland in May 1998, in a gesture of populism that would have given the typical consociational theorist cause for alarm. This is therefore one point, alongside the (planned, but never implemented) creation of a Civic Forum, the integration and equality agenda, and the external dimensions, that lead Dixon (2005, 363–64) to conclude that the GFA is not consociational.

The reading of the GFA in this section has not been undertaken to come to a position on whether the document is consociational or not: instead, it has sought to demonstrate that the GFA is a *contradictory* document. It contains elements of the 'competing national aspirations' understanding of 'the troubles', which views the conflict as driven by the conflicting political identifications of two ethno-national groups, while maintaining space for these identifications to be transformed; alongside elements of an 'ethnic' understanding of identity as fixed and unchanging, rooted in a 'two communities' binary, the placation of which must be placed at the centre of political life. The following two sections track the unfolding of these contradictions in the post-conflict politics of Northern Ireland, revealing the manners in which the GFA contains the seeds of its own deconstruction.

## THE 'TWO COMMUNITIES' SUPPLEMENT AND POST-CONFLICT POLITICS

The post-conflict electoral politics of Northern Ireland can be characterised by one overriding tendency: a continuity of dominance for parties representing the 'two communities', modified only by a transfer of pre-eminence *within* each of the blocs. While the more 'moderate' Unionist and Nationalist UUP and SDLP were the largest parties in the immediate post-GFA period, since 2003 this mantel has been taken on by the DUP and Sinn Féin, communal parties often considered as more 'extreme' proponents of Unionism and Nationalism. This section examines in detail how the party political and electoral system created by the GFA allows for a (re)enactment of a 'two communities' struggle. This performance of communal politics legitimises the understanding of the conflict embedded within the GFA, as this becomes retroactively justified when contemporary politics appears to follow the conflictual pattern assumed by the 'two communities' thesis. In this way, the 'two communities' supplement operates within the GFA to produce understandings of the 'conflict' and 'post-conflict' as the *différance* of each other.

## 1998–2006: From 'Creative Ambiguity' to 'Acts of Completion'

In the early elections to the Assembly, the ability of voters to use the STV electoral system to transfer votes across numerous parties may have had a moderating effect, as parties such as Sinn Féin sought transfers from more moderate voters within their bloc. However, there is little evidence of the transfer of votes *across* the divide (Reilly 2001, 137–39), and any such transfers that did take place in the first election in June 1998 may be explained, not by the 'centrapetalist' pressures of STV (Aitken 2007, 260), but by the willingness of 'Unionist' electors to transfer votes to Nationalist parties in order to ensure a pro-GFA majority in the Assembly by punishing 'anti-Agreement' Unionist parties such as the DUP and UKUP (Aughey 2005, 96). In any event, early elections saw the moderate UUP and SDLP returned as the largest Unionist and Nationalist parties respectively, with David Trimble and Seamus Mallon being elected to the positions of FM and DFM on 1 July 1998. However, out of the fifty-eight MLAs designating as Unionist, only thirty were from the pro-GFA UUP and PUP, giving them an 'uncomfortably slim majority' over anti-GFA Unionists (Tonge 2002, 191).

The functioning of the Assembly in this period was beset with difficulties, largely over the decommissioning of paramilitary weapons. According to Dixon (2013), Blair can be judged to have misled the people of Northern Ireland during the referendum campaign, by implying that the GFA required decommissioning before paramilitary prisoners could be released, and before Sinn Féin could sit in the Executive. When it became clear that this was not required by the text of the agreement, Dixon argues, Unionist opinion towards the GFA hardened. While the DUP refused outright to sit in the Executive alongside Sinn Féin before the PIRA disarmed, the UUP membership eventually authorised Trimble to take part in an Executive, conditional on acts of PIRA decommissioning within a set timeframe. The first Executive was therefore formed in November 1999, and inaugural meetings of the North/South Ministerial Council and British-Irish Council took place that December. This Executive lasted only seventy-two days, however, collapsing in February 2000 due to a failure to reach agreement on decommissioning. The Assembly as a whole was suspended by the UK government on 11 February 2000. Trimble secured support for the UUP to re-enter the Executive in May 2000, but the failure to make progress on decommissioning by July 2001 led to his resignation as FM (Tonge 2002, 192–95; Wilford 2010, 143). The inability of the parties to agree a route to the restoration of devolution led to another suspension of the Assembly in September 2001. This lasted until November 2001, when three Alliance Party MLAs re-designated as Unionist in order to secure Trimble's re-election as FM (a manoeuvre that is no longer possible after the SAA). This period of devolved government lasted until September 2002, when the police raided Sinn Féin's Assembly offices during investigations into an alleged PIRA spy ring at Stormont. This crisis over the continuing activities of the PIRA led to a long-term suspension of the Assembly between October 2002 and February 2007.

Blair (2011, 189–90) has since labelled this initial stage (up to 2002) as a period of 'creative ambiguity', riven by fudges and inconsistencies. He labels the period from 2002 to 2007, with its stronger focus on the decommissioning of paramilitary weapons, as the 'acts of completion' phase. During this latter period, with direct rule from Westminster being re-imposed, a shift in the electoral fortunes within each bloc took place. With no prospect of devolution being restored, the elections held in November 2003 (postponed from May) saw the DUP and Sinn Féin emerge as the largest parties in their respective blocs. This was unsurprising in the case of Sinn Féin given they had outpolled the SDLP in the 2001 Westminster elections (King 2008, 6), and by 2005 the DUP's electoral ascendency over the UUP was confirmed at all levels (Anthony 2008, 154). By September 2005, meaningful acts of PIRA decommissioning had been completed, providing the impetus for a fresh round of negotiations (McEvoy 2015, 94). When Blair, seeking to secure his legacy as a peacemaker in Ireland while being condemned as a warmonger in the Middle East, brought the DUP and Sinn Féin leadership together in October 2006, alongside the Irish government, the resulting SAA resolved the issues around policing and justice that had prevented joint DUP-Sinn Féin government in Northern Ireland (McEvoy 2015, 94–5; Patterson 2012, 242). The two governments made it clear that failure to reach agreement would have led to the creation of 'new British Irish partnership arrangements to implement' the GFA (HM Government 2006): a clear example of the threat of greater inter-governmentalism, perhaps approaching shared sovereignty, operating as an incentive to make the necessary compromises needed to restore devolved government.[14]

## 2006–2020: Consolidation and Crises

With the DUP and Sinn Féin toping the polls in the March 2007 elections to a restored Assembly, Ian Paisley and Martin McGuinness were appointed as FM and DFM. The two parties have maintained their electoral dominance ever since, creating a 'dyarchy' (Wilford 2010, 135), although there have been two major political disputes in the period since 2006. The first developed as a response to the UK government's austerity agenda, as implemented under the Conservative-Liberal Democrat coalition, in office from 2010 to 2015, and the subsequent Conservative government. Sinn Féin opposition to the implementation of welfare reform in Northern Ireland led to the UK and Irish governments holding talks with the five main parties on this issue. The parameters of these talks was soon expanded beyond austerity and welfare, however, incorporating a series of outstanding peace process issues that were the subject of stalled negotiations in 2013[15]: perhaps this says something about the structure of the political system, which is unable to contain political focus on 'normal' political issues, with such talks transforming into discussions on 'community' issues. The resulting Stormont House Agreement of December 2014, therefore, as well as providing additional welfare funding, also attempted to provide a framework for engaging with the long-running, contentious issues of flags,[16] parades[17] and the legacy of 'the troubles'. Sinn Féin withdrew their support from this agreement in March 2015 (BBC News 2015a), prompting another round of talks on the same issues, resulting in the November 2015 Fresh Start Agreement. Between September and October 2015 this crisis was accentuated by DUP ministers engaging in a cycle of resignation-then-reappointment-then-resignation over alleged PIRA involvement in the murder of Kevin McGuigan (BBC News 2015b). The Assembly passed a motion that month allowing the UK Parliament to implement the austerity agenda in Northern Ireland, with the cuts softened by a relief package worth £585million.

The normality restored by the Fresh Start Agreement did not last long, however, with Sinn Féin's Martin McGuinness resigning as DFM in January 2017, following a scandal about the gross financial mismanagement of the DUP-implemented RHI scheme, with estimates of the cost to taxpayers in the area of £490million (BBC News 2017). As the Executive Office, created under the terms of the 2015 Fresh Start Agreement as the successor to the 'Office of the First Minister and Deputy First Minister', is a joint institution, this resignation prefigured the collapse of the Executive. Under the terms provided by the SAA, the political void caused by this resignation did not lead straight to direct rule, but to new elections (Anthony 2008, 160). These were duly held in February 2017, in which Unionist parties lost their overall majority in the Assembly, with the DUP leading Sinn Féin by a single seat. As in 2014, the more 'normal' political issue (this time, of culpability for a financial scandal) was soon subsumed by disagreement over 'community' issues, largely over the Irish language: while Sinn Féin sought the legal protection of a stand-alone Irish Language Act, the DUP would only accept Irish being given a statutory footing as part of a wider 'culture' bill dealing with Ulster-Scots and other cultural matters alongside protection for Irish (Devenport 2018). Sinn Féin and the DUP also failed to agree a way forward on mechanisms for investigating unsolved murders during 'the troubles'. This impasse was to last for three years.

The failure of initial efforts at restoring devolved government was strongly influenced by two UK-wide contextual issues. First, the UK's protracted efforts to negotiate withdrawal from the EU polarised opinion in Northern Ireland further. While other parties campaigned in the 2016 referendum for a Remain vote, the DUP were ardent Leave supporters. The issues of a possible 'hard border' on the island of Ireland, or a new customs border between Northern Ireland and Great Britain, were particularly contentious, leading to years of discussion around the nature of the Irish 'backstop' that would negate the need for fresh border infrastructure in Ireland.[18] Second, after June 2017 the DUP propped-up the minority Conservative government that was returned after the early general election of that month,[19] through a confidence-and-supply deal. This election, under the non-proportional 'first past the post' system, saw the DUP and Sinn Féin record their best ever results, completely supplanting the UUP and SDLP at Westminster, and sharing seventeen out of the eighteen Northern Ireland seats between them (ten for the DUP, seven for Sinn Féin, with the final seat of North Down taken by the independent Unionist Silvia Hermon). While the UUP had been without MPs between 2010 and 2015, for the SDLP June 2017 marked the end of forty-three years of continuous Westminster representation (Tonge 2017). For Tonge and Evans (2017, 139–41), this resulted in an election in which 'unionist and nationalist voters overwhelmingly backed the dominant representative forces within their respective ethno-national blocs', with 'swings from the SDLP to Sinn Féin in all constituencies and from the UUP to DUP wherever both those parties contested a seat', and the highest correlation between religious affiliation and voter preference in Europe.

These two structural issues were swept away by the December 2019 general election, which returned a landslide victory for the Conservative PM Boris Johnson. With an eighty-seat majority in the House of Commons, Johnson gained Parliamentary approval for the UK to leave the EU on 31 January 2020, under the terms of the October 2019 Withdrawal Agreement. This election therefore removed both contextual issues preventing the restoration of devolved government in Northern Ireland, as the large majority means the Conservatives are no longer reliant on the votes of DUP MPs, removing the latter's influence at Westminster, as well as their veto over the inclusion of a 'Northern Ireland only' backstop in the Withdrawal Agreement. This means that, if the UK and EU do not agree a comprehensive trade agreement by the end of 2020 (when the 'transition period' comes to an end), 'Northern Ireland will apply many EU customs rules and there will effectively be a customs and regulatory border between Great Britain and Northern Ireland in the Irish Sea' (John Curtis et al. 2019, 30). The new Withdrawal Agreement also calls for the 'democratic consent' of the Northern Ireland Assembly to be provided, four years after the backstop comes into effect. What is interesting about this mechanism is that consent can be given 'on the basis of a majority of Members of the Northern Ireland Assembly, present and voting' (HM Government 2019, 323) which would allow the arrangements to continue functioning for another four years. While a cross-community vote would double the length of the extension granted, the Withdrawal Agreement allows this crucial issue, which could be considered as central as the items listed in the GFA as requiring cross-community support, to be decided by a simple majority vote.

The December 2019 general election results in Northern Ireland[20] were also damaging to the DUP and Sinn Féin, with both parties seeing a drop in their share of the vote (by 5.4% for the DUP, and by 6.7% for Sinn Féin), and both parties losing seats (two loses for the DUP, including their Westminster leader Nigel Dodds, with their overall tally down to eight; one loss for Sinn Féin, but their total remaining at seven after they gained Belfast North from the DUP), though they remained the top two in terms of votes and seats. Under the threat of fresh Assembly elections in which these losses could be compounded, and with the contextual issues at the UK level removed, the parties began a fresh round of negotiations on restoring devolved government. These talks were successful, with the contentious issue of the status of Irish being resolved through a compromise on the creation of an Irish Language Commissioner 'to recognise, support, protect and enhance the development of the Irish language in Northern Ireland and to provide official recognition of the status' of Irish (HM Government and Government of Ireland 2020, 15). The Executive was re-appointed (under the mandate provided by the February 2017 Assembly election) on 11 January 2020, with the DUP's Arlene Foster and Sinn Féin's Michelle O'Neill elected as FM and DFM, and all entitled parties taking an Executive position (meaning that the Alliance Party, the SDLP and the UUP joined the DUP and Sinn Féin in government).

This presentation of the post-conflict electoral politics of Northern Ireland has highlighted a pattern of development in which the two parties once considered at the 'extreme' end of the Unionist and Nationalist political spectrum have achieved and maintained electoral dominance (with minor but by no means terminal reversals in 2019). Whether this movement towards extremes was caused by a process of 'ethnic outbidding', in which elections are fought on the basis of who can best protect their 'community interest', by the moderation of positions due to the demands of government and power-sharing, or by some combination of these forces,[21] this has developed within the political framework of the GFA. This can therefore be seen as one manifestation of the operation of the 'two communities' supplement within the GFA, which has enabled post-conflict politics to (re)enact a 'two communities' struggle. The

power-sharing mechanisms, while designed to prevent one community dominating another, have institutionalised communal politics by basing the highest
political office and key aspects of the legislative process around the need to
gain agreement between the 'two communities', that the main political parties claim to represent. The modifications to this system brought about by the
SAA strengthen this tendency, by fixing in place the community designation
for the length of an Assembly term, and by ensuring that the largest Unionist
and Nationalist parties no longer have to vote across community lines for
both the FM and DFM, but can rather nominate a candidate from their own
party. The institutionalisation of division and power-sharing in Northern
Ireland can therefore be said to have perpetuated a system of communal politics, prefiguring the continuing dominance of communal parties and indeed
generating the conditions in which the more 'extreme' representatives of
community interests have entrenched their pre-eminent positions.

The supplementation of the GFA by a 'two communities' understanding
of the conflict has therefore transmitted this logic into the political present,
generating a political system structured around the divergent interests of
opposed groupings. Simultaneously, the 'two communities' understanding of
the conflict as driven by the historic presence of two competing communities
in Ireland is *itself* strengthened by this entrenchment of division, as the thesis is vindicated by the apparent fact that contemporary politics in Northern
Ireland is structured around this continuing division. This is how I understand
the 'conflict' and 'post-conflict' to be produced as the *différance* of each
other, meaning that, rather than being a post-conflict society in which the 'two
communities' struggle is over or annulled, Northern Ireland is, in this area
of electoral politics, more akin to a society in which the 'two communities'
struggle *continues* in a *differed* and *deferred* manner.

However, this is just one way of telling the story of the post-conflict
politics of Northern Ireland. One clue that this is a partial picture of the
political landscape comes from the electoral turnout figures.[22] From a high
watermark of 81.1% for the referendum in May 1998 on the GFA, turnout
immediately dropped below 70% for the first Assembly election in June
1998. There was then a period of steady and consistent decline, across both
Westminster and Assembly elections, until a low of 54.9% was reached in
the May 2016 Assembly election. If the literature suggesting a link between
voter turnout and citizen satisfaction with democracy, as summarised by
Ezrow and Xezonakis (2016, 1), is accepted, this decline in turnout may be
read as a sign of *dissatisfaction* with the political institutions in Northern
Ireland. Therefore, rather than interpreting the electoral dominance of the
DUP and Sinn Féin as an indication that division is an unchanging reality in
Northern Ireland, and a reality that the political system simply reflects, we are
alerted by the warning signs provided by turnout levels that large sections of

the population reject this politics, and register their rejection by disengaging from the formal political sphere. Of course, ascertaining political engagement from turnout levels is not a simple matter of direct correlation (as Ezrow and Xezonakis argue). The next section therefore looks for wider signs of a politics which seeks to challenge and subvert the 'two communities' binary, rather than treating it as fixed given by starting with, and then going beyond, the formal realm of electoral politics.

## DECONSTRUCTING THE GOOD FRIDAY AGREEMENT

### Electoral Politics beyond the 'Two Communities'

As suggested above, the near clear-sweep of the DUP and Sinn Féin in the 2017 Westminster elections does not tell the whole story of recent electoral politics in Northern Ireland. While those two parties have retained their dominant positions within the Unionist and Nationalist blocs since 2003, the record is not one of continual movement towards the 'extremes'. In the 2010 Westminster elections, for example, DUP leader Peter Robinson lost his East Belfast seat to the non-communal Alliance Party, in the aftermath of a scandal involving Robinson's wife and fellow DUP member Iris Robinson (McDonald 2010). That election also saw the UUP lose all its MPs: but more due to a misguided (and short-lived) alliance with the UK Conservatives, than due to a movement towards more hard-line Unionism. Indeed, the moderate Unionist Hermon retained her seat when running as an Independent, after resigning from the UUP over their dalliance with the Conservatives. While the DUP won back the East Belfast seat in 2015, this Westminster election saw Hermon retain her seat as an Independent, alongside the return of the UUP to the House of Commons, with two seats. To further complicate the picture, this UUP resurgence cannot be seen as purely the consequence of a moderation of Unionist electoral opinion. While the South Antrim seat was wrestled directly from the DUP, victory in Fermanagh and South Tyrone was achieved with the aid of a 'Unionist pact', whereby the DUP did not field a candidate. This was one of four constituencies in which the DUP and UUP agreed to put forward only one candidate between them, contributing to Tonge and Evans's (2015) characterisation of these elections as 'another communal headcount'. Tonge and Evans (2015, 119) also point out that the two-seat gain was only achieved on a 1% rise in votes for the UUP. The defeat of the Alliance Party in East Belfast can also be linked to this pact. In 2017, agreement was reached only for the DUP to stand aside in Fermanagh and South Tyrone, with the UUP reciprocating in North Belfast (ITV News 2017). Despite no electoral pact in East Belfast in 2017, the DUP retained the seat, with an increased majority (Tonge and Evans 2017, 141).

While this manoeuvring between the DUP and UUP to maximise Unionist representation at Westminster can be seen as a reflection of the bifurcation of Northern Irish politics in the post-GFA period, recent developments in Assembly, local and European elections, which utilise the more proportional STV system, indicate a more complex picture. In the May 2016 Assembly elections, the vote share of all the five main parties fell, while the left-wing PBP party won two seats, adding to the tally of non-communal parties (i.e. those designating as 'Other') in the Assembly. The Green Party also won their second seat in this election, building on their success in gaining representation for the first time in May 2011 (Tonge 2016, 14). As stated above, the UUP and SDLP formed the first ever Opposition in May 2016. When early elections were called in February 2017 over the RHI scandal, UUP leader Mike Nesbitt stated publicly his intention to transfer his second preference to his Opposition partners. While he did not directly call on UUP voters to do the same, and while the SDLP leader Colum Eastwood did not make a reciprocal gesture (beyond a less emphatic statement that he would transfer to the UUP at some point), the number of transfers between the UUP and SDLP did increase markedly at this election (McBride 2017). While this did not help either party gain seats (the UUP in fact lost six MLAs, in the first election to an Assembly reduced by eighteen to ninety members), it does illustrate the willingness of the electorate to vote across community lines, thus questioning the salience of the more rigid understandings of the 'two communities' thesis. The ability to form an official Opposition may therefore be seen as an example of what Horowitz (2014, 5) calls centrapetalist incentives, which encourage 'moderates to compromise on conflicting group claims, to form interethnic coalitions, and to establish a regime of interethnic majority rule'.

Two elections held in May 2019, to local councils and the European Parliament, provide further evidence of the advance of the 'Others' in votes using STV. In the 2 May local elections, the two main 'Unionist' and 'Nationalist' designating parties (i.e. who designate this way in the Assembly), though maintaining their position as the four biggest parties, either lost or (in the case of Sinn Féin) failed to gain seats (though the DUP saw a 1% increase in first preference votes), while the non-communal parties made gains: seven seats a piece for the Green Party and PBP, and twenty-one for the Alliance Party, achieved through a near 5% increase in first preference votes. The 23 May election for Members of the European Parliament (MEPs) produced an ever more remarkable result: while the Sinn Féin candidate topped the poll in terms of first preference votes (as they had in the previous vote in 2014), and the DUP candidate was the first elected on transfers, Naomi Long was returned as the first ever Alliance Party MEP, being elected before

Sinn Féin's Martina Anderson on transfers, and increasing first preference votes by nearly 138%.[23] One caveat is that both these results were achieved on substantially lower turnouts than the most recent Assembly and Westminster elections: 52.7% in the local elections, and 45% in the European election (BBC News 2019b; the Electoral Office for Northern Ireland 2019a).

The December 2019 Westminster elections also provided some extraordinary results. The election campaign itself was notable, with the 'Unionist pact' in Belfast North between the DUP and UUP being matched by a 'Remain alliance' between Sinn Féin and the SDLP, with the former not standing in Belfast South, Belfast East and North Down, while the latter did not contest Belfast North, Belfast East and North Down. The 'Other' designating Green Party followed suit by stepping aside in all four Belfast constituencies, with only the Alliance Party contesting all eighteen seats (McCormack 2019). This pre-election positioning helped produce some big shocks on election night: the SDLP won Belfast South from the DUP, while also defeating Sinn Féin in Foyle; Sinn Féin made up for this loss by defeating the DUP in Belfast North; and the Alliance Party gained their first MP since 2015 by winning North Down with a 35% increase in their vote share after Hermon stood down, beating the DUP into second place with a majority of nearly 3,000 votes. The Alliance Party also came close to pipping the DUP in Belfast East. On a reduced overall turnout of 62%, while the DUP and Sinn Féin remained the two biggest parties, the Alliance Party made history by coming third in terms of overall vote share: helped no doubt by the fact they were the only party standing in all eighteen constituencies.[24]

This alternative story of the post-conflict electoral politics therefore highlights the (limited) advances made in political representation by those who reject community identification. This has been stuttering and uneven, and until 2019 much more pronounced in elections within Northern Ireland than those to Westminster, but non-communal parties have made progress, albeit hesitant and reversible. The Alliance Party's electoral victories in 2010 and 2019 are of great significance, while the Assembly has seen steady increase from a low-point of only six 'Other'-designating MLAs in 2003 (following the demise of the Women's Coalition Party, who held two seats alongside the Alliance Party's seven in 1998). By 2016, this reached a high point of twelve MLAs, thanks to the presence of PBP and Green MLAs alongside the Alliance Party members. While in absolute terms this fell by one in the 2017 elections, due to the reduction in size of the Assembly to ninety members, this actually increased the overall proportion of 'Others' in the legislature: from 11.1% after the 2016 elections, to 12.2% in 2017. The march of the 'Others' has also been reflected in the 'New Decade, New Approach' agreement which the main parties signed-up to before re-entering the Executive in January 2020. This is the first formal document in which 'acknowledging and accommodating those within our community who define themselves as "other", and those from our ethnic communities and newcomer communities' is placed alongside 'the birthright of all the people of Northern Ireland to identify themselves and be accepted as Irish or British, or both, as they may so choose' (HM Government and Government of Ireland 2020, 15).

Two other aspects of the January 2020 agreement are worth considering here. First, it greatly extends the amount of time that can elapse between the resignation of an FM or DFM, or after an Assembly election, before a new FM and DFM must be appointed, 'from 7 and 14 days respectively to 6 weeks in each case'. The text also calls for provision to be made for 'Northern Ireland Executive Ministers to remain in office beyond the day of the poll to allow for greater continuity of decision making, until such a time as d'Hondt [i.e. the process for appointing an Executive] is run', with a maximum period of forty-eight weeks without a functioning Executive being provided for (HM Government and Government of Ireland 2020, 24). This serves to normalise and regularise the type of extended breakdown in government that has recently come to an end, by providing a legal framework for a prolonged period without an Executive or fresh elections: in other words, recognising that future crises may cripple the functioning of the devolved institutions. Second, the text states that the parties have agreed to reform the petition of concern by, amongst other means, committing to using the measure 'only in the most exceptional circumstances and as a last resort, having used every other available mechanism', and requiring two or more parties to support a motion before the petition can be triggered (HM Government and Government of Ireland 2020, 20). Such reform of the petition of concern, as noted above, has long been an aspiration of those dissatisfied with communal politics in Northern Ireland.

We can also identify such dissatisfaction with communal politics by examining opinion poll data. The most recent 'Northern Ireland Life and Times' survey, carried out between September 2018 and February 2019, found that, when asked whether 'you think of yourself as a unionist, a nationalist or neither', 50% of respondents answered 'neither', suggesting a very widespread rejection of the community designations amongst the electorate. The breakdown for people of different religions also demonstrated how denomination is not a simple predictor for political opinion: 48% of Catholics answered 'neither', as did 42% of Protestants (ARK 2019). Widespread support for the restoration of devolved government can also be inferred from responses to a question about 'the long-term policy for Northern Ireland', in which the most popular option, garnering 41% of support, was for Northern Ireland 'to remain part of the United Kingdom, with devolved government'. While the results in elections do not always map on to the data collected in opinion polls, my survey of party politics in Northern Ireland indicates a more complex picture than one of simple division between 'two communities'.

Therefore, while aspects of the GFA assume the existence of opposed identity groups that must be accommodated through a communal politics, it simultaneously creates the space for these identities to be transformed, and for a non-communal politics to emerge. This is apparent in the contrast between recent results for elections to Westminster and to the Northern Ireland Assembly: while the former suggests a near-complete carve up between the DUP and Sinn Féin (particularly in 2017), the latter, using the electoral system *prescribed by the GFA*, provides a much more fractured picture, with greater representation for parties who stand outside community designation. The GFA therefore simultaneously requires the existence of parties who designate as one of the 'two communities' for its key aspects, relating to Executive formation and voting, to function, while providing space for the existence and (albeit hesitant and reversible) advance of parties who reject these designations. This is therefore one example of the contradictions within the post-conflict political landscape of Northern Ireland, and a fault-line upon which the edifice is already deconstructing.

This means, therefore, that it cannot simply be stated that the political framework of the GFA has led to the solidification or fixing in place of a 'two communities' division, or that the dominance of opposed communal party blocs reflects the unchanging reality of political identification in Northern Ireland. Rather than a *simplification* of political life to a binary opposition between two competing communities, we see a *complication*, an enactment of undecidability at the centre of the political system. The presence of the 'two communities' supplement within the GFA allows for some aspects of contemporary politics in Northern Ireland to operate as a (re)enactment of a 'two communities' struggle, which in turn strengthens the historical validity of this analysis by presenting communal political competition as the 'natural' state of affairs. The current performance of communal politics, and the historical understanding of the conflict as driven by the mutual antagonism between the 'two communities', are thus tied through a process of supplementation, producing one as the *différance* of the other, in the same temporal moment. Yet, the presence of this supplement does not reduce politics purely to such a communal contest: as Derrida argues, the supplement does not fill-in the gaps completely, but highlights the continued undecidability of that which is supplemented. The 'two communities' supplement therefore *replicates* the contradictions of the GFA, *carrying them into* the present, producing a political system which contains its own contradictions in the 'Others' who are accommodated while marginalised and constrained, gaining electoral support at the same time as the communal parties become more entrenched.

This is therefore a political system in a process of deconstruction. It is partially filled by proponents of Unionism and Nationalism who are prone to irreconcilable disagreement over 'cultural' and 'legacy' issues such as the Irish language and investigations into murders during 'the troubles', while also providing space for political currents which seek to move beyond this communal politics. However, these 'Others' are only partially accommodated by the political system, being excluded from certain key votes, as discussed above. If there was no electorate for these 'Others', then there may still be a breakdown in the political institutions, but without dissatisfaction (as the logic of zero-sum would rule, and not losing out to the 'other side' would trump the lack of gain for one's own side). Yet these currents *do* exist and are accommodated and encouraged by certain aspects of the GFA: we therefore have dysfunction *and* dissatisfaction, as breakdown in governance is lamented for its damaging effects, provoking (albeit small scale) protests.[25] This is an instance of 'deconstruction in action' in the post-conflict politics of Northern Ireland: something that can be more strongly identified if we look outside the realm of formal electoral politics.

The rest of this section therefore discusses two examples of activity in the political sphere more widely understood: the artwork 'Temple', constructed and destroyed in 2015, and the Turas Irish language classes in East Belfast. These will be taken as exemplars of activities that seek to put into practice the aspects of the GFA which recognise identity as fluid and transformable, and thus seek to subvert and disrupt the 'two communities' understanding of politics. Their (again limited) popularity and durability is taken as evidence that political life in Northern Ireland cannot and must not be reduced to a fixed 'two communities' binary. However, their inability to challenge the prevalence of this 'two communities' understanding in the formal political sphere is understood as evidence of the limitations of this 'deconstruction in action', prefiguring the need for the deconstructive conclusion to the conflict that chapter 6 will argue for.

## Deconstruction beyond Electoral Politics

### Temple

In the west of Northern Ireland, near the border with Donegal in the Irish republic, lies the city known variously as Derry, Londonderry, or Derry~Londonderry. This is a city whose very name symbolises the 'two communities' dispute in Northern Ireland,[26] with Nationalists using 'Derry' (an Anglicised version of the Irish place name 'Doire'), while some Unionists prefer 'Londonderry', as the city is officially known by the UK state since a Royal Charter was granted by King James I in 1613, acknowledging the settlements' association with the City of London (BBC News 2007). In 2013, this city became the first 'UK City of Culture', a four-yearly event modelled upon the European 'Capital of Culture' programme. One of the biggest attractions, witnessed by nearly two hundred thousand people, was the four-night Lumiere festival, curated by the London-based art group Artichoke.[27] Artichoke also considered bringing the Californian artist David Best to the city, to construct, and then burn, one of his 'Temple' structures, but logistical difficulties prevented this. Two years later, however, building on the connections they had made through Lumiere and their earlier work 'Peace Camp' at nearby Mussenden Temple,[28] Artichoke were able to bring Best to (London)Derry and, with the help of the local arts and community group the Nerve Centre, a Temple was constructed, displayed and then set alight in March 2015.

Building on the Nerve Centre's outreach work, a range of schools and community groups (representing, for example, cancer survivors, people with mental health issues, and relatives of suicide victims) were invited to design panels for inclusion on the Temple. The ethos that Best envisioned for the project, as explained to me by the Nerve Centre's John Peto, was one of 'cleansing', whereby participants 'tell [their] story on a panel, and then [they] can see it being burnt', in a 'mass cathartic event for the city'.[29] Best was keen to bring his artwork to Northern Ireland, Peto told me, in order to engage with wider political issues around loss and mourning, in a departure from his usual work with individuals who have been bereaved or experienced traumatic events. Artichoke also sought to play on, and subvert, the traditional bonfires held in Northern Ireland, that are very much celebrations of one community, and very often events which replicate and multiply ill-feelings and acts of violence across community fault lines.[30] In Loyalist areas, bonfires are lit on 11 July, on the eve of the Orange marches that take place the next day on 'The Twelfth', in commemoration of the victory of King William III over the deposed Catholic King James II in 1690, and in August on the eve of 'Apprentice Boy' parades, which mark the 'Siege of Derry' which occurred earlier in the conflict between King William and King James. In Republican areas, bonfires are held in August, to mark both the Catholic Feast of Assumption, and the introduction of internment in 1971.

After the fabrication of intricate panels based on designs produced by members of the local community, the Temple structure was put in place on the 'Top of the Hill' park, next to the Gobnascale estate, in the Waterside district. Situated in a Nationalist area with some notoriety due to a pub shooting, attributed to Loyalist paramilitaries, which killed five civilians in December 1972 (Derry Journal 2012), the park enjoys panoramic views of the city. While the park is perceived as belonging to one of the 'two communities', it was accessible to everyone in the city and surrounding locale. According to Peto, a buzz started to develop once the Temple structure began to be put in place, with the scale of the project generating great interest on social media and attracting the attention of local, national and international news outlets.[31] The completed construction stood for seven days (Culture Northern Ireland 2015), allowing visitors to add their own mementos or write messages on the structure, and attracting interest from across Ireland. By the time it was ready for immolation, 65,000 people had visited, filling the structure with 'many thousands of intimate confessions of regret, hope, love and longing' (Harper 2015, 81). The Temple was then set alight on the night of 21 March, in front of a crowd of 15,000 spectators.[32]

My interest in this event arises from its contrast with the forms of ritualised commemoration and celebration linked to one or other of the 'two communities' in Northern Ireland. While the obvious target, and the one Artichoke consciously had in mind, comes from the annual bonfires, and the attendant burning of symbolic representations of the 'other side' (whether that is effigies, flags, election posters, or religious icons), the Temple can also be seen as a counterpoint to the permanent, physical memorials to victims of 'the troubles'. There are countless plaques, engravings, memorial stones and other structures commemorating those killed in terrorist incidents, by security forces, or during their participation in 'armed struggle'.[33] While serving as focal points for remembrance services, and vehicles for the creation of narratives about specific aspects of the conflict, such memorials regularly attract violent attack from those opposed to the stories they seek to tell. One exemplar of this tendency is the James McCurrie Robert Neill Memorial Garden on the Lower Newtownards Road, East Belfast, which commemorates two Protestant men shot dead by the PIRA in June 1970, during a gun battle centred on St Matthew's Church, in the Short Strand interface area. The presentation of this memorial, with the use of terms such as 'Remember the Fallen' borrowed from British Army war memorials, the flying of the Union flag from the garden, and the wording of the plaque and a poem mounted on the walls, clearly links the memorial to the Unionist community, meaning it operates as much as an indictment of Republicans and, by implication, the wider Nationalist community, as a commemoration to the murdered men. It does so by writing the deaths into a historical narrative of unprovoked Republican attacks, which obscures competing historical claims about such violence being in self-defence, while simultaneously speaking to a future of continued vigilance against threats to Unionist culture and identity (Pinkerton 2012, 146–7). This memorial garden continues to attract violent attack, most recently in January 2019 when the Union flag was stolen from the garden (Belfast Telegraph 2019). By marking out this part of Belfast as a space for one specific community, and by commemorating specific deaths represented and remembered in a specific way, this memorial garden replicates division, standing as a Union-flagged, walled-and-gated symbol of defiant identity, and a target for the hatred of others.

The Temple, on the other hand, attempted to create a temporary shared public space, was dedicated to a generalisable conception of loss, and is now nothing but ash scattered across the earth. Its destruction was a constructive act that, while leaving no physical trace, nor attempting to crystallise particular understandings of the past or present to be carried into the future, created singular memories in those present at the burning, free of all claims of central ownership or official sanction, and incapable of being inscribed into a particular narrative of history, or becoming a target for violence aimed at heightening tension, fear or mistrust. Rather than remaining as a physical structure to be argued over, possessed and dispossessed, the Temple 'lives on in the experience of everyone who contributed to it and witnessed it going up in smoke' (Harper 2015, 82). As Best has put it, 'You don't destroy the temple when you burn it. You burn it to protect it' (Harper 2015, 82). This is the sense in which I understand the Temple to be an example of 'deconstruction in action'. It provided a vessel for individuals to engage with their past, and a shared experience of engaging with some form of loss encountered in their lives. As Peto experienced first-hand, participation in the project had a profound and transformative impact for some individuals, in terms of dealing with traumatic incidents in their lives. However, the wider, political impact is much harder to measure, and Peto was not aware of any long-term implications: indeed, he noted that in 2017 the illegal 15 August Republican bonfire attracted a much bigger crowd than the safe bonfire held elsewhere in the city, with the proscribed event escalating into violent clashes with police (The Guardian 2017). This indicates how the 'deconstruction in action' represented by the burning of the Temple is only partial: it challenges the *impact* of the 'two communities' supplement in the political present, by subverting the traditions of exclusive and divisive commemoration and celebration, without overcoming the *source* of that supplementation in the understandings of the conflict embedded in the GFA, and replicated through its political structures into the post-conflict period.

While the burning of the Temple can be seen as a deconstructive subversion of the 'two communities' thesis, it did not originate from inside either of these 'two communities'. Rather, it was something brought to (London) Derry from 'outside': by a Californian artist and a London-based art group. The project was not something internal to the city, something brought forth as a means of healing and reconciliation, and was therefore in no real sense 'owned' by the locale. It may demonstrate what is possible in terms of alternative forms of commemoration, which aim to bring people together not in an artificial 'cross-community' spirit but as humans who have experienced or will experience loss; but this was only made possible by Best's substantial charisma and energy, and Artichoke's logistical and project management skills. Even the media attention that sparked pride amongst local people, who became eager to show off their area to outsiders, did not come about spontaneously, but through the work of Artichoke's communications team. However, if we look elsewhere in Northern Ireland, to East Belfast, we can see an organisation that is very much 'owned' by locals, that also transcends and subverts traditional understandings of what it means to be part of one of the 'two communities' in Northern Ireland. It is to this example, of the Turas Irish language classes, that I will now turn.

## Turas

East Belfast is strongly associated with the Loyalist or Unionist community. The landscape is dominated by the giant cranes of the Harland and Woolf ship-yards, symbols of Belfast's former industrial might, with East Belfast being home to the largely Protestant working-class communities that this industrial growth generated in the nineteenth and twentieth centuries (Johnson 2008). The area retains a reputation as a Loyalist heartland, with the streets closest to the city centre marked out as such with prominent displays of Union flags, red-white-and-blue bunting and wall paintings. While many of these murals glorify the Loyalist paramilitary groups active in the area, more recent addi-tions commemorate cultural and sporting icons from East Belfast, such as C. S. Lewis, Van Morrison and George Best (Belfast Telegraph 2017).

Dispute this recent diversification in street art and local cultural display, this area is still one of the last places one would expect to find an Irish language class. Irish, or Gaeilge, has been strongly associated with the Republican or Nationalist community, since at least the 'Gaelic Revival' of the nineteenth century, becoming tied up with the struggle for Home Rule, and then inde-pendence, for Ireland. As stated above, the status of the Irish language in Northern Ireland was one of the major stumbling blocks preventing the resto-ration of devolved government after the collapse of power-sharing in January 2017, though this issue goes back at least as far as the GFA. The 'Economic, Social and Cultural Issues' subsection of the 'Rights, Safeguards and Equality of Opportunity' chapter of the GFA pledges participants to 'recognise the importance of respect, understanding and tolerance in relation to linguistic diversity, including . . . the Irish language, Ulster-Scots and the languages of the various ethnic communities' (HM Government 1998a), while making aspirational statements about actions which could be undertaken to promote and encourage the Irish language, including through Irish medium education, and Irish television and film production. The 2006 SAA seemingly puts in writing a stronger commitment on behalf of the UK government to 'introduce an Irish Language Act reflecting on the experience of Wales and Ireland and work with the incoming Executive to enhance and protect the development of the Irish language', alongside a pledge of the UK government's support for 'a Single Equality Bill', and 'the need to enhance and develop the Ulster Scots language, heritage and culture' (HM Government 2006). Former DUP leader Peter Robinson has since accused Blair's government of wilfully misleading Sinn Féin during these negotiations, and of telling the DUP team that the pledge was meaningless, as it would be superseded by the expected (and subsequently achieved) restoration of devolved government to Northern Ireland (Breen 2017). This lack of clarity has thus contributed to a situation in which the status of the Irish language is highly politicised. There have been regular accusations of Republicans using the Irish language as a 'weapon' in a 'culture war' against Unionist communities (McCausland 2014; McEvoy 2015, 99; Swann 2017); meanwhile, Unionists are accused of denying Irish speakers their rights to equal recognition and support (Mac Giolla Bhéin 2019). This wider political context makes the presence of the Turas (which means 'journey' in Irish) language centre, located within the East Belfast Mission (EBM), even more remarkable.

The key figure behind Turas is Linda Ervine. Ervine, while a member of the EBM congregation and working as an English teacher in an East Belfast secondary school, attended a six-week taster session in Irish at the EBM, and was inspired to attend Irish classes elsewhere in Belfast. Local media was alerted to the story (The Irish Times 2011) as Ervine's husband Brian was the leader of the PUP at the time, following in the footsteps of his brother David Ervine (the former Loyalist paramilitary prisoner and PUP leader who, before his death in 2007, campaigned in support of the GFA). In a radio interview Ervine mentioned the sessions at the EBM, and this exposure lead to inquiries from service users at the EBM hoping to attend their Irish class. However, there was no permanent class, just the taster session that had taken place six months beforehand. The EBM therefore approached Ervine, and asked if she would facilitate a more permanent Irish language programme. Ervine agreed to do so, on a voluntary basis at first, before helping the EBM secure funding for the creation of Turas. Ervine is now the centre's Irish Language Development Officer, as well as campaigning for the creation of an Irish language nursery and primary school in the area.[34]

What this indicates, and what marks Turas as distinct from the Temple and other consciously 'cross-community' endeavours, is the fact that it grew from the bottom up, from the local area. It was persons living in and around East Belfast who became curious about the Irish language, and Turas was set up in response to that demand. While the central goal of Turas is to facilitate a deep engagement in the Irish language for their learners, and encourage them to gain formal language qualifications, Ervine told me she also sees their role as one of 'raising awareness', and 'introducing people to the language who will never learn the language but will hopefully have a more positive attitude towards it'. Central to this is the work of Gordon McCoy, who researches the Gaelic history of East Belfast, with the aim of 'indigenising Irish', and demonstrating that the classes do not import something that is external to East Belfast, but facilitate engagement with something that was always part of the history of the area. As Ervine put it, the people participating in Turas 'are embracing something that's probably regarded as not theirs'. It does not seek to take people from one community, and expose them to the culture that belongs to the 'other' community: rather, it builds on the idea that the Irish language does not 'belong' to one community or the other, but is something that can be possessed by anyone in Northern Ireland. As Ervine recognised during our conversation, this may be why Turas attracts so much media attention.[35] 'I think people like our story', she told me, as 'there is a novelty about it . . . I hadn't really thought about it but I suppose that is why [there is so much interest in Turas] because it came from inside rather than outside'.

This ethos also informs Ervine's resistance to traditional 'cross-community' initiatives, in which representatives from across the community divide are brought together: in the case of language, this would usually involve inviting one Irish speaker and one Ulster-Scots speaker to an event. For Ervine, such actions entrench polarisation, by presenting certain characteristics as belonging to one community rather than the other, when her agenda is to highlight the common ownership and inter-mingled nature of the languages. Ervine therefore has a mirror image in her friend Liam Logan, an Ulster-Scots enthusiast whose work with the Nationalist SDLP defies the stereotypes which associate that language with the Unionist community. For Ervine, attending events with Logan is a way of demonstrating that the two languages 'overlap with each other' and 'borrow [from] each other'. They travel to such functions together to show they 'both have respect for Irish and Ulster-Scots, rather than . . . staring over the hedge at each other' from their opposed and separate communities. Like the Temple project, these linguistic projects transcend and disrupt binary understandings of the presence of 'two communities' in Northern Ireland. However, the fact that Turas is a truly 'local' project, and not something imported from outside, makes it an even stronger example than the Temple of 'deconstruction in action', of a cultural practice that subverts the 'two communities' understanding of political identity in Northern Ireland. However, despite the positive engagement with the Irish language undertaken at this local level in East Belfast, the status of the language remains controversial at the elite political level, even after the January 2020 restoration of devolved government in Northern Ireland.

## CONCLUSION

This chapter has traced the presence of the ethno-national account, and its 'two communities' supplement, within the text of the GFA and the political framework it created. The presence of this supplement was seen as transmitting the contradictions of the ethno-national account into the GFA and the post-conflict period, thus producing the 'conflict' and 'post-conflict' as the *différance* of each other. The contradictions within the text of the GFA were then traced across two competing tendencies of the post-conflict politics of Northern Ireland. First, the elements of the GFA that specifically seek to accommodate the opposed political manifestations of the 'two communities' were seen as allowing for politics to (re)enact a 'two communities' struggle, even if this does not map onto the 'reality' of 'the troubles' (which was not only a struggle between 'two communities', but something driven by a range of actors with diverse motivations). Second, the elements of the GFA that seek a transcendence or transformation of the 'two communities' binary were seen as creating space for a non-communal politics, that was identified both in the formal political sphere of electoral competition, and in the exemplary artistic and cultural practices of the Temple and Turas projects, which seek to subvert and disrupt the 'two communities' understanding, and show that political life in Northern Ireland cannot and must not be reduced to a fixed 'two communities' binary. These contradictory tendencies were both seen as rooted in the GFA, as arising from the internal contradictions of the GFA, thus generating a political system marked by inconsistency and dysfunction: in other words, one already in a process of deconstruction.

However, the case of the Irish language demonstrates that this deconstruction has not yet gone far enough. Although the (limited) success of Turas shows that opinion on the Irish language does not divide neatly along community axes, by demonstrating that some of those at certain grassroots levels expected to scorn or fear the language in fact seek to learn it, Irish remains caught up in communal political division at the elite political level. This speaks to the central problem of the GFA: as long it embodies the 'two communities' understanding of the conflict, even while it simultaneously allows for the disruption and subversion of that thesis, it cannot provide the basis for a politics that goes beyond the 'two communities' binary. Chapter 6 therefore consider how this deconstruction can be completed, through a deconstructive conclusion which challenges the sources of the 'two communities' supplement at the same time as challenging its effects in the present. First, I will return to the BiH case, and consider its post-conflict political situation.

# Chapter 5

# Post-Conflict Bosnia and Herzegovina

## Différance *and Ethnic Politics*

Like Northern Ireland, contemporary BiH is commonly considered a post-conflict society. The physical scars of war remain visible in some places, whether in the still-ruined buildings on the old frontline in Mostar, or in the 'Sarajevo roses' which mark the spots of deadly mortar attacks during the siege of that city. The legacy of the violence is still contested in war crimes tribunals, while the genocide at Srebrenica is marked every year in a remembrance ceremony on 11 July, usually accompanied by the burial of recently uncovered human remains. The political, institutional and territorial structures of the country also bear the imprints of war, being bequeathed to the country by the DPA. In these ways, therefore, BiH can be considered an exemplar of a post-conflict society.

Following from the analysis in chapter 4, this chapter interrogates and unsettles what it means to say that BiH is a post-conflict society. Rather than viewing the post-conflict period as separate from the time of the conflict, in the sense of being marked by the passage from one specific temporal period to another, I view one as the *différance* of the other. While recognising the qualitative differences brought about by the peace settlement, I argue that both the 'conflict' and 'post-conflict', as they are understood from the perspective of contemporary politics, are constituted by the DPA. The post-conflict period is thus tied to the time of the conflict, not through a dichotomous or oppositional logic as the war ended or annulled, but through a relationship of *différance*, which produces the post-conflict period as the conflict *differed* and *deferred*. I demonstrate this by identifying the contradictory conflict framings discussed in chapter 3 within the DPA, to illustrate the key role this text plays in the continued salience of these two understandings of the war. I argue that these contradictory framings are made to work together as the basis for the current political system of BiH through the presence of the 'Balkans' supplement, which allows the DPA to embody an undecidable understanding of BiH as a Balkans space in which politics is determined by the reality of ethnic difference, while *simultaneously* being a place where manipulative politicians exacerbate and mobilise ethnic identity for their own ends. The DPA therefore generates an 'ethnic politics' through the internal territorial and institutional divisions put in place as the basis for power-sharing government between Bosniacs, Croats and Serbs, allowing for a (re)enactment of a 'Balkans' struggle, in which ethnic identity is valorised as the central locus of political debate, in a manner which gives strength to the historical understandings which view the conflict as an 'ethnic war'.

However, and crucially, this performance of contemporary politics as a (re)enactment of a 'Balkans' struggle is not the only effect of the 'Balkans' supplement within the DPA. As I argue, the supplementation enables the continuing presence of the 'international aggression' discourse within the text of the DPA. This framing, which views the war as an international conflict sparked by the political machinations of elite leaders willing to mobilise ethnicity towards violent ends, gives strength to certain transformational currents within the DPA, enabling a 'non-ethnic politics' which seeks to challenge and overturn ethnic division. As the final section of the chapter highlights, the embedding of numerous references to human rights and equality into the DPA allows for forms of politics which contest the ethnic basis of politics in BiH. Importantly, I stress how these legal and political challenges derive from the same source (the DPA) as that which they seek to challenge. As with my highlighting of contradictory logics within the GFA (see chapter 4), I am not the first to make this observation. Bieber (2006, 22) notes the contradiction in the DPA which 'recognized the principle of ethno-territorial autonomy as the "building block" of the state, but at the same time introduced the principle of human rights and equality, which ran counter to the ethno-territorial autonomies'. By focusing on the source of these contradictions within the DPA, and on the manner in which this source is supplemented by a 'Balkans' framing which connects the post-conflict politics to the conflict through a relation of *différance*, I go beyond the analysis of scholars like Bieber by arguing that the DPA is already in a process of deconstruction.

The first section of the chapter provides a close reading of the DPA, in order to locate within the text the contradictory conflict framings of the 'ethnic war' and 'international aggression' discourses, and the productive supplement of the 'Balkans' understanding (as discussed in chapter 3). The second section then describes how the post-conflict electoral politics of BiH, and the various attempts at reforming the political institutions, can be seen as a (re)enactment of a 'Balkans' struggle, using the same understanding of '(re) enactment' set out in chapter 4. This term is used to highlight how this post-conflict politics is not a simple re-enactment of the conflict in its totality, as the war was not a simple 'Balkans' struggle, but something driven by a range of social, political, economic and military factors, and prosecuted by multiple actors with diverse motivations (as chapter 2 sets out); and to demonstrate how the performance of this 'Balkans' struggle in the post-conflict period gives retroactive strength to historic understandings of the conflict framed in this way. The third section then considers how this is only a partial picture of the post-conflict political landscape, by examining some high-profile challenges to the ethnic logics of the system. After examining the Sejdić-Finci court case, in which BiH's constitution was found to be incompatible with the ECHR, I analyse the various protest movements which, over the last several years and demonstrate that a non-ethnic politics is possible in BiH. By emphasising how the DPA produces both an ethnic politics in BiH, and a politics which contests this, I argue that the DPA is already in a process of deconstruction.

## RECONSTRUCTING THE DAYTON
## PEACE AGREEMENT

The DPA represented the culmination of the US's renewed efforts in the summer of 1995 to end the conflict in BiH. The massacre at Srebrenica, followed by the Bosnian Serb mortar attack on a Sarajevo market on 28 August 1995, provoked the US to lead military action against Bosnian Serb positions, and in the context of a two-week NATO air campaign, beginning on 31 August, negotiations were renewed by the Clinton administration from a position of strength. National Security Advisor Anthony Lake toured Europe that month, gaining support for a new effort based on the old ideas of maintaining BiH within its current borders, but divided into two entities. Another key development in August 1995 came when Milošević asserted his authority over the Bosnian Serb leadership by forcing them into what became known as the 'Patriarch Agreement', which allowed Milošević to represent the Bosnian Serbs at future peace negotiations. This paved the way for all sides to agree to a set of 'Basic Principles', which were to structure future negotiations, and for agreement to be reached on a ceasefire on 5 October (Daalder 2000, 128–9; Silber and Little 1996, 361–68). Izetbegović, Milošević and Tuđman then travelled to the Wright-Patterson air force base in Dayton, Ohio. In protracted talks, lasting between 1–21 November, the three presidents agreed on a settlement that was to end the war. The memoires of some of those involved highlight the many twists and turns in the process, with prospects for agreement building and fading as the mediators attempted to maintain the support of the different factions (Chollet 2005; Holbrooke 1999). Such accounts also stress the clashing personalities of the Balkan delegates. Milošević is characterised as hard drinking and gregarious, enjoying his exchanges with the waitresses in 'Packy's sports bar', the main eating establishment in the nearby Bob Hope Hotel that delegates frequented. Izetbegović, by contrast, is seen as quiet and withdrawn, spending more time alone or arguing with his own delegation. Much attention is also placed in these accounts on wrangling over the final maps, and the delineation of what became the 'Inter-Entity Boundary Line'. After the deal was agreed at Dayton, the final text was formally signed in Paris on 14 December by the three presidents, and witnessed by delegates from the EU, France, Germany, Russia, the UK and the US.

The signatories to the DPA declared they would refrain from using force in BiH and respect its independence. The eleven Annexes flesh out the detail of this, covering a range of topics including regional stability, human rights, elections, refugees and national monuments. As Malik (2000, 311) observes, the DPA was signed by three sovereign states: BiH, Croatia and FRY, while the Annexes were agreed between BiH and the two entities. The very structure of the DPA therefore embodies the split between the 'ethnic war' account, with its focus on internal conflict within BiH (as represented by the signatories to the Annexes) and the 'international aggression' discourse, with its recognition of wider regional causes to the conflict (as represented by the signatories to the DPA). However, this is immediately complicated in a number of ways. First, the signatories to the Annexes represent the two entities: there is thus no representation specifically for Croats in BiH. The 'ethnic war' reflected here is thus the latter stages of the conflict, when the ARBiH and HV joined forces to fight the Bosnian Serbs (the period of the conflict when, as chapter 3 argued, the 'Balkans' supplement operated most strongly to merge together the 'ethnic war' and 'international aggression' discourses). Second, looking through the annexes reveals that 1 and 10 required signatures from Croatia and FRY before entering into force, while Annex 2 is endorsed by them. Finally, the 'Patriarch Agreement' indicates that the RS delegates were mere proxies for the government of FRY, their signatures reflecting the will of Milošević. Therefore, as Zahar (2005, 123) notes, 'of the three Bosnian warring factions, only one – the Bosniak community – was a full partner to the peace talks. Presidents Slobodan Miloševiç and Franjo Tudjman stood for the Bosnian Serbs and Bosnian Croats, respectively, although it is to be doubted whether these two men truthfully represented the interests of these communities'.

I now go through the text[1] of the Annexes to the DPA in detail, examining how they embody both the 'ethnic war' and 'international aggression' understandings of the conflict discussed in chapter 3, and exploring how these contradictory discourses have been made to work together in the post-conflict period through the presence of an undecidable 'Balkans' supplement. This undecidability is to be seen as generating the contradictory political currents discussed later in the chapter – that is, those which allow politics to become a (re)enactment of a 'Balkans' struggle in which ethnic identity is seen as innate, and those which view the conflict as a product of a 'Balkans' tendency to mobilise and manipulate ethnic belonging for political purposes – thus demonstrating how the DPA contains the source of its own deconstruction.

## Security, Boundaries and Elections

Annex 1-A deals with 'Military Aspects of the Peace Settlement', as relating to the territory of BiH alone. One major aspect of this annex is the creation of the NATO Implementation Force (IFOR).[2] The signatories for the two entities of BiH also pledge in this annex that neither will 'threaten or use force against the other entity, and under no circumstances shall any armed forces of either entity enter into or stay within the territory of the other Entity' without due consent. This was relevant only while separate entity armies existed: since 2006 there has been one unified BiH army. While this focus on stability between entities chimes with the 'ethnic war' understanding of the conflict, the annex also goes beyond this by highlighting the importance of international human rights standards: the first of many such references to human rights in the DPA. Annex 1-B then embodies more strongly the 'international aggression' discourse, through its focus on the wider regional security environment. The recognition here that 'progressive measures for regional stability and arms control is essential to creating a stable peace in the region' implies an understanding of the war in BiH as more than a purely internal matter, as something arising from wider regional disputes (and thus needing regional solutions). To this end, the annex sets out regional confidence-building measures, such as restrictions on arms imports, fixed ratios of armaments between BiH, Croatia and FRY, and the acceptance of an assistance and supervisory role for the OSCE.

Annex 2 returns to a focus on internal BiH matters, by setting the framework for delineating, enforcing and modifying the Inter-Entity Boundary Line, including the authority of IFOR on such matters, and the Brčko arbitration process. Annex 3 then deals with the 'Agreement on Elections', which provided the basis for running elections until 2001, when an 'Election Law' was passed (Coles 2007b, 10; Friedman 2004, 72). While this is again an internal BiH issue, the OSCE is given a major role in organising and supervising elections, in one of many examples of the hybrid nature of the peace settlement, with competencies and enforcement powers shared between international and local actors. However, the most important aspect of this annex is the article on 'Eligibility', which states that a 'citizen who no longer lives in the municipality in which he or she resided in 1991 shall, as a general rule, be expected to vote, in person or by absentee ballot, in that municipality'.

In other words, those displaced by the fighting are given the right to vote in their pre-war place of residence. This right to vote is then linked to the issue of refugee return (which is discussed in more detail in Annex 7) when the article states that the 'exercise of a refugee's right to vote shall be interpreted as confirmation of his or her intention to return' to BiH. This aspect of the DPA is thus based on a determination to reverse the carving out of ethnically pure territories through killing and violent expulsion (Malik 2000, 305–17). As such, it runs counter to the 'ethnic war' idea that the violence in BiH was a consequence of innate and opposed ethnic identities, being compatible instead with the 'international aggression' notion of ethnic difference in BiH as a construction, exacerbated and mobilised by manipulative elites for their own politics ends. Thus, while other parts of the DPA cemented 'ethno-political partition', the election rules 'held out the prospect of resisting the reality of ethnic cleansing for those determined and brave enough to try to turn back the tide' of the war (Gow 2006, 53).

## The Constitution, Arbitration and Human Rights

Annex 4 then details the constitution of BiH. Like the DPA as a whole, this constitution embodies both an 'ethnic war' and 'international aggression' understanding of the conflict. As such, it is a key location where the 'Balkans' supplement can be identified in the DPA, allowing the 'ethnic war' and 'international aggression' discourses to operate together. Some elements of the constitution are a pure reflection of the 'ethnic war' discourse, with its emphasis on three opposed ethnic groups that must be accommodated if BiH is to remain peaceful, while the territorial division of BiH contains traces of the 'international aggression' discourse, as the continued existence of the RS entity carries traces of what many saw as Milošević's political goal of carving out a 'Greater Serbia' from the ruins of SFRY.

The Preamble to the constitution makes references to concepts such as pluralism, international law and human rights, which suggest the constitution will be based on liberal principles of individual freedom and equality before the law, rather than any understanding of politics in BiH as ethnically determined. However, the last point of the Preamble introduces an ethnicising thread that runs throughout the constitution. This passage states that 'Bosniacs, Croats, and Serbs, as constituent peoples (along with Others), and citizens of Bosnia and Herzegovina hereby determine' the constitution of BiH. This sentence thus both privileges three ethnic groups as 'constituent peoples' in BiH, while relegating 'Others' to a parenthesised after-thought. Yet, even the act of relegating the 'Others' to parenthesises can be seen as evidence of the instability and contradiction within the DPA, as the presence of those who do not fit into the ethnic logic that is central to the DPA is recognised, even while these 'Others' are denied full participation rights. The complexity of the institutional frameworks bequeathed by the constitution, and by constitutional reforms undertaken in the subsequent decades (discussed in the next section), follow from the definition here of the three 'ethnic' communities (Bosniacs, Croats, and Serbs) as 'constituent peoples'. When I refer to 'ethnic politics' in BiH, I therefore refer to the internal divisions (both territorial and institutional) which seek to accommodate all three of these 'constituent peoples'. Conversely, I use 'non-ethnic politics' to refer to that which rejects or seeks to supplant these divisions. I will describe the parties who claim to speak for one of these 'constituent peoples' as 'nationalist parties', as they all look beyond this internal division of BiH to a wider national constituency: Croat and Serb nationalists aspire to connect parts of BiH with territory beyond the borders of BiH, while Bosniac nationalists seek an undivided, unitary BiH[3]. 'Non-nationalist parties' will be used to describe those who pursue a non-ethnic politics.

The constitution enshrines the separation of BiH into two entities, RS and FBiH. The fact that BiH is divided into only *two* entities, and not three, indicates how the 'ethnic war' discourse is only partially present in the constitution. Despite regular attempts by Croat nationalist parties to put a third entity on the political reform agenda, the structure of BiH still follows the 51–49 split first mooted in 1993. As discussed in chapter 3, this two-way split provided the strongest indication of how the 'Balkans' supplement operated to shape the concrete decisions taken over the future of BiH in the closing stages of the war, when the HV and ARBiH were encouraged to push back the Serb aggressors, but only *up to a point*, so as not to disturb the fine ethnic balance that could be created by a two-entity solution on this specific ratio. The continued presence of this territorial split, alongside the criss-crossing patterns of ethnic division that I will go on to detail, indicates that the undecidable 'Balkans' supplement continues to operate, allowing the contradictory elements of the DPA to function together as the basis of the current political system. These elements of the constitution also demonstrate how the undecidability functions across temporal barriers, gaining strength from historic accounts of the conflict as a 'Balkans' war, while strengthening these historical accounts by allowing for the performance of a 'Balkans' politics in the present, with one being produced as the *différance* of the other.

The RS entity corresponds roughly to the territory of the enclave declared in January 1992, and largely 'cleansed' of its pre-war Muslim and Croat populations by Bosnian Serb forces. Granting this entity a large degree of autonomy, including the right to its own flag and police force (Osland 2004, 549), can be seen as a de facto legitimisation of the war-time actions of the Bosnian Serb leadership (Campbell 1998, 151). The FBiH entity, meanwhile, was the product of the Washington Agreement of March 1994, and was institutionally designed to accommodate both Bosniacs and Croats (Silber and Little 1996, 321–23). To this end, it is divided into ten cantons, five of which are designated as Bosniac majority cantons, three as Croat-majority cantons, and two as mixed. The dilemmas posed by the existence of two mixed cantons influences the distribution of powers to the municipal level. The FBiH constitution stipulates that when a municipality has a majority ethnic composition different from that of the canton it resides in, the cantonal government are obligated to delegate functions regarding areas such as education, culture, radio and television to the municipality (Bose 2002, 80–81). This facet of the entity constitution embodies the desire to delegate power to the lowest appropriate level in order to guard against the possibility of one ethnic group dominating another. As Stjepanović (2015, 1046) puts it, the system of canton and municipality government in FBiH was driven by a logic that 'was to descale and decentralise powers so as to reach the territorial level at which a strong ethnic majority would be exhibited', meaning that 'territories were simply used as proxies for ethnicity and ethnic representation rather than as an expression of genuine democratic demands and cross-cutting interests with spatial boundaries'.

The two entities, as well as the cantonal governments in FBiH, are vested with a wide range of competencies, making BiH a highly decentralised state. This decentralisation has decreased somewhat in the post-conflict period, with the number of central state ministries growing from three in the immediate post-war period to nine (Keil and Perry 2015, 83). The constitution affirms the right of the entities to provide citizenship, with an automatic right to BiH citizenship following from the possession of entity citizenship. There is no reference to an ability to hold citizenship of both entities, or delineation of a process for changing entity citizenship. This has created some complications in the Brčko District. While Annex 5 of the DPA commits the two entities to engage in arbitration to resolve disputes as a general principle, a specific arbitration process for Brčko is set out in Annex 2. This resulted in the district becoming simultaneously part of both entities, with residents required to choose one entity or the other for their citizenship, in order to avoid being disenfranchised from national elections, which are run on the basis of entity membership (Stjepanović 2015, 1046–47). Brčko itself can be seen as a challenge to the ethnic logic present elsewhere in BiH's political structures, as its institutions do not employ the same formal, institutionalised ethnic power-sharing. Instead, key decisions such as the election of the District Mayor require a three-fifths majority: something which necessitates 'cooperation between ethnic elites' while assuring 'representation of major ethnic groups but also the inclusion of political representation and engagement of non-dominant ethnicities' (Stjepanović 2015, 1047). The complications thrown up by the Brčko anomaly indicate the contradictions inherent in attempting to apply a strict ethnic logic to Bosnian politics.

The article of the constitution on 'Human Rights and Fundamental Freedoms' secures the direct application in BiH of no less than fifteen international human rights agreements, listed in Annex I to the constitution. This article also affirms the right of refugees and displaced persons to return to their homes. Annex 6 of the DPA gives more details on how human rights are to be protected, through institutions such as a Commission on Human Rights, a Human Rights Ombudsman, and a Human Rights Chamber. Membership of these bodies is divided between appointees of international organisations such as the OSCE and the Council of Europe (CoE), and the two entities of BiH. The articles on institutional organisation embody more of an ethnic determination of politics in BiH. The upper house of the Parliamentary Assembly, the House of Peoples, 'shall comprise 15 Delegates, two-thirds from the [FBiH] (including five Croats and five Bosniacs) and one-third from the [RS] (five Serbs)', with the Croat and Bosniac Delegates elected indirectly by their respective ethnic delegates in the House of Peoples of FBiH, while the Serb Delegates are selected by the National Assembly of RS. The lower house, the House of Representatives, is directly elected without strict ethnic quotas. However, it is still divided along the (ethnically determined) territorial division of BiH, with two-thirds of the forty-two members being elected from FBiH, and one-third from RS. This 2:1 ratio between FBiH and RS representation is repeated in the Constitutional Court and Central Bank of BiH, augmented in both cases by internationally-appointed members. The tripartite state Presidency is to be shared between one Bosniac, one Croat, and one Serb. The Presidency is authorised to nominate the Chair of the Council of Ministers, who serves as de facto prime minister, with the candidate requiring approval by the House of Representatives. The Chair may then appoint further ministers, who serve as head of the state-level ministries. According to the constitution, no more than two-thirds of the ministers may be appointed from the FBiH territory. Deputy ministers must also be appointed, who must 'not be of the same constituent people as their Ministers'.

The rules regarding elections to the Presidency have led to numerous political problems. The Croat and Bosniac members of the Presidency are elected by voters residing in FBiH, and the Serb member by those living in RS. This means that individuals living in the 'wrong' entity are barred from voting for a candidate corresponding to 'their' ethnicity. Furthermore, as there is no mechanism for checking ethnicity at polling stations, residents in FBiH can vote for either the Croat or Bosniac member. This anomaly in the strict ethnic quota system resulted in the election in 2006, 2010 and 2018 of Željko Komšić, to the position of Croat member of the Presidency on the back of Bosniac votes (Kasapović 2016), generating complaints from Croat nationalists 'about an institutional structure that, in their view, marginalizes them' (Belloni 2009, 355). The stipulation that candidates for the Presidency must declare their ethnicity makes it impossible for those who feel affinity for more than one of the major ethnic groupings to stand for political office, as well as barring minority groupings (such as those from the Jewish or Roma communities) from standing, as potential candidates are required to designate as a member of one of the three 'constituent peoples' before putting themselves forward for election. As discussed in detail below, in December 2009 this stipulation was judged by the European Court of Human Rights (ECtHR) in the Sejdić-Finci case to be in violation of the ECHR. The challenges and contradictions thrown up by the attempt to run the Presidency on the basis of a tri-ethnic division provides one illustration of how the DPA provides the grounds for its own deconstruction.

These complex rules around power-sharing between 'constituent peoples' mean that many analysts define BiH as a consociational political system (Belloni 2009; Eralp 2012; Keil and Perry 2015; Stroschein 2014; Weller and Wolff 2006). As O'Halloran (2005, 108) puts it, the BiH constitution, with its mechanisms of checks and balances, 'develops a federal system of power-sharing that fractions both the parliamentary assembly (House of Representatives and House of Peoples) and the presidency into ethnic blocs'. Central to these countervailing measures are the ethnic veto powers inserted at various points into the political system (Bose 2002, 63). Delegates of each ethnic group in the House of Peoples are given authority to declare a decision to be 'destructive of a vital interest' of their group, if a majority (i.e. three out of five) of them think this is the case. If such a declaration is challenged the proposal comes under the consideration of a special Joint Commission, made up of one Delegate from each group. If this Commission fails to resolve the issue, it must be referred to the Constitutional Court. Within the articles on the Presidency, veto powers are first couched in terms of 'entity' interest, not ethnic interest, in that a 'dissenting Member of the Presidency may declare a Presidency Decision to be destructive of a vital interest of the Entity' from which they were elected. The fact that this is a de facto ethnic veto point, however, is revealed by the process for ratifying this declaration. The article goes on to state that '[s]uch a Decision shall be referred immediately to the National Assembly of the [RS], if the declaration was made by the Member from that territory; to the Bosniac Delegates of the House of Peoples of the [FBiH], if the declaration was made by the Bosniac Member; or to the Croat Delegates of that body, if the declaration was made by the Croat Member'. The three-way ethnic divisions that cascade throughout the political institutions of BiH therefore operate here to translate the vital interest of the entity into the vital interest of an ethnic group, in that only elected officials of the same ethnic designation as the dissenting president are given a role in determining whether a 'vital interest' is at stake (Gow 2006, 53).

Ethnic division was thus inscribed into various aspects of the Dayton constitution: between the two entities, within the FBiH entity, and within the state-level political institutions. Politicians from nationalist parties defend these arrangements, arguing that their removal would threaten the very survival of their ethnic group (Hemon 2014, 60). This has operated to transfer political legitimacy from the level of the individual or citizenry as a whole to a reified ethnic level (Mujkic 2007, 112–15), and has led to frequent institutional deadlock (Belloni 2009, 360; Sebastián 2010, 323). It belies the notion of an integrated and united political structure by giving power to sub-groups of elected representatives, based on their ethnic affiliation, and providing no incentive for cross-ethnic co-operation (Donais 2013, 196–202; Keil and Perry 2015, 84; Manning 2004, 75; O'Halloran 2005, 108).

## Refugee Return and Civilian Implementation

Annex 7 of the DPA details the procedures for promoting the return of refugees and displaced persons. The thrust of this policy runs counter to the idea of the conflict as an inevitable 'ethnic war', by seeking to return BiH to the state of inter-ethnic mixing seen as present before the outbreak of violence. The return process is thus driven by the rejection of the idea that different ethnic groups require different and distinct political spaces, but views them as capable of living together peacefully. As well as making statements on the right to return to their 'homes of origin', which, as Toal and Dahlman (2011, 163) argue, is something 'unique in international law' (what they term 'domicile return'), the annex provides for institutional support to make this possible. The BiH and entity governments pledge to give 'full and unrestricted access' to the UNHCR, the International Committee of the Red Cross, and the UN Development Programme, and a 'Commission for Displaced Persons and Refugees' is also created, empowered to adjudicate on conflicts over property rights or compensation. As with many other bodies constituted by the DPA, membership of this commission is split between appointees of the two entities (in a 2:1 ratio in favour of FBiH) and international organisations: in this case, the president of the ECtHR is empowered to appoint three members, and designate one as the chair. The strength of the provisions for the rights of refugees contained in this annex are the strongest trace of the 'international aggression' understanding of the war in the DPA, in that it attempts to counter-act the violent mobilisation of ethnic identity by manipulative political leaders that the 'international aggression' discourse views as responsible for the conflict. The empowering of refugees and displaced persons to return, not just to BiH, but to their pre-war homes, was a clear attempt to reverse some of the effects of ethnic cleansing, and reject the mono-ethnic nature of certain communities that had been produced through violence. As Toal and Dahlman (2011, 7) put it, this annex 'contained provisions that threatened the ethnoterritorial separatism' that actors in the war had attempted to create. While those promoting this agenda recognise it can never completely reverse the demographic effects of ethnic cleansing during the war, over one million refugees and displaced persons have returned to their former homes (Toal and Dahlman 2011, 286).

The final annexes deal with a range of issues, including the designation of National Monuments in Annex 8, the establishment of Public Corporations in Annex 9, and the creation of an International Police Task Force in Annex 11. Annex 10, unassumingly titled 'Agreement on Civilian Implementation', has been one of the most important annexes, particularly in the early years of the post-conflict period. This annex set out the mandate of the OHR, which became one of the most powerful actors in post-war BiH and, at times, a de facto executive authority. The annex states that the High Representative shall '[m]onitor the implementation of the peace settlement', and facilitate, as they judge necessary, 'the resolution of any difficulties arising in connection with civilian implementation', and that the OHR is 'the final authority in theater regarding interpretation of this Agreement on the civilian implementation' of the DPA. This allows holders of the OHR to interpret their own mandate (Chandler 2006, 132), which for Knaus and Martin (2003, 61) produces 'essentially unlimited legal powers' of self-interpretation. After a December 1997 meeting of the Peace Implementation Council[4] in Bonn, the OHR was given new authority (the so-called Bonn powers) to remove major obstacles to the implementation of the DPA (Bougarel, Helms and Duijzings 2007, 9), which Cousens and Cater (2001, 131, emphasis in original) describe as the '*creative authority* to develop and enact laws otherwise blocked by the Bosnian leadership and *enforcement powers* to take action against any public party . . . who were not abiding by the terms of the Dayton implementation'. These powers were used by High Representatives to sack elected officials, suspend and remove judges, and impose decisions on a new flag and national anthem for BiH (Bougarel, Helms, and Duijzings 2007, 9; Knaus and Martin 2003, 65–66; Office of the High Representative 1998; 1999; 2002), when local politicians were unable to finalise agreement themselves.

Across its different Annexes, the DPA therefore traverses the two contradictory framings of the war discussed in chapter 3, alternating between an understanding of the violence as an 'ethnic war', and as one driven by 'international aggression'. This generates a contradictory document, based on contradictory understandings of the war, and with contradictory visions of how post-conflict politics in BiH should unfold. Some aspects build on an understanding of a civil war driven by ancient and innate ethnic hatreds, presupposing the existence of opposed ethnic groups who must be balanced by complex territorial and institutional divisions, constituted through quotas and safeguarded by mutual veto points; while others build on an understanding of an international conflict driven by the mobilisation of ethnic identity by manipulative political elites, demanding a pluralist polity where individual human rights are guaranteed, and the damaging effects of ethnic cleansing can be reversed by electoral mechanisms and the 'domicile return' of refugees and displaced persons. The following two sections trace these contradictions into the post-conflict politics of BiH.

## THE 'BALKANS' SUPPLEMENT AND POST-CONFLICT POLITICS

The institutions designed in the DPA have produced the conditions over the last two decades in which nationalist parties, in one form or another, have been able to maintain their positions of dominance despite endemic failures in their governance. This section argues that the Dayton constitution allows for post-conflict politics in BiH to (re)enact a 'Balkans' struggle. This performance highlights the temporal dimensions of the 'Balkans' supplement contained within the DPA, in that it gives strength, in a retroactive movement, to the historical understandings of the conflict as a typical 'Balkans' war, as the success of the nationalist parties can be read as demonstrating the salience and accuracy of the 'Balkans' analysis of the conflict. The presence of the 'Balkans' supplement in the DPA thus unsettles the idea that post-conflict BiH is temporally distinct from the period of the conflict, showing that one is in fact the *différance* of the other, meaning that post-conflict politics in BiH is not the 'Balkans' struggle ended or annulled, but the 'Balkans' struggle *differed* and *deferred*.

### 1995-2006: Nationalist Politics and International Reform Efforts

In the first post-war elections held in September 1996, the parties involved in the conflict were able to entrench their position within Bosnian politics. The SDA, the HDZ and the SDS swept to victory in a climate of political mistrust, with war-time tensions still very much on the agenda, due to the physical divisions that still existed (i.e. the former front lines), and the fact that there were no other established parties that could challenge the nationalists (Bose 2002, 90). The speed with which these elections were held, which Manning (2004, 63) attributes to the US's military exit strategy, also contributed to massive irregularities around factors like voter turnout, suggesting widespread voter fraud and questioning the legitimacy of the vote (Malik 2000, 340–41). For Manning (2004, 66), these irregularities were so severe that the 1996 election results are discounted from her analysis. The 1997 municipal election results indicate, according to Malik (2000, 344–48), that 'the 80% of the electorate that voted did so along ethnic and national lines', leading him to conclude that these early elections 'not only failed to reverse the consequences of ethnic cleansing, but they entrenched and consolidated the consequences of cleansing' and 'reinforced the country's territorial divisions'. Manning (2004, 75) links this to the 'constitutional peculiarities' of BiH which allow nationalist parties to carve out separate territorial spheres (RS for Serb parties, and Bosniac- and Croat-majority cantons for Bosniac and Croat parties, respectively) 'in which they can maintain their economic as well as political power'.

The dominance of these nationalist parties lasted until the aftermath of the November 2000 elections, when a coalition of opposition parties were brought together by international actors, under the umbrella of the 'Alliance for Change'. This group, building on the successes of the Bosniac Party for Bosnia and Herzegovina (SBiH) and non-nationalist Social Democratic Party (SDP), formed an administration in January 2001, excluding the three wartime parties from government for the first time (McEvoy 2015, 121). A fresh general election was held in 2002, after BiH passed its Election Law, allowing for self-administration of the electoral process for the first time (rather than OSCE administration, as with the previous elections). Due to losses by the SDP, the Alliance for Change was unable to form a new administration, and the nationalist parties regained control (Burwitz 2004, 330).

The end of this short-lived exclusion of the war-time parties coincided with an important change in the institutional set-up of the entities in BiH. A Constitutional Court decision in July 2000 had ruled that the entity constitutions were in violation of the state constitution, in that they did not provide the same guaranteed representation to the three 'constituent peoples'. The ruling was implemented through the decision of the High Representative Wolfgang Petritsch, leading to changes to the entity constitutions in April 2002. The FBiH government must now include eight Bosniac, five Croat, and three Serb ministers (with the PM having the right to appoint one 'Other' in place of a Bosniac), while the RS executive must include eight Serb, five Bosniac, and three Croat ministers (with the PM having the right to appoint one 'Other' in place of a Serb) (Bieber 2005, 86; McEvoy 2015, 27–28). The decision also guarantees a minimum of four seats to ethnic minorities within the National Assembly of RS and the House of Representatives of the FBiH (Burwitz 2004, 330). As Bieber (2006, 21–22) notes, the way in which the court decision was implemented had the effect of cascading the logic of power-sharing and veto rights from the state level down to the entities and cantons, 'thus increasing the degree of ethnic representation in the political system, rather than reducing it', and rendering BiH 'more, rather than less, complex'. This greater fragmentation proceeded alongside a consolidation and strengthening of the powers of the state-level government, however. Starting from a low base of three central ministries, by 2004 this had grown to nine, with key areas such as justice and defence now being administered through the Council of Ministers.[5] An integrated tax system was also created, and new state-level regulatory bodies, such as the State Border Service and the Regulatory Agency for Communication, have been formed (Bieber 2006, 19; Jenne 2009, 280; Sebastián 2010, 323). This centralisation at the state-level thus provides something of a counter-weight to the fragmentation at the entity and local levels, moving BiH closer to an approximation of a 'normal' political system.

This period also saw a major attempt to reform the Dayton constitution. After the CoE's 'Venice Commission' made recommendations for reform in March 2005, talks amongst seven major political parties began in April 2005, as a private initiative of Donald Hays, a former Deputy Principal in the OHR (Sebastián 2007, 4). Talks were centred around the 'premise of streamlining the state structure and preventing blockages, while recognizing that national identities matter in the political system' (Bieber 2006, 28). After initial conclusions were reached in November 2005 about the transfer of powers from the Presidency to the Council of Ministers, a more comprehensive reform package was agreed by March 2006 (Arvanitopoulos and Tzifakis 2008, 19). The proposals included 'a new format for the election of the Presidency along with a reduction of its powers; new competences granted to the state; the creation of two new ministries, namely agriculture and technology; the strengthening of the Council of Ministers; and an increase in the number of MPs in both parliamentary chambers' (Sebastián 2007, 4). These proposals, which became known as the 'April package', were put to a vote in the state-level House of Representatives. However, with last-minute opposition from SBiH, who withdrew from the process, and a split in the HDZ over the proposals, the package failed to achieve the required two-thirds majority by just two votes (Arvanitopoulos and Tzifakis 2008, 19–20; Hays and Crosby 2006, 10).

The 2006 general elections were held in the context of this failed reform effort. SBiH and the newly formed splinter party 'HDZ 1990' 'built their electoral platform for the 2006 October elections around the opposition to the constitutional package and the vilification of the party leaders who supported it' (Sebastián 2010, 337). Thus while the war-time nationalist parties were again marginalised, in the case of the SDA and SDS, their usurpers in this election were not proponents of a non-ethnic politics, but rival nationalist parties from *within* their own blocs. Milorad Dodik's Alliance of Independent Social Democrats (SNSD) came to power while warning about the threats posed to the existence of the RS entity, while Haris Silajdžić's SBiH countered Dodik's rhetoric by describing RS as a 'genocidal creation' (Arvanitopoulos and Tzifakis 2008, 20; Weber 2014, 99). Dodik also questioned the future of BiH as a state during the 2012 local election campaign, although in this case losing votes to the SDS (Karić 2013, 210–4). The performance of HDZ 1990 in October 2006 served only to split the 'Croat' vote, allowing the SDP's Komšić to gain the Croat seat in the Presidency for the first time (Sebastián 2010, 339). The victory of this non-nationalist candidate indicates that the election results were not solely the continuation of ethnic politics in the guise of new parties: a sign of the complication and contradiction carried into the post-conflict political landscape by the DPA.

## 2006–2020: Integration and Disintegration

While further attempts at constitutional reform in 2008 and 2009 broke down without agreement (Belloni 2009, 366; McEvoy 2015, 140–43), the 2010 general elections appeared to signal a change when the strongly pro-EU and non-nationalist SDP emerged as the largest parliamentary group in the FBiH entity and the strongest party at the state level. However, the SDP's attempt to form a government on the basis of an EU-integration agenda led to a fifteen-month political crisis, with the main parties unable to agree on the formation of a government. Indeed, for Keil and Perry (2015, 83–85), one of the problems reaching agreement in this period was that the SDP's success upset the usual balance formed by nationalist parties in governing institutions, whereby they attempt to support each other's interests in order to thwart the emergence of a non-ethnic politics. When an agreement was reached, the compromises maintained fidelity to the vision of European integration, but jettisoned the practical details in favour of strengthening party control over the decentralised BiH state (Weber 2014, 103–104). The 2014 elections punished the SDP, which lost over half its vote in FBiH (Keil and Perry 2015, 84), but also served to return to power the parties who had dominated politics in BiH before 2010. The SNSD was returned in 2014 as the governing party at entity level in RS, however (Keil and Perry 2015, 85), although it failed to gain representation on the state-level government (Lippmann 2015), and the HDZ's Dragan Čović was returned as the Croat member of the Presidency, replacing Komšić (who was now standing for the Democratic Front party, after splitting from the SDP) (Keil and Perry 2015, 85). These results, which had been foreshadowed by the success of the three major nationalist parties in the 2012 local elections (Karić 2013; 2015), provided, in the words of Florian Bieber (2014a), 'change without change', producing another tortuous post-election negotiation period, with six months passing before a new government was formed, with SDA, SDS and HDZ re-emerging in power (Lippman 2015,

3). According to Keil and Perry (2015, 82), the 2014 election campaign was 'one of the dirtiest and most divisive' in recent years, 'further polarizing an environment characterized not only by the lack of reform, but by stagnation and even regression since 2006'.

The 2016 local election campaign was overshadowed by Dodik's decision to hold a referendum in RS, less than two weeks before polling day, on the entity's disputed and contentious national holiday (which falls on the day RS was declared in 1992, in the period preceding the outbreak of war). This limited the ability of rival Serb parties to oppose the SNSD, and allowed parties in FBiH to play-off heightened fears of the threat posed by Dodik to state unity. This context helped the SNSD regain its dominant local position in RS politics (Kapidžić 2016, 128–30). The long-run up to the October 2018 elections saw debates in RS about a possible referendum on the jurisdiction of BiH-level courts over the entity, and calls from Croat politicians for the creation of a third, Croat entity (Kovacevic 2017; Lakic 2018a). In the election itself, the main talking point was Dodik's victory in his run for the state-level Presidency. As well as stating that he will 'work above all and only for the interests of Serbs' in this new role, Dodik is shunning the Presidency building in Sarajevo for a new office in East Sarajevo, within RS territory (Lakic 2018c; 2018d). In doing so, he is following the example of the Croat member of the Presidency Dragan Čović, who opened a Presidency office in Mostar. Čović himself lost his seat on the Presidency to Komšić, who held the position between 2006 and 2014. As on previous occasions, the election of Komšić provoked protests from some Croats, who argue that Komšić has been elected on the back of Bosniac votes (Lakic 2018e). It took until December 2019 for a state-level government to be formed following the October 2018 elections, after protracted debates over issues including BiH's progress towards NATO membership (Kovacevic 2019a; 2019b).

The story of post-conflict politics told here suggests that, despite some alterations in the political structures and the dominant parties, post-conflict politics in BiH has been a (re)enactment of a 'Balkans' struggle. This tendency is highlighted by the numerous academics who view the institutional framework of the DPA as operating to reify and strengthen the ethnic identities mobilised during the conflict (Jenne 2009, 280; Weller and Wolff 2006; Zahar 2005, 129). Belloni (2009, 360) is not atypical in charging the DPA with 'reversing Clausewitz' by turning politics in BiH 'into the continuation of war by other means'. Furthermore, this performance gives strength to historical readings of the conflict as a 'Balkans' war, as these accounts are vindicated after the event by the apparent fact that politics in BiH remains structured around ethnic division. This is how I understand the conflict and post-conflict to be produced as the *différance* of each other: rather than the post-conflict being a new temporal state where the conflict is over or annulled, it remains tied to the conflict, through a chain of supplementation, which produces the post-conflict as the conflict *differed* and *deferred.*

However, the next section shows that is only a partial picture of the contemporary political landscape in BiH. By first considering the legal challenges brought by citizens of BiH who do not identify with any of the 'constituent peoples', and then examining the protest movements that have emerged over the last decade or so, I show how the transformative elements of the DPA provide a basis for forms of non-ethnic politics which challenge the mobilisation of ethnicity seen as the peculiar predilection of Balkan political leaders in BiH. Crucially, both these trends are seen as arising from within the DPA, demonstrating how this political system is already in a process of deconstruction.

## DECONSTRUCTING THE DAYTON
## PEACE AGREEMENT

### Legal Challenges to Ethnic Politics

As discussed above, the institutional and territorial set-up of BiH has long been recognised as making 'political representation dependent upon ethnic belonging and thus discriminat[ing] against individuals who do not identify themselves ethnically or, even if they do, might not be able to exercise a variety of rights because they reside in an area where they constitute a minority' (Belloni 2009, 360). This is most apparent in relation to the House of Peoples and the Presidency, elections to which are governed both by territorial and ethnic stipulations. This means that Bosniacs and Croats living in RS, or Serbs living in FBiH, cannot run for these offices from their home entity, 'while any person unwilling to identify with one of the three main groups is effectively excluded altogether' (Zahar 2005, 128–29). A similar anomaly exists due to the status of Brčko as simultaneously a part of the RS and FBiH entities. As entity citizenship is the only route to national citizenship, residents in Brčko must choose citizenship of one or other of the entities, if they wish to vote in state-level elections. Refusing to choose means they will be disbarred from voting at the national level. Non-entity citizens in Brčko thus join non-ethnically identified citizens in FBiH as having restricted opportunities for formal engagement with the political institutions of BiH (Stjepanović 2015, 1047).

These exclusionary stipulations were challenged in a landmark court case, brought against the state of BiH by two prominent public figures from the Roma and Jewish community, Dervo Sejdić and Jacob Finci. In 2006, the two men attempted to stand in the October 2006 general elections, for the House of Peoples and the Presidency. As Eralp (2012, 6-7) puts it, the 'Bosnian Central Election Commission turned down their applications on the grounds that [they] did not belong to any of the constituent peoples . . . and thus were not eligible to run for a seat in the House of Peoples and the Council of the Presidency'. Sejdić and Finci therefore took their case to the ECtHR, where it was heard in 2009. The ECtHR judged the constitution of BiH to be in violation of the protocols of the ECHR that prohibit discrimination. Two further rulings in the ECtHR have re-affirmed the decision in the Sejdić-Finci case. Firstly, the rights of Azra Zornic were ruled to be infringed by her unwillingness to declare as anything other than a citizen of BiH; secondly, Ilijas Pilav was ruled to be unfairly treated by the requirement to declare himself as a Serb in order to stand for the Serb position on the Presidency (Perry 2019, 113). In these decisions, the ECtHR ruled that no matter why you do not identify with one of the three 'constituent peoples' (i.e. whether through identification with a minority, or refusal to ascribe to a particular identity), you should be able to run for all political offices (Stojanović 2018, 351).

While implementation of the Sejdić-Finci case was once a precondition for progress on the accession of BiH to the EU, the persistent failure of political parties to agree on how exactly to generate compliance has led to the EU no longer insisting on this reform (Bieber 2014b). These efforts where complicated by the election of Komšić to the Croat position on the Presidency in 2006 and 2010. Croat nationalist parties argued that Komšić did not truly represent the views of their constituency, due to his election being secured by non-Croat votes, and therefore demanded that any resolution of the issues thrown up by the Sejdić-Finci case also resolves this perceived issue (Bieber 2014b, 186–87). These troubles mean that, over ten years after the original ruling, the BiH constitution is still held to be in conflict with the ECHR.

The Sejdić-Finci case, and its follow-ups, are therefore interesting not because of the transformative effect they have had on politics in BiH, but because of what they say about the Dayton constitution. While not yet successful in annulling the discriminatory sections of the constitution, the fact these challenges have been launched demonstrate that politics in BiH does not divide neatly into the three 'constituent peoples'. Furthermore, the rulings of the ECtHR must not be seen as holding the constitution against exterior standards of judgement: rather, they are important in highlighting *contradictions within* the constitution. As legal scholar Marko Milanovic (2010, 640) has argued, the cases arise from 'an unresolvable norm conflict between different parts of the Constitution, with one part prohibiting discrimination and the others institutionalizing it', meaning that the constitution itself was 'irrevocably fragmented'. The cases are possible because the DPA embodies a contradiction, between an ethnically determined account of political identity in BiH, and a transformative agenda based on human rights and equality. One reason why the claimants were able to take their cases to the ECtHR is because the ECHR is one of the international human rights agreements which, according to the constitution, apply directly in BiH (as discussed above). The cases thus highlight the in-built contradictions of the constitution, which reflect and retroactively reconstruct the contradictory understandings of the conflict as simultaneously an internal 'ethnic war' and a regional conflict brought about by 'international aggression', and demonstrate the Dayton political system to already be in a process of deconstruction.

The court cases also highlight a more general point about the political activity of 'Others' in BiH: that is, those who do not (or refuse to) ascribe themselves to one of the three 'constituent peoples'. As discussed above, the Preamble to the constitution recognises the presence of 'Others' in BiH, though they are relegated to parentheses after Bosniacs, Croats and Serbs. While they are legally banned from running for the state Presidency and the state House of Peoples, there are no restrictions on many other offices of state. As Stojanović (2018, 350) notes, 'between 2006 and 2010 the Bosnian foreign minister was of Jewish background'. I discussed above how the entity constitutions now make allowance for 'Others' in some cases, and the 2008 amendments to the Election Law guarantee seats for national minorities at the local level if, according to the 1991 census, they make up more than 3% of the municipality population (Hodžić and Stojanović 2011, 55). Bieber (2006, 23) highlights how this system is abused on occasion, however, with those holding seats as 'Others' in fact being self-declared representatives of dominant nationalist parties.

The reference to the 1991 census in the Election Law is also worthy of more consideration, as it is just one instance of a widespread practice. Before 2013, the 1991 census, conducted across the territory of the former Yugoslavia, was the last to be held in BiH. After years of wrangling, a new census was held in 2013, with the results not released until 2016. The 1991 census was referenced in the DPA in the annex on elections, which ruled:

> Any citizen of Bosnia and Herzegovina aged 18 or older whose name appears on the 1991 census for Bosnia and Herzegovina shall be eligible, in accordance with electoral rules and regulations, to vote. A citizen who no longer lives in the municipality in which he or she resided in 1991 shall, as a general rule, be expected to vote, in person or by absentee ballot, in that municipality. (Organisation for Security and Co-operation in Europe 1995)

While citizens can apply to vote elsewhere, and those not counted in the 1991 census can register to vote, the 'general rule' is that citizens vote in the municipality in which they resided at the time of the 1991 census – in other words, in their *pre-war locations*. In tandem with the policy of refugee return discussed above, this stipulation was governed by a desire to reverse the effects of ethnic cleansing through electoral politics, by allowing those who had fled or been forced from their homes to vote in their pre-war locations, to help ensure that areas made (entirely or largely) ethnically homogenous through violence would not overwhelmingly elect the political representatives of the now-dominant group. This is therefore a strong example of how the DPA political system, while in other parts accepting ethnic difference as a reality to be accommodated, simultaneously suggests an understanding of ethnic differences as constructed through violent mobilisation (as proponents of the 'international aggression' discourse put forward), by installing mechanisms to re-create the more pluralistic ethnic mix seen in the 1991 census data.

When this annex was supplanted by the Election Law in 2001,[6] reference to the census was retained, and indeed used more extensively. The law states that the composition of an election commission or Polling Station Committee should reflect the multi-ethnic balance of the electoral unit for which it is formed, based upon the information provided by 'the most recent national Census'. If the appropriate ethnic balance is not realised, the Election Commission of BiH are empowered to annul the appointment of the members. Further articles re-affirm the use of the census in the original annex on elections, by linking permanent residence to 'either the citizen's residence according to the most recent national Census, or the municipality where a citizen is registered as a permanent resident in accordance with law', and by providing for the right of refugees and displaced persons to vote in the municipalities in which they resided at the time of the last census. While the wording of this law indicates that the 2013 census data should replace reference to the older census, the entity-level constitutions[7] in BiH both make specific reference to the '1991 census'. The FBiH constitution requires that representation in governments and courts, at the cantonal and municipal level, must be apportioned according to the information provided by the 1991 census, while the RS constitution was amended in 2002 to include a new article, which states: 'Constituent peoples and members of the group of Others shall be proportionally represented in public institutions in [RS]; As a constitutional principle, such proportionate representation shall follow the 1991 census'. As Perry (2015, 59–61) notes, the references to either the 1991 census or 'the last census' in these stipulations is problematic, as this ambiguity may lead to different measures being used in different parts of BiH. Perry (2015, 61–62) also raises the issue of which question from the 2013 census would be used as a measure of 'national' or 'ethnic' balance. The census contained questions on nationality/ethnicity, religion, and mother tongue, but only the last of these was mandatory, and citizens were not told that their answers to this question would be used as proxy for their nationality or ethnicity.

Census data is therefore used in BiH not just to divide political positions between the three 'constituent peoples', but also, in some cases, to provide representation for the 'Others' who do not fit into the three-way division of the population. When reference is made to the 1991 census, the figure for 'Others' could include the 6% of the BiH population who classified themselves as members of the pan-national identity of 'Yugoslav' (Campbell 1998, 79). While this identity died along with the SFRY, meaning that the most recent census contained no direct equivalent, the 2013 exercise recorded 3.7% of citizens as belonging to the general category of 'Others': a population of over 130,000 (Stojanović 2018, 349). Focusing in on the data therefore highlights an instability, a sense in which the political system of BiH is built on contradictions between allowing a (re)enactment of a 'Balkans' struggle, while also containing space (no matter how small) for a transformative politics which rejects ethnic labels. This split-screen politics was even enacted while the 2013 census was carried out. Cooley (2019, 1–2), following Horowitz, discusses how the census was run like an election campaign. He notes that 'politicians and civil society organisations associated with each of the country's three largest ethnic groups' campaigned 'to ensure the maximisation of their share in the population statistics', while 'organisations that stressed citizens' rights to self-identification, free from political pressure' ran counter-campaigns, with some even urging citizens to opt out of identifying as Bosniac, Serb or Croat and 'instead declare themselves to simply be "Bosnians"'. While the final results showed that a crushing majority (96.3%) chose to identify with one of the 'constituent peoples', the activity of the political campaigns opposing this identification indicate that politics in BiH is more than a simple reflection of ethnic identity. Cooley also notes that many of the individuals involved in the civic campaigns around the census had taken part in earlier protest movements, indicating continuity between those who have taken to the streets to demonstrate their dissatisfaction with the political process, and those rejecting the ethnic division of the population. It is to these protest movements that I now turn.

## Protesting against Ethnic Politics

Commentators have long noted the dysfunction of politics in BiH, which is either blamed on the activities of competitive and uncooperative nationalist parties, or seen as an outworking of the decentralised and fragmented political system itself.[8] Examples of dysfunction abound in the literature. Perry (2019, 122) notes how 'there is not a single election in the country in which all citizens vote on the same slate of candidates', while an International Crisis Group (2014, 19) report records how 'at one point in 2013 all parliamentary parties were in opposition'. Political parties are regularly viewed in surveys as corrupt institutions (Donais 2013, 202), leading to a lack of support for their reform efforts (Søberg 2008, 730). A further indication of popular discontent with the political system is the low levels of turnout. As noted in chapter 4, it is possible to read low or declining turnout as a sign of dissatisfaction with electoral party politics. Discounting the early elections due to allegations of massive irregularities, we see a sharp decline in turnout after 2000, with the figure of 64.4% in the general election of that year being followed by one of 55% in the 2002 general election (Organisation for Security and Co-operation in Europe 2000; 2003). The highest point reached after 2000 was the 56% turnout in the October 2010 local elections[9] (Karić 2013, 212). This can be read as evidence of the disengagement of large sections of a frustrated and demoralised electorate (Belloni 2009, 360).

Popular dissatisfaction with the post-conflict political system has been even more visible, in the last decade or so, through various protest movements. As Belloni, Kappler and Ramovic (2016, 47) recount, '[c]ultural and social movements of resistance have existed in [BiH] for some time', but as they 'were barely channelled into official political processes' they were 'often overlooked [as] processes of political mobilisation'. After several small-scale industrial protests were held in the early to mid-2000s, without attracting much media attention, a wave of larger protests took place in Sarajevo in 2008, after the murder of teenager Denis Mrnjavac. In a pattern that was to be repeated in later protests, the demonstrators initially 'demanded improved security but the focus quickly shifted on to the incompetence of ruling elites and their unwillingness to address issues which were of importance for the majority of the population', such as high levels of unemployment. These protests endured for three months and can be seen as playing a role in the poor performance of the local governing party in municipal elections in October 2008 (Belloni, Kappler and Ramovic 2016, 52–53). The year 2012 then saw numerous protests over threats to valued public spaces: in Sarajevo, activists fought to prevent the closure of the National Museum and other cultural institutions (Kesby 2012); while in Banja Luka protesters opposed the development of the Pica Park into a residential and business complex (Belloni, Kappler, and Ramovic 2016, 53). The summer of 2013 then saw widespread protests over the death of the three-month-old girl Berina Hamidovic, who was unable to travel to Serbia for medical treatment due to a dispute over the issuing of identity cards (Dedovic 2013). After initial reticence, politicians eventually adapted a new law which allowed for the issuance of identity card numbers (Belloni, Kappler, and Ramovic 2016, 54). The protests of February 2014, however, were the most visible in the international media.

Beginning as an industrial dispute in the city of Tuzla, with protesters expressing anger at the privatisation and asset-stripping of once-productive factories, the action soon developed into a widespread movement against the political system in all the major cities of BiH (including the de facto capital of RS, Banja Luka). The attention of the global media focused largely on the violent emanations of these protests, reporting on the fires that were started at the cantonal government offices in Tuzla, Mostar and Sarajevo, and in the state archives and the presidency building in the capital. Contrary to these publicised images, the majority of protesters looked for peaceful and productive ways to channel their anger over unemployment, poverty and the growing divide between the connected elites and ordinary people. The protests quickly developed into a political forum, with 'plenums' or councils being set up in the major cities, allowing citizens to develop and publicise their demands for re-evaluations of the privatisation deals, reductions of the salaries of high-ranking government officials, and the provision of free health services (Pasic 2015).

These plenums attempted to build on the earlier protests and social movements to articulate a new style of democratic and non-ethnic politics, freed from a dependence on political parties, non-governmental organisations and the myriad international agencies operating in BiH. According to Heather McRobie (2014), the February protests arose from 'frustration at the unworkable political structure of post-war Bosnia and how it chews into the daily lives of Bosnian citizens, as well as anger at politicians who have capitalised on [them] to further their own interests'. The political institutions dating to the DPA were thus seen by many as the cause of the political stagnation and gridlock that has paralysed the country and stunted its development, producing the environment within which the protests developed (Gordy 2014; Smale 2014; The Guardian 2014). As argued by the Bosnian academic Damir Arsenijević (2014), who was involved in the plenums, the anger and dissatisfaction of citizens was directed at the dual-level of the 'local and international politicians [who] have exhausted the citizens of Bosnia and Herzegovina' since the outbreak of war. According to Murtagh (2016, 149–50), this 'ideological rejection of the postwar political regime' meant that the plenum movement 'chose to refrain from entering the fray of institutional politics', and instead pursued 'demands for political accountability' while 'resisting invitations to engage with political actors, institutions, or matters of high politics'.

Despite the marginalisation of the movement after catastrophic flooding hit the region in May 2014, and the victory of nationalist parties in the October 2014 elections, the energy and enthusiasm which characterised the early days of the plenums pointed to a clear and widespread dissatisfaction with how nationalist politicians have been able to entrench themselves into positions of power within the post-Dayton regime. The plenums have been described as 'practicing the democracy that has been denied to Bosnians by the postwar framework', as embodying a rejection of the nationalist discourse and articulating through their very existence a vision of social justice (McRobie 2014). The legacy of the protests and plenums can also be seen in the ongoing struggles for justice after the unexplained deaths of two young men, David Dragičević and Dženan Memić, which have again become focal points for anger with the governing parties (Lakic 2018b; Sarajevo Times 2019). Finally, the threat provided by the plenums to the nationalist parties is seen in the documented cases of intimidation of participants: but always intimidation of persons from the *same* ethnic group that the coercive party claims to represent (Murtagh 2016, 160). This fits an earlier trend identified by Manning (2004, 71–72), whereby most serious cases of voter intimidation recorded by the OSCE (such as beatings, arson and bombings) occurred *between* parties fighting to represent the same ethnic group. For Belloni, Kappler and Ramovic (2016, 56), the pressure put on participants, as well as negative coverage in nationalist party-dominated media, 'showed how big the stakes were for political elites and how much they felt threatened by the citizens' actions'. This intimidation indicates how the link between national parties and 'their' ethnic population is not natural, but must be policed and maintained, sometimes through violence.

The centrality of the rejection of ethnic division in the February 2014 movement can be seen in the slogan 'We are hungry in three languages', which was displayed on banners at various protest sites in BiH. Images containing this slogan were widely circulated on social media, and the phrase even found its way into the title of an article written by the former High Representative for BiH Wolfgang Petritsch (2014).[10] The 'three languages' in the slogan refers to the three de facto official 'languages' of BiH – Bosnian, Croatian and Serbian – which emerged from the Serbo-Croat language spoken in the days of SFRY. Despite being mutually comprehensible, each of these languages is claimed by a different 'constituent people'.[11] The slogan also echoes one of the few definitions Derrida (1989, 15, italics in original) ever proffered for deconstruction, when he wrote that if he 'had to risk a single definition of deconstruction, one as brief, elliptical, and economical as a password, I would say simply and without overstatement: *plus d'une langue*–both more than a language and no more of *a* language'. Discussing this elsewhere, Derrida (2001a, 28–29) describes deconstruction as 'more than one language . . . that is, several languages, more than one language, more than language'. Derrida (1995, 27–28) admitted this 'definition', being 'the only definition I have ever in my life dared to give of deconstruction', is neither a statement nor a sentence, but something that highlights the centrality to deconstruction of translation, of transference amongst and within languages. In his playful style, it is a definition to be put into use, to be inserted into language and discourse as a destabilising gesture. What would it mean, then, to put this definition 'into use' in the context of the slogan referenced above?

The slogan can be read simply as a demand, aimed at the various levels of BiH government, to ensure the material well-being of the people, no matter which of the three languages they speak. While such a reading of the slogan, as a simple embodiment of the protesters focus on everyday issues such as employment, welfare and health care, which were seen as 'blurred by the continual focus on ethnonational matters in Bosnian politics' (Murtagh 2016, 156), is possible, I read the slogan as making a critical *connection* between ethnic division *and* the social and economic issues facing citizens of BiH. This is because it disrupts the division of BiH into three distinct ethno-linguistic groups by introducing an element of undecidability between them. The slogan is simultaneously saying 'we are hungry no matter what language we speak' *and* showing how the statement 'we are hungry' can be written *once* in 'all three languages', thus challenging the division of BiH on an ethno-linguistic basis. If this was merely a protest about living standards or a call to universal solidarity the banner need only have read 'We are hungry'. The playful and subversive addition of 'in three languages' (the text is only written once, not 'translated' into the other languages) makes it clear that no translation is needed between the 'three languages'. It is a slogan written in Bosnian, Croatian, Serbian and the now-defunct Serbo-Croat, all at once. It is any one of these languages, and all of them, and therefore cannot be appropriated solely by any one language. To say 'we are hungry in three languages' in Bosnian, in Croatian or in Serbian is to reveal the fiction of that language's uniqueness, by making it clear that the slogan would be the same in any of the other languages. Even if rendered in the Cyrillic script in an attempt to fix its meaning in Serbian, the slogan would break free again when chanted at a protest march or read aloud by those who view it in person, on television or online. The slogan therefore reveals the emptiness of claims to the immanent reality of ethnic difference in BiH that rest upon the assertion of linguistic difference. I therefore read it as an example of 'deconstruction in action'.

However, the slogan does not address the source of the ethnic division that it seeks to displace: in other words, it targets the *effects* of the supplementation of the DPA with the 'Balkans' understanding of war, *without challenging the supplement itself*.[12] To do so, more is needed than a deconstruction of the contemporary iterations of ethnic division, no matter how much they are seen as the cause of current hardship and alienation by those engaging in protest. Rather, a deconstruction which challenges *both* the present ethnic divisions *and* their basis in historical conceptualisations must be enacted: a deconstruction which radiates its effects both backwards and forwards in time. The development of such a 'deconstructive conclusion' is the goal of the following chapter.

## CONCLUSION

This chapter has traced the presence of two contradictory accounts of the war in BiH, as either an internal 'ethnic war' or a conflict started by 'international aggression', into the text of the DPA. These accounts were seen as giving rise to two central, but contradictory, elements of the post-conflict landscape: the complex system of territorial and institutional divisions designed to placate the formerly warring 'constituent peoples'; and a transformative agenda based on individual human rights that could counteract the destructive mobilisation of ethnic difference during the conflict. The post-conflict electoral politics was seen to follow from the first of these, allowing a (re)enactment of a 'Balkans' struggle, while simultaneously giving strength to the historical accounts of the conflict that view the violence in such a manner. Yet, this was seen as only a partial picture of the post-conflict political landscape. By examining legal challenges to the ethnic basis of the political system, and the various protest movements of the last decade that have expressed dissatisfaction with governing elites, I highlighted some of the ways in which the ethnic elements of the Dayton system are already politically contested. Crucially, the legal cases were seen as arising from within the DPA, in that they utilise the transformational language of human rights embedded within the text as the basis for their challenge to the ethnic logics of the political institutions. In other words, they highlight the central and irresolvable contradictions within a political structure that attempts to simultaneously foreground group rights and protect individual rights. Some aspects of the protest movement, particularly the slogan 'We are hungry in three languages', were then read as examples of 'deconstruction in action', through the manner in which they present ethnic division in BiH as inseparable from social and economic difficulties.

However, the inability of the recent protest and plenum movements to have long-term political effects must also be considered. I connect this to the protesters' focus on the current situation in BiH, and their reticence to engage in debates on institutional reform. While I agree that the plenum movement risks being caught in fresh failures to agree meaningful constitutional change, I urge them to go *further* in their political demands, and avoid retreating into the immediate and the quotidian. In other words, I urge them to challenge not just the *effects* of the ethnic division written into the political structures of BiH, but the *source* of this division, and its divisive and contradictory effects, which I locate in the contradictory understandings of the conflict and the way in which they are made to work together through the operation of the 'Balkans' supplement. The manner in which such a deconstructive gesture could be put in practice will be the focus of the next chapter, where I argue for a deconstructive conclusion to the conflicts in Northern Ireland and BiH.

*Chapter 6*

# A Deconstructive Conclusion to the Conflicts in Northern Ireland and Bosnia and Herzegovina

For much of the time I was writing this book, one thing that Northern Ireland and BiH had in common was their lack of functioning government. In Northern Ireland, the devolved Assembly and Executive were suspended between January 2017 and January 2020, brought down by the financial mismanagement of a renewable energy scheme, but with restoration held up in a context of division over the UK's relationship with the EU, the legal status of the Irish language in Northern Ireland, and mechanisms for engaging with the legacy of 'the troubles'. In BiH, the three largest parties after the October 2018 elections took until December 2019 to agree to the formation of a state-level government. The level of dysfunction in this period is not atypical of the post-conflict political experience of Northern Ireland and BiH. Devolved government has been absent from Northern Ireland for over eight of the twenty years since powers were first handed down in December 1999, while the record for a post-election period without government in BiH was reached in 2011, when a state-level government formed fifteen months after the previous elections.

In chapters 4 and 5, I charted the development of this dysfunctional politics in post-conflict Northern Ireland and BiH. I argued that the peace agreements in both cases embedded specific understandings of the conflicts into the post-conflict political structures. However, as set-out in chapters 2 and 3, these understandings were seen as contradictory, and thus only capable of working together with the addition of the undecidable 'two communities' and 'Balkans' supplements, respectively. This supplementation, traced in the wording and workings of the peace agreements, has two simultaneous effects, as examined in chapters 4 and 5. First, it allows the post-conflict electoral politics of Northern Ireland and BiH to (re)enact the 'two communities' and 'Balkans' struggles, presenting Northern Ireland and BiH as political spaces where irreconcilable identity groups can, at best, be accommodated by a division of power across political institutions, with breakdowns in this system acceptable as an alternative to violence. In this sense, I argued that the post-conflict period is not truly *different* from the conflict, in the sense of being defined as the opposite or the absence of conflict, but as the *différance* of the conflict, the conflict *differed* and *deferred* through the detour of the peace agreements. The (re)enactments of the 'two communities' and 'Balkans' struggles in the post-conflict period thus gives strength to these analyses of the conflicts, making it seem self-evident that the conflicts were driven by the clash of historically constituted, irreconcilable groups, as this remains the apparent structure of contemporary politics in Northern Ireland and BiH. Second, I argued that these (re)enactments of the 'two communities' and 'Balkans' struggles do not capture everything about contemporary politics in Northern Ireland and BiH. Instead, I highlighted the political currents that contest the accommodation of innately opposed groups, taking strength from the elements of the peace agreements that view identity as capable of transformation. These aspects of formal and informal politics, from the electoral success of 'Others' in Northern Ireland to legal challenges to the privileged position of 'constituent peoples' in the BiH constitution, and from the Temple and Turas projects in Northern Ireland to the protest and plenum movements in BiH, were seen as examples of 'deconstruction in action'.

Chapters 4 and 5 therefore argued that the post-conflict political systems in Northern Ireland and BiH are already undergoing a process of deconstruction. The central question that remains, and what this chapter considers, is why this deconstruction does not generate a more positive and open politics in these places. In other words, why are the challenges to the political systems discussed in chapters 4 and 5 not 'successful', and how can politics in Northern Ireland and BiH be characterised as a dysfunctional (re)enactment of the divisions associated with the conflicts? This chapter argues that the failures thus far, and the continued possibility of dysfunction, are rooted in the peace agreements themselves, and how the understandings of the conflicts contained within these agreements are transmitted simultaneously into the historical analyses of the conflicts, and the political present and future of Northern Ireland and BiH. A more 'successful' response therefore requires challenging the historical understandings contained within the supplements of the 'two communities' and 'Balkans' accounts *at the same time* as challenging the effects produced by these supplements in the present. I now suggest how a Derridean 'deconstructive conclusion' can achieve these goals.

## ENDING CONFLICT, ENDING PEACE

Everyday thought and life depend upon concepts of linear temporality, of endings and beginnings, with the meaning of events and things arising in part from their placement on a straight line of causality (Edkins 2003b, xiii–xiv, 14–16). Conclusions play a key part in the construction of such linear temporalities. They provide an ending, while also pointing to new beginnings, to new questions, to new lines of thought. They provide a juncture within a linear temporal schema, an ending that also signals a new beginning, as time continues its inexorable onwards march. A full stop does not just denote the end of a sentence, but usually signifies the beginning of a new one as well. A conclusion, however, can do more than this, can perform more than such a Janus-faced looking-forwards and looking-backwards in a manner which reinforces dominant understandings of time as the linear progression from past-to-present-to-future. A conclusion can aspire to disrupt and unsettle these norms. Such a conclusion should therefore do more than just mark an ending and simultaneously signal a new beginning – it should upset settled notions of linearity, alter how ending (and beginning) are conceived, push time backwards, allow the whole to be expressed in one temporal instant. Following Derrida, a conclusion that works to question the ontology of beginnings and endings by putting linear temporality 'out of joint', and that shows time to be 'off its hinges' by making it apparent that 'no time is contemporary with itself' (Derrida 1994, 139), could be called a 'deconstructive conclusion'. What would it mean to provide such a deconstructive conclusion to the conflicts in Northern Ireland and BiH?

To say something has 'concluded', to move on from it, we must know what it was, and when it ended. Derrida makes this point in relation to the work of mourning: to mourn, we must first know *who* has died, and *when* they have died. Derrida (1994, 9, emphasis in original) writes that mourning 'consists always in attempting to ontologize remains, to make them present, in the first place by *identifying* the bodily remains . . . One has to know. *One has to know it. One has to have knowledge* . . . one *has to know* who is buried where'. Mourning 'presumes above all a knowledge, the knowledge of the date. One must indeed know *when: at what instant* mourning began. One must indeed know *at what moment* death took place' (Derrida 1995, 20, emphasis in original). We must move here from the intimate realm of mourning the death of a loved one, to the question of moving on from a conflict, of moving into a post-conflict time period. Following Derrida, we can say that to 'mourn' a conflict, in the sense of declaring it over and attempting to move on from its violence, requires 'ontologising' it, giving it presence by containing it within certain dates, dates which mark the beginning and ending of the conflict. This 'mourning' would also require providing certainty about what the conflict was, what its causes were, who the combatants were, and why they were fighting: for only when you have certain knowledge of what the conflict *was*, can you know for certain that it has *ended*. This ontologising of conflict attempts to provide a secure ground from which to say that we are now in a post-conflict period, when the violence has passed and the work of peacebuilding and reconciliation has begun.

It is just this secure ground that Derrida's (1995, 23) deconstructive ethos seeks to challenge, by demonstrating 'the impossibility of an objective and stable reference to . . . the founding event'. Derrida (1994, 48) argues that what is located in the past does not stay in the past, but returns as a spectral presence in the present, disrupting the 'linear succession of a before and an after, between a present-past, a present-present, and a present-future', and casting doubt on 'the reassuring order of presents', and the opposition of presence to absence. This is what Derrida (1994, 10) calls *hauntology*, the 'logic of haunting' that disrupts every ontology or thinking of Being. Naming a moment of 'ending' that is a simultaneous 'beginning' of peace is thus unstable and unsustainable: the attempt to contain the conflict within certain dates fails, as the conflict continues to make its presence felt in the present, re-appearing as a spectral presence to haunt the present. This is not the same as stating that post-conflict politics simply re-stages the conflict by other means, but must be a way of challenging the understanding of the conflict itself, of showing how the conflict escapes classification, how it refuses to stay contained within the dates ascribed to it.

In taking up Derrida's call to refute the myth of an 'origin' on which the present is founded, to refuse all search for a rightful 'beginning' on which to base our present politics, a deconstructive conclusion must inhabit the undecidability between conflict and post-conflict. It must show that post-conflict does not follow naturally from an objective reference to a self-contained conflict, that there is no secure or stable ground of conflict, with an end date that is simultaneously the beginning of a contemporary post-conflict period. This is what I have argued in this book: that the conflict and the post-conflict periods are constituted at the same time, through the detour and delay of the peace agreements, and that the understandings of the conflicts contained within the peace agreements radiate their effects forwards and backwards in time. The undecidability thus crosses temporal boundaries: the understandings of post-conflict politics as a 'two communities' or 'Balkans' struggle, which are themselves undecidable in the sense of generating contradictory political currents, depend upon undecidable 'two communities' or 'Balkans' accounts of the conflicts. The inability to resolve the undecidability in the present is sidestepped through reference to the past, through arguments that defend the current status of the political institutions on the grounds that they prevent a resumption of hostilities. Yet when we look at the conflicts themselves, we see a lack of consensus as to what drove them: was 'the troubles' an ethnic or a national conflict; and was BiH destroyed by an ethnic war or acts of international aggression? The undecidability of the present institutions is thus founded on undecidable understandings of the conflicts, generating a temporal nexus that is unstable and deconstructing.

It is this undecidable temporal nexus, where an undecidable past produces an undecidable present, and through which an undecidable present is founded on an undecidable past, that must be the target of a deconstructive conclusion to the conflicts in Northern Ireland and BiH. Such a deconstructive conclusion would inhabit the undecidability of understandings of the conflict, pushing such contradictory accounts even further, rather than seeking supplementary understandings that attempt to resolve these contradictions. Simultaneously, a deconstructive conclusion would inhabit the undecidability of the post-conflict politics, pushing further the contradictory manifestations of political identity and belonging in the present. It must do so because these two aspects of undecidability *cannot be separated*. In this sense, a deconstructive conclusion to the conflict would *also* be a deconstructive conclusion to the post-conflict, or a deconstructive conclusion to the *peace agreements* which produce the conflict and post-conflict as the *différance* of each other.

The peace agreements in Northern Ireland and BiH are commonly taken as shorthand for the 'end' of the conflict in the respective cases. 'Post-Agreement' or 'post-Dayton' are regularly used to indicate the post-conflict period. In Derridean terms, the peace agreements can be considered as the 'hinges' on which the conflicts turn, the hinges which mark the threshold from a time of conflict, to a time of post-conflict (see chapter 1). As I have argued in previous chapters, these agreements do more than simply reflect the nature of the conflicts: instead, they play a role in the constitution of these understandings of the conflicts, through the operation of the 'two communities' and 'Balkans' supplements, generating these as common-sense understandings of the conflicts that can then be read backwards into the historical record. The 'success' of the peace agreements, the fact they do mark a threshold to a much less violent time period, is central to this (though they came after ceasefires, of a more extended duration in Northern Ireland than in BiH, where the process was condensed into four months): it allows for supporters of the agreements, and of the political systems they created, to argue that they succeed due to the accuracy of their diagnoses and analyses of the conflicts. Yet, this process is not just backwards looking: the agreements do more than provide a historical structure upon which post-conflict politics plays out. Instead, they also (simultaneously) transmit the historical understandings of the conflicts into the present through the political structures they generate, which depend upon the same 'two communities' and 'Balkans' supplements, to function (as argued in chapters 4 and 5).

I have also argued in previous chapters that this supplementation produces a contradictory and contested political environment, in which post-conflict politics both (re)enacts a 'two communities' or 'Balkans' struggle based on fixed identities, while simultaneously allowing for a politics which sees these identities as fluid and capable of transformation. Yet these two politics are bound together, as both arise from the same undecidable 'two communities' or 'Balkans' account embedded in the peace agreements. Thus when the non-communal or non-ethnic political movements push against the door of the political structures designed to accommodate community or ethnic identities, they find this door opens onto a door they have already passed through: the door that opens onto the peace agreements that the non-communal or non-ethnic politics themselves depend upon.[1]

This is where a deconstructive conclusion must come in: to push the door back on its hinges, and allow the undecidability of the 'two communities' and 'Balkans' understandings to be recognised; and to then swing back on its hinges to the present, to erase and undo the political structures that build upon these undecidable understandings of the conflicts. Such a deconstructive conclusion would show how the political present in Northern Ireland and BiH is built around an absence that requires supplementation by discourses which see the past in terms of a clash of 'two communities' or a 'Balkans' war; and that this past is itself marked by absence, by the absence of any certainty that the conflict unfolded in the manner that contemporary politics depends upon. A deconstructive conclusion to the conflicts, if it is to provide an 'ending' that does more than essentialise and ontologise particular understandings of the violence, must bend backwards, in the sense of allowing the conflicts to be understood as something other than a 'two communities' or 'Balkans' struggle. The effects of such a deconstructive conclusion to the conflicts must therefore radiate backwards in time, to the years of attempted peace efforts during the conflicts, to how the conflicts are understood and to how the terms 'two communities' and 'Balkans' are understood. This signals an 'opening' towards the conflicts, in the sense of allowing them to be re-engaged with and re-understood, rather than an 'ending' which closes them off between specific dates of commencement and cessation.

However, the effects of a deconstructive conclusion must not be limited to one direction on a linear temporal schema. As well as showing how the GFA and DPA are dependent upon undecidable understandings of the conflicts, a deconstructive conclusion must show how these understandings are given presence in the present through the political systems, designed to keep opposed groups from resuming violence, that the peace agreements created. It is not a case of doing one, and then the other, but doing *both*, *simultaneously*. Linear temporality *itself* must be targeted by a deconstructive conclusion, as that which suggests that the conflict and the post-conflict are separate. A deconstructive conclusion to the conflicts would not be achieved in one temporal moment: rather, it would be a *process*, an engagement with understandings of the conflicts *alongside* an engagement with current political arrangements. Such an unsettling of linear temporality is central to the deconstructive conclusion that can bring an end to the divisive and dysfunctional politics enacted through the GFA and DPA. Through a backwards- and forwards-looking movement, such a deconstructive conclusion would seek to challenge the historic understandings of the conflict contained within the peace agreements, at the same time as challenging their effects in the present.

## A DECONSTRUCTIVE CONCLUSION IN PRACTICE

In practical terms, a deconstructive conclusion would challenge and contest simplistic accounts of the conflicts contained in media reports, historical texts, memorials and art works. This would not require denying all efforts to explain the conflicts, or attempts to place them into a narrative to aid understanding: but it would require refusing those endeavours which present their explanations as full and complete, or fail to make clear the practices of 'emplotment' that surround the narratives being presented. In other words, this is not a call to reject all historical investigations into the conflicts, or deny all practices which seek solace and meaning in reminiscence and remembrance: but to refuse those performances which present one understanding of the past as the 'true', singular or objective account of historical reality. There are examples that show how such an approach to the past is possible. The 'Decade of Centenaries' project, which brings together various governmental and non-governmental organisations to mark the key moments in Irish history that occurred in the years 1912–1922, is in part guided by 'Principles for Remembering in Public Space' which state 'that different perceptions and interpretations exist' of the events commemorated (Community Relations Council 2020). Such guidelines allowed the 2016 remembrance events for the Easter Rising (lauded by Republicans as the foundational moment in their struggle for Irish independence) and the Battle of Somme (lauded by Loyalists as a blood sacrifice for the Crown that demands their continued inclusion within the British state) to be carried out peacefully.[2] This perhaps provides a model that can be followed in other, wider engagements with the past.

A deconstructive conclusion would operate through forms of political critique that do not simply challenge the political institutions of Northern Ireland and BiH for their delimiting effects in the present, but also for the manners in which they sustain specific understandings of the past. This could mean, for instance, challenging the community and ethnic designations or veto points in the political institutions, not (just) because they transfer political authority from an individual level to a reified community or ethnic level, but because they depend upon and sustain accounts of the conflicts as driven by community or ethnic difference and interest. Such a deconstructive conclusion can therefore work to challenge the strongest manifestations of the 'two communities' and 'Balkans' supplements that this book has identified. In Northern Ireland, this would mean critiquing the way in which the GFA translates universal, individual rights into group rights through the petition of concern and cross-community voting measures, or the manner in which the undecidability of national identity (i.e. the right to be British, Irish or both) does not find an equivalent in the Northern Ireland Assembly, where only those MLAs who designate as Unionist or Nationalist have full voting rights. The recognition in the January 2020 agreement on restoring devolution of the need to acknowledge and accommodate 'those within our community who define themselves as "other", and those from our ethnic communities and newcomer communities', alongside the long-enshrined rights to identify and be accepted as Irish or British, or both (HM Government and Government of Ireland 2020, 15), is perhaps a first step in this direction. Contesting these manifestations of the 'two communities' supplement in the present, meanwhile, would be strengthened by simultaneously highlighting the contradictory understandings of the conflict they depend upon. With the constitutional future of the UK threated by the process of leaving the EU, an ability to focus critique on attempts to translate fluid national identification into rigid community identity remains vitally important. In BiH, this could mean highlighting the instability of placing three 'constituent peoples' into two entities: not so as to strengthen arguments for a third entity, but to demonstrate how that anomaly arises from the closing stages of the war, when the HV and ARBiH were allowed to gain territory in order to bring the situation on the ground closer to the 51–49 territorial split that was favoured by outside mediators. Making this connection can demonstrate how two key aspects of BiH's current political reality (the division of its territory into two entities, and the division of its population into three 'constituent peoples') arise from the contradictions in the understandings of the conflict contained in the DPA. Such political critique is crucial in a context in which the tripartite presidency and entity structures remain subjects of contentious debate.

These are indications of how the political challenges discussed in chapters 4 and 5 could be more 'successful' in contesting the dominant communal or nationalist parties, and in offering an alternative to communal or ethnic politics. The political critique suggested by the deconstructive conclusion must therefore not be interpreted simply as a call to re-open the peace agreements, to re-negotiate them or to reform the political structures contained within them. Such attempts can only ever be partial, as they too will push up against the door of the peace agreements, and the historical narratives contained within them. I am advocating a harder path, but one that I genuinely believe could prove more fruitful: a path which involves reworking the agreements while *simultaneously* challenging the historical understandings that inform them.

## AGAINST CONCLUSIONS

It is now over twenty years since the peace agreements in Northern Ireland and BiH were signed. The institutions they created have become entrenched in this time, being modified by reforms rather than reworked entirely. They have also proved resilient in the face of political challenges, and must be praised for their role in preventing any return to large-scale violence. However, the agreements are *themselves* a key cause of the political issues facing Northern Ireland and BiH, in terms of both the political institutions they bequeathed, and the understandings of the conflicts these institutions depend upon. The need to deconstruct the conclusion of these conflicts is therefore as pressing as ever.

This book has presented a deconstructive reading of the GFA and DPA, as a form of affirmative critique of their impacts on the post conflict politics of both places. I have argued that the peace agreements are already in a process of deconstruction, in that they create institutions which operate on the basis that community or ethnic division is a reality to be accommodated, while simultaneously generating a politics which seeks the transformation of this division. I view these fault lines, which are rooted in contradictory understandings of the conflicts, as the sources of the persistent dysfunction of the political systems. This is something internal to the peace agreements, and the consequences are already identifiable in both cases (as chapters 4 and 5 demonstrate). I am not seeking an exogenous intervention into the politics of Northern Ireland and BiH, therefore, but merely arguing for the intensification of processes that are already unfolding, through a deconstructive conclusion to the conflicts which furthers the transformative agendas the peace deals enable, alongside a sustained challenge to the understandings of the conflicts contained within the agreements.

This deconstruction conclusion is not meant to deny the impact that the conflicts continue to have on peoples' lives in Northern Ireland and BiH, nor to demean or denigrate the understandings of history that individuals cherish and hold dear (even when those understandings generate negative or exclusive political positions), in the belief that a simple re-interpretation of the conflicts can allow new, less oppositional identities and belongings to emerge. Instead, I am arguing for a recognition that the understandings of the conflicts contained in the peace agreements and manifestations of community or ethnic difference in contemporary politics are rooted in each other, and must therefore be challenged *together*, by a politics that rejects attempts to put in place specific narratives of the conflicts in the central political documents of Northern Ireland and BiH. Such refusal is the crucial first movement in the building of a politics that overcomes the dysfunction that post-conflict Northern Ireland and BiH have witnessed.

Furthermore, I do not deny that hatred or fear of a community or ethnic group played a role in the conflicts. This is all too apparent from even the most cursory examination of first-hand accounts of the violence, or investigation into some of the many heinous acts of murder, ethnic cleansing and genocide. The Shankhill butchers, the Kingsmill killings, the Srebrenica massacre, the Krajina expulsions: in these and other cases, acts of violence were undoubtedly motivated by such prejudice. Similar motivations can also be identified in ongoing acts of desecration (such as attacks on memorials), intimidation (whether through formal marches and parades, or in the marking of space with flags or places of worship), and segregation (in housing and education) witnessed in parts of Northern Ireland and BiH: acts which also undoubtedly play a role in replicating such prejudice in the minds of future generations. These historic acts were real, and they have real resonances in the present: I would not deny that. What I *do* deny, what I argue *must* be refused, is the conflation of certain acts of violence motivated by hatred or fear of another group with 'the conflicts' as a whole, in a manner which ignores other (non-communal or non-ethnic) ways of understanding the violence. My point is that multiple and at times contradictory understandings must be allowed to co-exist *as contradictions*, not made to work together through the addition of the 'two communities' or 'Balkans' supplements. I am not arguing to replace the 'two communities' or 'Balkans' understandings with more 'accurate' or 'true' narratives of the conflicts, therefore, but to highlight the *lack* of consensus around what caused the violence. A deconstructive conclusion would therefore challenge the peace agreements on the grounds that they fix in place narratives of the conflicts, rather than arguing that they embody *incorrect* understandings (as this implies there is a *correct* explanation waiting to be uncovered).

The politics that recognises this, and which contests the 'two communities' and 'Balkans' accounts of political life in Northern Ireland and BiH, already exists. I am not arguing for the inauguration of a new form of political critique, therefore, but the completion of trends that are already existent. To allow this politics to flourish, the categories of the 'two communities' and 'Balkans' must be challenged in the present as well as being shaken and unsettled backwards in time. This is what is required of the deconstructive conclusion of the peace agreements. It is not enough to stop or overturn the divisive practices in the present and attempt to build a new politics beyond these practices. Rather, the constraining understandings need to be excised backwards in time, as well as prevented from taking root in the present and future. A deconstructive conclusion that ends the conflicts while undoing the beginnings of the peace, can therefore help Northern Ireland and BiH move beyond the constraining patterns of their post-conflict politics.

# Notes

## CHAPTER 1

1. This is referred to by the UK government as the Belfast Agreement, and both terms are used by politicians and commentators.

2. Officially known as The General Framework Agreement for Peace in Bosnia and Herzegovina.

3. See, for example, Kim (2018), Radin (2014), Stravidis (2015) and White (2014).

4. For examples of such arguments see Aitken (2007), Burg and Shoup (1999, 317–87), Chollet (2005, 183–202); Little (2004, 9–32), McGrattan (2010a, 156–80; 2010b).

5. The international status of these countries is recognised in association football, where the four parts of the UK compete as individual nations. International football is in fact another area of commonality between Northern Ireland and BiH, in that they are two national teams that do not attract the support of their entire football-supporting populations: many Irish Nationalists in Northern Ireland follow the Republic of Ireland football team, while Bosnian Croats and Bosnia Serbs may favour the Croatian and Serbian national teams, respectively.

6. For a detailed discussion of the emergence of the civil rights movement in Northern Ireland, placed in the context of the 'long '68' in the US, France, Germany and elsewhere, see Prince 2018.

7. For exhaustive accounts of the road to war in BiH, see Woodward (1995) and Silber and Little (1996); for Northern Ireland, see McKittrick and McVea (2012).

8. See, for example, Zalewski (2008), Edkins (2008), Vaughan-Williams (2008) and Conrad (2008).

9. Elsewhere Derrida (1993, 15) calls these 'quasi-concepts', in order to distinguish them from the (apparently) rigid concepts of metaphysical philosophy.

10. For other examples of Derrida stressing the inherently political and constructive nature of his philosophy see Derrida (2001c, 68; 2005b, 39).

11. While the official name of this country (in English) is simply 'Ireland', it is commonly referred to as the Republic of Ireland in the UK.

12. This is how Derrida sought to clarify the meaning of the (in)famous phrase *il n'y a pas de hors-texte*. Originally translated as '*There is nothing outside of the text* [there is no outside-text . . .]' (Derrida 2016, 172, emphasis in original), Derrida (1988, 136–37) later states that it means 'there is nothing outside context', because things 'always appear in an experience, hence in a movement of interpretation which contextualizes them according to a network of differences and hence of referral to the other'. Elsewhere, Derrida (2001b, 48) provides a slightly different clarification, stating that the phrase refers to the idea that there is no external reference outside the text that can be drawn upon in a reading, 'that there is no other, non-textual domain which harbours secret answers to the problem of reading'. The multiple clarifications of this phrase perhaps speak to Derrida's playful use and deployment of concepts and ideas, rather than to a failure to systematise his thought.

13. Another of the 'analogous motifs' Derrida (1988, 117) employs throughout his opus, the 'interminable list of all the so-called undecidable quasi-concepts' (Derrida 1993, 15) which include the supplement and *différance*.

# CHAPTER 2

1. The name of this city is controversial, and is often officially rendered as Derry~Londonderry, as Nationalists tend to use the term Derry, while Unionists may prefer the term Londonderry.

2. Released Cabinet minutes indicate that Labour and Conservative governments in the 1940s and 1950s did express a strategic interest in maintaining sovereign control over Northern Ireland. See McKittrick and McVea (2012, 27–28).

3. For more on parity of esteem see Aughey (2005, 49–50), Hayes and McAllister (1999) and Thompson (2003, 47). I will also discuss the term in chapter 4.

4. I will return to these aspects of the GFA in chapter 4.

5. While parties can and do define themselves as Unionist, defining a section of the electorate in such simplistic terms is less straightforward, as it assumes a degree of uniformity and fixity amongst voters that may not exist.

6. This group held numerous peace rallies after its formation in 1976, and its two founding members received that year's Nobel Peace Prize. For more information see Darraj (2006) and Maguire (2010).

7. As Edwards (2009) recounts, the Northern Ireland Labour Party, founded in 1924, operated in the early years of 'the troubles' before winding down in 1987. The Alliance Party was formed in 1969, and continues to operate today. Chapter 4 will cover its contemporary influence in detail, but for information on the Alliance Party during 'the troubles' see Eggins (2015) and Mitchell (2018).

## CHAPTER 3

1. For a richly detailed version of this account, see Silber and Little (1996).

2. For more examples of this see Hansen (2006, 107–109, 124–25, 133–36).

3. For all Resolutions see United Nations 2020. Resolutions up to January 1995 are also listed in Woodward (1995, 401–24).

4. See also Zarkov (1995, 113) and Orford (2003, 175–85).

5. See also Mulaj (2005, 16) and Woodward (1995, 283). The Security Council gave their support to this proposal through Resolution 752, which explicitly references the 'three communities' of Bosnia, thus contributing to the essentialisation of ethnic identities. See United Nations (1992a).

6. That is, the armed forces of the independent Croatian state, previously known as the Croat National Guard, not the armed forces of the Herceg-Bosnia region within BiH.

7. That is, the armed forces controlled by Izetbegović's Bosnian government.

8. The fascination with PowerScene as a means of visualising the territory of BiH, and allowing users to virtually 'fly over' this territory, is noted by some accounts of the Dayton negotiations. See Chollett (2005, 166) and Holbrooke (1999, 283).

9. For more detailed discussions of the political debates within the US on this policy option see Hansen (2006, 133–43) and Owen (1995, 160–97).

10. Different accounts give different casualty figures: Silber and Little (1996, 309) say sixty-nine, while Daalder (2000, 25) and Hansen (2006, 120) say sixty-eight.

11. Again, different accounts give different casualty figures: Silber and Little (1996, 365) and Hansen (2006, 12) say thirty-seven, while Daalder (2000, 130) says thirty-eight.

12. These will be discussed in more detail in chapter 5. For the full text of the DPA see Organisation for Security and Co-operation in Europe 1995.

13. For examples of such strategic actions during the war see Chollet (2005, 160), Silber and Little (2016, 202–203, 245–46, 257, 337) and Woodward (1995, 236–37, 269–70).

14. For more on this see Daalder (2000, 95, 127).

15. For an account of this see Silber and Little (1996, 226–28).

## CHAPTER 4

1. There is a huge amount of work on this for both Northern Ireland and BiH. For a first step into this literature, see Shirlow and McEvoy (2008) on the role of paramilitary prisoners in conflict transformation, and Toal and Dahlman (2011) on the attempts to reverse ethnic cleansing in BiH.

2. For a sample of this diversity, see: Richard English (2003, 109–23) on the impact of Republican family traditions on the personal motivation to join the PIRA, even for key figures such as Gerry Adams; Peter Taylor (1999, 152–54) on the notorious murder gang known as the 'Shankhill Butchers', who seemingly took pleasure

in killing, being more akin to a group of serial killers than participants in an armed conflict; and Edward Burke (2015) on the influence of colonial conflicts in places like Cyprus, Aden and Kenya on the tactics of the British Army.

3. According to McGarry and O'Leary (2016, 506) the two parties 'played no role in the key discussions on the rules of executive formation: the DUP boycotted the negotiations, while Sinn Féin focused on the release of IRA prisoners and other subjects'.

4. For the DUP, the label 'extreme' may be used due to the flirtations with Loyalist paramilitaries during 'the troubles' by key party figures such as Ian Paisley and Peter Robinson, to the evangelical Protestantism of many in the party, which leads them to oppose liberalising access to abortion and marriage equality, and to their historic rejectionist politics; the label may be applied to Sinn Féin due to their reputation as being, historically, at least, the political wing of the PIRA.

5. For the full text see HM Government (1998a). Subsequent references in this section will be to this text, unless otherwise stated.

6. The author included. Leading DUP politician Ian Paisley Jr. publicly stated in August 2016 that he was 'very relaxed' about people in Northern Ireland applying for an Irish passport. See Belfast Telegraph (2016).

7. Despite the number of MLAs being reduced by eighteen to ninety members, from the February 2017 election, as per the 2014 Stormont House Agreement, the threshold of thirty MLAs for lodging a petition of concern remains in place.

8. This is what McGarry and O'Leary (2004, 32–34) describe as the non-corporate, more liberal aspects of the GFA, and what Ruane and Todd (1999, 16) characterise as its 'strong egalitarian and liberal dimensions'.

9. Under the 1998 Northern Ireland Act the Assembly cannot pass legislation that is 'incompatible with any of the Convention rights' contained within the ECHR. See HM Government (1998b).

10. Marriage law in Northern Ireland was changed in October 2019, alongside the law on abortion, after votes in the UK Parliament. See Page (2019).

11. See BBC News (2015c), Naomi Long quoted in Gordon (2013), and Alliance Party member Tennyson (2018) writing on the blog site Slugger O'Toole.

12. While taking inspiration from the Stormont House Agreement, and the follow-up Fresh Start Agreement of 2015, this bill was introduced by an independent MLA, rather than by a member of the Executive.

13. One amusing anecdote in Blair's autobiography recounts how he thought Unionists were asking for the destruction of Murrayfield, the home of Scottish rugby in Edinburgh. According to Blair (2011, 174), 'it was a measure of our now complete isolation in the negotiating cell that I neither asked why Unionism might want to erase a rugby pitch, nor was unprepared to do it'.

14. As discussed in chapter 2. See O'Duffy (2004, 422), and also McEvoy (2015, 33, 94, 97).

15. The so-called 'Haass' talks, named for the US mediator Richard Haass. See BBC News (2013b).

16. The flying of flags has been a particularly contentious issue since the Belfast City Council decision in December 2012 to fly the Union flag from Belfast City Hall only on certain 'designated days', rather than all year round. This sparked a series

of protests, which continue to the time of writing, though no longer producing the violent disorder seen in 2013. See BBC News (2013a).

17. Parading has long been a major issue, with the decision to allow, or reroute, Orange Order and related parades, sparking riots on several occasions. The Stormont House Agreement talks took place in the context of the Twaddell Avenue protest, which was ongoing from July 2013 to September 2016, over the rerouting of an Orange march in North Belfast. See BBC News (2016).

18. For a discussion of the impact of the vote to leave the EU on the Irish border see Gormley-Heenan and Aughey (2017).

19. With echoes of 1974, a Conservative government called a snap Westminster election in the midst of a political crisis in Northern Ireland, without considering the debilitating effects this would have on attempts to resolve the impasse.

20. See The Electoral Office for Northern Ireland (2019a).

21. McGrattan (2010a, 171) notes that by 2001 the DUP had moderated their position from 'smashing' the Assembly to 'renegotiating' the GFA. See also McGlynn, Tonge and McAuley 2014 and Mitchell, Evans, and O'Leary (2009).

22. Data available at The Electoral Office for Northern Ireland (2019b).

23. The full results are available at The Electoral Office for Northern Ireland (2019a).

24. All data from The Electoral Office for Northern Ireland (2019a).

25. See, for example, BBC News (2019a) and McCann (2019).

26. The same could be said for the name 'Northern Ireland': many Republicans and Nationalists prefer the term 'the north' or the 'north of Ireland', in order to deny legitimacy to what they see as the partitioned statelet. The term 'occupied six counties' may also be used, to link Northern Ireland to continued British colonial presence.

27. See Artichoke (2013).

28. Part of the 2012 London Olympics celebrations. See Artichoke (2012).

29. Interview with John Peto, Derry, 17 May 2018.

30. For examples, see BBC News (2019c) and The Irish News (2019).

31. See, for example, Bennhold (2015).

32. Visitor figures from interview with Helen Marriage, London, 21 March 2019.

33. For a detailed discussion and survey see Viggiani (2014).

34. Interview with Linda Ervine and Gordon McCoy, Belfast, 15 May 2018. See also Meredith (2018).

35. While I was at Turas, a news crew from the UK national broadcaster Channel 4 visited the centre, and filmed part of the Irish singing class. This then featured in a television news item on opinion in Northern Ireland towards leaving the EU

# CHAPTER 5

1. For the full text see Organisation for Security and Co-operation in Europe (1995). Subsequent references in this section will be to this text, unless otherwise stated.

2. This has since been superseded, first by the Stabilization Force, or SFOR, and then by the EU Force, or EUFOR.

3. These are often referred to in the literature as 'ethno-national' parties. However, after my extended critique of the term 'ethno-national' in relation to Northern Ireland (see chapters 2 and 4), I will not use this term uncritically here. I therefore refer to the dominant parties who claim to speak for a 'constituent people' in BiH as 'nationalist' parties. This will be the equivalent of the term 'communal parties' used in chapter 4. However, I will still refer to the internal division of BiH to accommodate these 'constituent peoples' as signs of 'ethnic politics' in BiH. For examples in the literature of the use of the term 'nationalist parties' see Bieber (2006), Burwitz (2004), Eralp (2012), Heimerl (2005), Jenne (2009), Keil and Perry (2015), Malik (2000), Murtagh (2016) and Søberg (2008).

4. A body which grew out of the 'Peace Implementation Conference' that was held in London on 8-9 December 1995, to mobilise international support for the DPA. See Office of the High Representative (2015a).

5. The latter reform was made possible by the unification of the armed forces of the two entities in 2006: though, as Belloni (2009, 367) notes, 'the Army still maintains nine ethnically based infantry battalions'.

6. For the full text see Office of the High Representative (2015b).

7. For the full text of both see Office of the High Representative (2015c).

8. For the former tendency see Belloni (2009, 360) and O'Halloran (2005, 109); for the latter see Keil and Perry (2015, 87).

9. For turnout date from 2002 onwards see Central Election Commission Bosnia and Herzegovina (2018).

10. Petritsch acted as High Representative between August 1999 and May 2002.

11. While the Dayton constitution does not specify the 'official languages' of BiH, Article 11 of the DPA gives de facto recognition to the three languages by stating the text is written in 'the Bosnian, Croatian, English and Serbian languages, each text being equally authentic'. The fact that the 2013 census question on 'mother tongue' listed the three languages, as well as an open text box, is indicative of their quasi-official status (see Cooley 2019, 6). For a discussion of the disintegration of Serbo-Croat into its successors see Greenberg 2008.

12. For a discussion of the limited engagement with controversial issues relating to the war in the plenums, see Lai (2020, 177–78).


## CHAPTER 6

1. This is a paraphrasing of Derrida (1996, 68–69).

2. For a detailed discussion of the importance of these two historical events in the Republican and Loyalist imaginaries see Graff-McRae (2010).

# Bibliography

Ahern, Bertie. 2009. *The Autobiography.* London: Random House.

Aitken, Rob. 2007. Cementing Divisions? *Policy Studies* 28(3): 247–67.

Alliance Party. 2006. Response to the 'St. Andrews Agreement'. 10 November. Available at: https://www.allianceparty.org/publications.

Anthony, Gordon. 2008. The St Andrews Agreement and the Northern Ireland Assembly. *European Public Law* 14(2): 151–64.

ARK. 2019. Northern Ireland Life and Times Survey 2018, 'Political Attitudes'. Available at: https://www.ark.ac.uk/nilt/2018/Political_Attitudes/.

Artichoke. 2013. Lumiere Derry~Londonderry. Available at: https://www.artichoke.uk.com/project/lumiere-derrylondonderry/.

Artichoke 2012. Peace Camp. Available at: https://www.artichoke.uk.com/project/peace-camp/.

Arsenijević, Damir. 2014. After 22 Years of Being Bullied Bosnians are Desperate, and Must Protest. *The Guardian.* 28 February. Available at: http://www.theguardian.com/commentisfree/2014/feb/28/bosnia-protest-citizens-change-corruption.

Arvanitopoulos, Constantine and Nikolaos Tzifakis. 2008. Implementing Reforms in Bosnia and Herzegovina: The Challenge of the Constitutional Process. *European View* 7(1): 15–22.

Aughey, Arthur. 2005. *The Politics of Northern Ireland: Beyond the Belfast Agreement.* Abingdon: Routledge.

Bakić-Hayden, Milica and Robert M. Hayden. 1992. Orientalist Variations on the Theme 'Balkans': Symbolic Geography in Recent Yugoslav Cultural Politics. *Slavic Review* 51(1): 1–15.

Balkan Insight. 2015. Bill Clinton Celebrates Bosnia Peace Deal Anniversary. 20 November. Available at: http://www.balkaninsight.com/en/article/bill-clinton-celebrates-bosnia-peace-deal-anniversary-11-20-2015.

BBC News. 2007. Stroke City to Remain Londonderry. 25 January. Available at: http://news.bbc.co.uk/1/hi/northern_ireland/6297907.stm.

BBC News. 2013a. Union Flag Dispute: Riot Breaks out in East Belfast. 15 January. Available at: https://www.bbc.co.uk/news/uk-northern-ireland-21020296.

BBC News. 2013b. Northern Ireland: Richard Haass talks end without Deal. 31 December. Available at: https://www.bbc.co.uk/news/uk-northern-ireland-255 56714.

BBC News. 2015a. Sinn Féin Blocks Welfare Bill in Northern Ireland Assembly. 9 March. Available at: https://www.bbc.co.uk/news/uk-northern-ireland-31798766.

BBC News. 2015b. DUP Ministers Resume Northern Ireland Executive Posts. 20 October. Available at: https://www.bbc.co.uk/news/uk-northern-ireland-34583021.

BBC News. 2015c. Same-Sex Marriage: Proposal Wins Assembly Majority but Fails over DUP Block. 2 November. Available at: https://www.bbc.co.uk/news/uk-north ern-ireland-politics-34692546.

BBC News. 2016. Twaddell: Agreement Reached over Long-Running Parade Dispute. 24 September. Available at: https://www.bbc.co.uk/news/uk-northern-ireland-37458065.

BBC News. 2017. Martin McGuinness Resigns as NI Deputy First Minister. 10 January. Available at: https://www.bbc.co.uk/news/uk-northern-ireland-38561507.

BBC News. 2018. Good Friday Agreement was 'Work of Genius'. 10 April. Available at: https://www.bbc.co.uk/news/uk-northern-ireland-43660970.

BBC News. 2019a. Stormont Deadlock: Dylan Quinn's 90-mile Protest from Enniskillen to Belfast. 5 January. Available at: https://www.bbc.co.uk/news/uk-northern-ireland-46769670.

BBC News. 2019b. European Elections: Dodds, Anderson and Long Elected. 28 May. Available at: https://www.bbc.co.uk/news/uk-northern-ireland-politics-48428491.

BBC News. 2019c. Londonderry: PSNI Treat Bonfire Material as 'Hate Incident'. 16 August. Available at: https://www.bbc.co.uk/news/uk-northern-ireland-49363571.

BBC News. 2020. Stormont Deal: Arlene Foster and Michelle O'Neill New Top NI Ministers. 12 January. Available at: https://www.bbc.co.uk/news/uk-northern-ireland-51077397.

Belfast Telegraph. 2016. Ian Paisley on Irish Passports: It's a European Document with an Irish Harp Stuck on Posing as a Passport. 8 August. Available at: https://www.belfasttelegraph.co.uk/news/northern-ireland/ian-paisley-on-irish-passports-its-a-european-document-with-an-irish-harp-stuck-on-posing-as-a-passport-3494 9658.html

Belfast Telegraph. 2017. Mural Tribute to the Heroes of East Belfast. 23 March. Available at: https://www.belfasttelegraph.co.uk/news/northern-ireland/mural-tribute-to-the-heroes-of-east-belfast-35556507.html.

Belfast Telegraph. 2019. Union Flag Stolen from Belfast Memorial to Men Killed by IRA. 2 January. Available at: https://www.belfasttelegraph.co.uk/news/northern-ireland/union-flag-stolen-from-belfast-memorial-to-men-killed-by-ira-37675865 .html.

Belloni, Roberto. 2009. Bosnia: Dayton is Dead! Long Live Dayton! *Nationalism and Ethnic Politics* 15(3–4): 355–75.

Belloni, Roberto, Stefanie Kappler, and Jasmin Ramovic. 2016. Bosnia-Herzegovina: Domestic Agency and the Inadequacy of the Liberal Peace. In *Post-Liberal Peace*

*Transitions: Between Peace Formation and State Formation*, edited by Oliver P. Richmond and Sandra Pogodda, 47–64. Edinburgh: Edinburgh University Press.

Bennhold, Katrin. 2015. Healing Fire in Londonderry: The Temple Was Built to Burn. *The New York Times*. 27 March. Available at: https://www.nytimes.com/2015/03/28/world/europe/using-flames-to-soothe-a-northern-ireland-city-scarred-by-fire.html.

Bhabha, Homi. 1994. *The Location of Culture*. Abingdon: Routledge.

Bieber, Florian. 2005. Power Sharing after Yugoslavia: Functionality and Dysfunctionality of Power Sharing Institutions Post-War Bosnia, Macedonia and Kosovo. In *From Power Sharing to Democracy: Post-Conflict Institutions in Ethnically Divided Societies*, edited by Sid Noel, 85–103. Montreal: McGill-Queen's University Press.

Bieber, Florian. 2006. After Dayton, Dayton? The Evolution of an Unpopular Peace. *Ethnopolitics* 5(1): 15–31.

Bieber, Florian. 2014a. Elections in Bosnia – Business as Usual? *Balkan Insight*. 15 October. Available at: http://www.balkaninsight.com/en/blog/elections-in-bosnia-business-as-usual.

Bieber, Florian. 2014b. Ungovernable Bosnia? From the Ruling of the European Court of Human Rights on the Sejdić-Finci Case to the Government Crisis. *IEMed*. Mediterranean Yearbook, 186–88.

Bildt, Carl. 1998. *Peace Journey: The Struggle for Peace in Bosnia*. London: Weidenfeld and Nicolson.

Blair, Tony. 2011. *A Journey*. London: Arrow Books.

Bose, Sumatra. 2002. *Bosnia After Dayton: Nationalist Partition and International Intervention*. London: Hurst and Company.

Bougarel, Xavier, Elissa Helms, and Ger Duijzings. 2007. Introduction. In *The New Bosnian Mosaic: Identities, Memories and Moral Claims in a Post-War Society*, edited by Xavier Bougarel, Elissa Helms and Ger Duijzings, 1–35. Aldershot: Ashgate Publishing Limited.

Boutros-Ghali, Boutros. 1999. *Unvanquished: A U.S.–U.N. Saga*. London: I.B. Tauris.

Bowcott, Owen. 2019. Northern Ireland Citizens Must Register to Identify as Irish, Tribunal Told. *The Guardian*, 10 September. Available at: https://www.theguardian.com/world/2019/sep/10/northern-ireland-citizens-must-register-to-identify-as-irish-tribunal-told.

Breen, Suzanne. 2017. Tony Blair Deceived Sinn Fein on Irish Language at St Andrews, Says ex-DUP Chief Robinson. *Belfast Telegraph*. 28 June. Available at: https://www.belfasttelegraph.co.uk/news/northern-ireland/tony-blair-deceived-sinn-fein-on-irish-language-at-st-andrews-says-ex-dup-chief-robinson-35872919.html.

Bryan, Dominic. 2008. The Politics of Community. In *Intervening in Northern Ireland: Critically Re-Thinking Representations of the Conflict*, edited by Marysia Zalewski and John Barry, 125–39. London: Routledge.

Burg, Steven L. and Paul S. Shoup. 1999. *The War in Bosnia-Herzegovina: Ethnic Conflict and International Intervention*. Armonk, NY: M.E. Sharpe.

Burg, Steven L. and Paul S. Shoup. 2000. *Ethnic Conflict and International Intervention: Crisis in Bosnia-Herzegovina*. London: Routledge.

Burke, Edward. 2015. Counter-Insurgency against 'Kith and Kin'? The British Army in Northern Ireland, 1970–76. *The Journal of Imperial and Commonwealth History* 43(4): 658–77.

Burwitz, Bernd. 2004. The Elections in Bosnia-Herzegovina, October 2002. *Electoral Studies* 23(2): 329–38.

Bush, George H.W. 1992. Containing the Crisis in Bosnia and the Former Yugoslavia. *US State Department Dispatch*. 10 August. Available at: http://dosfan.lib.uic.edu/ERC/briefing/dispatch/1992/html/Dispatchv3Sup7.html.

Campbell, David. 1998. *National Deconstruction: Violence, Identity, and Justice in Bosnia*. Minneapolis, MN: University of Minnesota Press.

Central Election Commission Bosnia and Herzegovina. 2018. Statistics and Elections' Results. Available at: http://www.izbori.ba/Default.aspx?CategoryID=421&Lang=6.

Chandler, David. 2006. *Empire in Denial: The Politics of State-Building*. London: Pluto Press.

Chollet, Derek. 2005. *The Road to the Dayton Accords: A Study of American Statecraft*. New York: Palgrave MacMillan.

Christopher, Warren. 1998. *In the Stream of History: Shaping Foreign Policy for a New Era*. Stanford, CA: Stanford University Press.

Clayton, Pamela. 1998. Religion, Ethnicity and Colonialism as Explanations of the Northern Ireland Conflict. In *Rethinking Northern Ireland: Culture, Ideology and Colonialism*, edited by David W. Miller, 55–69. Boston, MA: Addison Wesley Longman.

Clinton, Bill. 2005. *My Life*. London: Arrow Books.

Coles, Kimberley. 2007a. Ambivalent Builders: Europeanization, the Production of Difference, and Internationals in Bosnia-Herzegovina. In *The New Bosnian Mosaic: Identities, Memories and Moral Claims in a Post-War Society*, edited by Xavier Bougarel, Elissa Helms and Ger Duijzings, 255–72. Aldershot: Ashgate Publishing Limited.

Coles, Kimberley. 2007b. *Democratic Designs: International Intervention and Electoral Practices in Postwar Bosnia-Herzegovina*. Ann Arbor, MI: University of Michigan Press.

Community Relations Council. 2020. Principles for Remembering in Public Space. Available at: https://www.community-relations.org.uk/sites/crc/files/media-files/Decade%20Principles.pdf.

Conrad, Kathryn. 2008. Queering Community: Reimagining the Public Sphere in Northern Ireland. In *Intervening in Northern Ireland: Critically Re-Thinking Representations of the Conflict*, edited by Marysia Zalewski and John Barry, 114–24. London: Routledge.

Cooley, Laurence. 2019. To be a Bosniak or to be a Citizen? Bosnia and Herzegovina's 2013 Census as an Election. *Nations and Nationalism* 25(3): 1065–86.

Cousens, Elizabeth M. and Charles K. Cater. 2001. *Towards Peace in Bosnia: Implementing the Dayton Accords*. London: Lynne Rienner.

Cox, Lloyd and Steve Wood. 2017. 'Got Him': Revenge, Emotions, and the Killing of Osama bin Laden. *Review of International Studies* 43(1): 112–29.

Critchley, S. 2005. Jacques Derrida. *Theory and Event.* 8(1). Available at: https://muse.jhu.edu/article/180066.

Culture Northern Ireland. 2015. How We Built Temple. 3 March. Available at: https://www.culturenorthernireland.org/features/visual-arts/how-we-built-temple.

Curtis, John, Sylvia de Mars, Stefano Fella, Daniel Ferguson, Jonathan Finlay, Suzanna Hinson, Ilze Jozepa, Matthew Keep, Anthony Seely, David Torrance, and Dominic Webb. 2019. The October 2019 EU-UK Withdrawal Agreement. *House of Commons Library Briefing Paper*, No. CBP 8713. 17 October. Available at: https://researchbriefings.parliament.uk/ResearchBriefing/Summary/CBP-8713.

Daalder, Ivo H. 2000. *Getting to Dayton: The Making of America's Bosnia Policy.* Washington D.C.: The Brookings Institute.

Darraj, Susan Muaddi. 2006. *Mairead Corrigan and Betty Williams: Partners for Peace in Northern Ireland.* New York, NY: Chelsea House Publishers.

Dauphinee, Elizabeth. 2007. *The Ethics of Researching War: Looking for Bosnia.* Manchester: University of Manchester Press.

Dedovic, Edin. 2013. Bosnia's Baby Revolution: Is the Protest Movement Coming of Age? *Open Democracy.* 26 June. Available at: https://www.opendemocracy.net/edin-dedovic/bosnia%E2%80%99s-baby-revolution-is-protest-movement-coming-of-age.

Derrida, Jacques. 1978. *Writing and Difference.* Translated by Alan Bass. Abingdon: Routledge.

Derrida, Jacques. 1982. *Margins of Philosophy.* Translated by Alan Bass. Chicago, IL: University of Chicago Press.

Derrida, Jacques. 1988. *Limited Inc.* Evanston, IL: Northwestern University Press.

Derrida, Jacques. 1989. *MEMOIRES for Paul de Man* (Revised Edition). Translations edited by Avital Ronnel and Eduardo Cadava. New York: Columbia University Press.

Derrida, Jacques. 1992. Force of Law: The 'Mystical Foundation of Authority'. In *Deconstruction and the Possibility of Justice*, edited by Drucilla Cornell, Michel Rosenfeld and David Gray Carlson, 3–67. London: Routledge.

Derrida, Jacques. 1993. *Aporias.* Translated by Thomas Dutoit. Stanford, CA: Stanford University Press.

Derrida, Jacques. 1994. *Spectres of Marx: The State of the Debt. The Work of Mourning and the New International.* Translated by Peggy Kamuf. Abingdon: Routledge.

Derrida, Jacques. 1995. The Time is Out of Joint. Translated by Peggy Kamuf. In *Deconstruction Is/In America: A New Sense of the Political*, edited by Anselm Haverkamp, 14–38. New York, NY: New York University Press.

Derrida, Jacques. 1996. *Archive Fever: A Freudian Impression.* Translated by Eric Prenowitz. London: The University of Chicago Press.

Derrida, Jacques. 2001a. Deconstructions: The Impossible. In *French Theory in America*, edited by Sylvère Lotringer and Sandre Cohen, 13–32. London: Routledge.

Derrida, Jacques. 2001b. Spectres of Media. In *Deconstruction Engaged: The Sydney Seminars*, edited by Paul Patton and Terry Smith, 43–53. Sydney: Power Publications.

Derrida, Jacques. 2001c. Time and Memory, Messianicity and the Name of God. In *Deconstruction Engaged: The Sydney Seminars*, edited by Paul Patton and Terry Smith, 57–69. Sydney: Power Publications.

Derrida, Jacques. 2005a. *Positions* (Second Edition). Translated by Alan Bass. London: Continuum.

Derrida, Jacques. 2005b. *Rogues: Two Essays on Reason.* Translated by Pascale-Anne Brault and Michael Naas. Stanford, CA: Stanford University Press.

Derrida, Jacques. 2016. *Of Grammatology, 40th Anniversary Edition.* Translated by Gayatri Chakravorty Spivak. Baltimore, MD: John Hopkins University Press.

Derry Journal. 2012. Annie's Bar–40 Years On. 20 December. Available at: https://www.derryjournal.com/news/annie-s-bar-40-years-on-1-4598034.

Devenport, Mark. 2018. Arlene Foster: 'No Stand-Alone Irish Language Act'. *BBC News.* 13 February. Available at: https://www.bbc.co.uk/news/uk-northern-ireland-43048025.

Dixon, Paul. 2005. Why the Good Friday Agreement in Northern Ireland is Not Consociational. *The Political Quarterly* 76(3): 357–67.

Dixon, Paul. 2008. *Northern Ireland: The Politics of War and Peace* (Second Edition). Basingstoke: Palgrave MacMillan.

Dixon, Paul. 2013. An Honourable Deception? The Labour Government, the Good Friday Agreement and the Northern Ireland Peace Process. *British Politics* 8(2): 108–37.

Donais, Timothy. 2013. Power Politics and the Rule of Law in Post-Dayton Bosnia. *Studies in Social Justice* 7(2): 189–210.

Edkins, Jenny and Maja Zehfuss. 2005. Generalising the International. *Review of International Studies* 31(3): 451–72.

Edkins, Jenny. 2003a. Humanitarianism, Humanity, Human. *Journal of Human Rights* 2(2): 253–58.

Edkins, Jenny. 2003b. *Trauma and the Memory of Politics.* Cambridge: Cambridge University Press.

Edkins, Jenny. 2008. The Local, the Global and the Troubling. In *Intervening in Northern Ireland: Critically Re-Thinking Representations of the Conflict*, edited by Marysia Zalewski and John Barry, 21–33. London: Routledge.

Edwards, Aaron. 2009. A *History of the Northern Ireland Labour Party: Democratic Socialism and Sectarianism.* Manchester: Manchester University Press.

Eggins, Brian. 2015. *History and Hope: The Alliance Party of Northern Ireland.* Dublin: The History Press Ireland.

English, Richard. 2004. *Armed Struggle: The History of the IRA.* Oxford: Oxford University Press.

Eralp, Doğa Ulaş. 2012. *Politics of the European Union in Bosnia-Herzegovina: Between Conflict and Democracy.* Washington, D.C.: Lexington Books.

Ezrow, Lawrence and Georgois Xezonakis. 2016. Satisfaction with Democracy and Voter Turnout: A Temporal Perspective. *Party Politics* 22(1): 3–14.

Filic, Goran. 2018. Rejection of Radical Nationalism in Wartime Yugoslavia: The Case of Tuzla (1990–1995). *Journal of Peacebuilding and Development* 13(3): 55–69.

Friedman, Francine. 2004. *Bosnia and Herzegovina: A Polity on the Brink.* London: Routledge.

Gagnon Jr., V.P. 1994/95. Ethnic Nationalism and International Conflict: The Case of Serbia. *International Security* 19(3): 130–66.

Gagnon Jr., V.P. 2004. *The Myth of Ethnic War: Serbia and Croatia in the 1990s.* London: Cornell University Press.

Glynn, Patrick. 1993. The Age of Balkanization. *Commentary* 96(1): 21–24.

Gordon, Gareth. 2013. Petitions of Concern: Is Stormont's Safeguard System Being Abused? *BBC News.* 9 July. Available at: https://www.bbc.co.uk/news/uk-northern -ireland-23247074.

Gordy, Eric. 2014. Bosnia's Protests: Made in Dayton, *UCL SSEES Research Blog.* 10 February. Available at: http://blogs.ucl.ac.uk/ssees/2014/02/10/bosnias-protests -made-in-dayton/.

Gormley-Heenan, Cathy and Arthur Aughey. 2017. Northern Ireland and Brexit: Three Effects on 'The Border in the Mind'. *British Journal of Politics and International Relations* 19(3): 497–511.

Gow, James. 2006. The ICTY, War Crimes Enforcement and Dayton: The Ghost in the Machine. *Ethnopolitics* 5(1): 49–65.

Gowing, Nik. 1996. Real-Time TV Coverage from War: Does it Make or Break Government Policy? In *Bosnia by Television*, edited by James Gow, Richard Paterson and Alison Preston, 81–91. London: British Film Institute.

Graff-McRae, Rebecca. 2010. *Remembering and Forgetting 1916: Commemoration and Conflict in Post-Peace Process Ireland.* Dublin: Irish Academic Press.

Greenberg, Robert. 2008. *Language and Identity in the Balkans: Serbo-Croatian and its Disintegration.* Oxford: Oxford University Press.

Hameiri, Shahar and Lee Jones. 2017. Beyond Hybridity to the Politics of Scale: International Intervention and 'Local' Politics. *Development and Change* 48(1): 54–77.

Hansen, Lene. 2006. *Security as Practice: Discourse Analysis and the Bosnian War.* Abingdon: Routledge.

Harper, Phineas. 2015. Let it Burn: Temple in Derry, Northern Ireland by David Best/ Artichoke. *The Architectural Review.* 22 April. Available at: https://www.architectural -review.com/today/let-it-burn-temple-in-derry-northern-ireland-by-david-best- /-artichoke/8681529.article.

Hayes, Bernadette C. and Ian McAllister. 1999. Ethnonationalism, Public Opinion and the Good Friday Agreement. In *After the Good Friday Agreement: Analysing Political Change in Northern Ireland,* edited by Joseph Ruane and Jennifer Todd, 30–48. Dublin: University College Dublin Press.

Hays, Don and Jason Crosby. 2006. From Dayton to Brussels: Constitutional Preparations for Bosnia's EU Accession. *United States Institute of Peace.* Special Report 175. October. Available at: https://www.usip.org/sites/default/files/reso urces/SRoct06_2.pdf.

Heathershaw, John. 2013. Towards Better Theories of Peacebuilding: Beyond the Liberal Peace Debate. *Peacebuilding* 1(2): 275–82.

Heimerl, Daniela 2005. The Return of Refugees and Internally Displaced Persons: From Coercion to Sustainability? *International Peacekeeping* 12(3): 377–90.

Hemon, Aleksander. 2014. Beyond the Hopelessness of Survival. In *Unbribable Bosnia and Herzegovina: The Fight for the Commons*, edited by Damir Arsenijević, 59–64. Baden-Baden: Nomos.

Hennessy, Thomas. 2000. *The Northern Ireland Peace Process: Ending the Troubles*. Dublin: Gill and Macmillan Ltd.

HM Government. 1973a. Northern Ireland Constitution Act 1973. Available at: https ://www.legislation.gov.uk/ukpga/1973/36/pdfs/ukpga_19730036_en.pdf.

HM Government. 1973b. Northern Ireland Assembly Act 1973. Available at: http:// www.legislation.gov.uk/ukpga/1973/17/pdfs/ukpga_19730017_en.pdf .

HM Government. 1998a. The Belfast Agreement. 10 April. Available at: https://www. gov.uk/government/publications/the-belfast-agreement

HM Government. 1998b. Northern Ireland Act 1998. Available at: http://www.legis lation.gov.uk/ukpga/1998/47.

HM Government. 2006. The St Andrews Agreement. 16 July. Available at: https://www.gov.uk/government/publications/the-st-andrews-agreement-october-2006.

HM Government. 2019. Agreement on the Withdrawal of the United Kingdom of Great Britain and Northern Ireland from the European Union and the European Atomic Energy Community. 19 October. Available at: https://www.gov.uk/govern ment/publications/new-withdrawal-agreement-and-political-declaration.

HM Government and Government of Ireland. 1985. Agreement between the Government of the United Kingdom of Great Britain and Northern Ireland and the Government of the Republic of Ireland. 15 November. Available at: http://cain.ulst. ac.uk/events/aia/aiadoc.htm.

HM Government and Government of Ireland. 2020. New Decade, New Approach. 9 January. Available at: https://www.gov.uk/government/news/deal-to-see-restored -government-in-northern-ireland-tomorrow.

Hodžić, Edin, and Nenad Stojanović. 2011. *New/Old Constitutional Engineering? Challenges and Implications of the European Court of Human Rights Decision in the Case of Sejdic and Finci v. BiH*. Sarajevo: Analitika Center for Social Research.

Holbrooke, Richard. 1999. *To End a War*. New York: Random House.

Horowitz, Donald L. 2002. Explaining the Northern Ireland Agreement: The Sources of an Unlikely Constitutional Consensus. *British Journal of Political Science* 32(2): 193–220.

Horowitz, Donald L. 2014. Ethnic Power Sharing: Three Big Problems. *Journal of Democracy* 25(2): 5–20.

Hume, John and Gerry Adams. 1993. First Joint Statement. 24 April. Available at: http://cain.ulst.ac.uk/events/peace/docs/ha24493.htm.

Hume, John and Gerry Adams. 1994. Second Joint Statement. 28 August. Available at: http://cain.ulst.ac.uk/events/peace/docs/ha28894.htm.

Hurd, Douglas. 1992. Presidency Intervention, London Conference General Debate, 26 August. *Balkan Odyssey CD-ROM* Academic Edition v1.1. London: The Electric Company.

Husanović, Jasmina. 2004. 'In Search of Agency': Beyond the 'Old/New' Biopolitics of Sovereignty in Bosnia. In *Sovereign Lives: Power in Global Politics*, edited by Jenny Edkins, Veronique Pin-Fat, and Michael J. Shapiro, 211–38. London: Routledge.

Hutchings, Kimberly. 2008. *Time and World Politics: Thinking the Present.* Manchester: Manchester University Press.

International Crisis Group. 2014. Bosnia's Future. *Europe Report* 232. 10 July.

ITV News. 2017. No Agreement on Unionist Pact. 8 May. Available at: https://www .itv.com/news/utv/2017-05-08/no-agreement-on-unionist-pact/.

Jenne, Erin. 2009. The Paradox of Ethnic Partition: Lessons from de facto Partition in Bosnia and Kosovo. *Regional and Federal Studies* 19(2): 273–89.

Johnson, Kevin. 2008. Sectarianism and the Shipyard. *The Irish Times.* 29 November. Available at: https://www.irishtimes.com/news/sectarianism-and-the-shipyard-1.9 16936.

Kapidžić, Damir. 2016. Local Elections in Bosnia and Herzegovina. *Contemporary Southeastern Europe* 3(2): 127–34.

Kappler, Stephanie and Oliver P. Richmond. 2011. Peacebuilding and Culture in Bosnia and Herzegovina: Resistance or Emancipation? *Security Dialogue* 42(3): 261–78.

Karić, Mirsad. 2013. Critical Analysis of 2012 Local Elections in Bosnia-Herzegovina. *Epiphany: Journal of Transdisciplinary Studies* 6(1): 203–18.

Kasapović, Mirjana. 2016. Lijphart and Horowitz in Bosnia and Herzegovina: Institutional Design for Conflict Resolution or Conflict Reproduction? *Croatian Political Science Review* 53(4): 174–90.

Kaufmann, Chaim. 1996. Possible and Impossible Solutions to Ethnic Civil Wars. *International Security* 20(4): 136–75.

Keil, Soeren and Valery Perry. 2015. Back to Square One?: An Analysis of the 2014 General Elections in Bosnia and Herzegovina. *Electoral Studies* 38: 82–87.

Kent, Gregory. 2013. Genocidal Intent and Transitional Justice in Bosnia: Jelisic, Foot Soldiers of Genocide, and the ICTY. *East European Politics and Societies* 27(3): 564–87.

Kesby, Rebecca. 2012. Who Can Protect Bosnia-Hercegovina's Cultural Heritage? *BBC News.* 23 February. Available at: https://www.bbc.co.uk/news/world-europe -17132141.

Kim, Dong Jin. 2018. Sharing Lessons between Peace Processes: A Comparative Case Study on the Northern Ireland and Korean Peace Processes. *Social Sciences* 7(3): 48.

King, Steven. 2008. In From the Cold: The Rise to Prominence of the Democratic Unionist Party since 2003. *Irish Review* 38: 1–12.

Knaus, Gerald and Felix Martin. 2003. Lessons from Bosnia and Herzegovina: Travails of the European Raj. *Journal of Democracy* 14(3): 60–74.

Kovacevic, Danijel. 2017. Bosnian Serb Leader Puts Justice Referendum on Hold. *Balkan Insight.* September 20. Available at: http://www.balkaninsight.com/en/ article/bosnian-serb-leader-puts-justice-referendum-on-hold-09-20-2017.

Kovacevic, Danijel. 2019a. Bosnia Fails again to Form New State Government. *Balkan Insight.* 27 August. Available at: https://balkaninsight.com/2019/08/27/bosnia-fails-again-to-form-new-state-government/.

Kovacevic, Danijel. 2019b. Bosnia Parliament Confirms Tegeltija as New State PM. *Balkan Insight.* 5 December. Available at: https://balkaninsight.com/2019/12/05/bosnia-parliament-confirms-tegeltija-as-new-state-pm/.

Lai, Daniela. 2020. Practicing Solidarity: 'Reconciliation' and Bosnian Protest Movements. *Ethnopolitics* 19(2): 168–87.

Lakic, Mladen. 2018a. Bosniak War Victims Condemn Croat Entity Call. *Balkan Insight.* February 1. Available at: http://www.balkaninsight.com/en/article/new-declaration-for-third-entity-in-bosnia-01-30-2018.

Lakic, Mladen. 2018b. Bosnians Stage Simultaneous Protests over Youngsters' Deaths. *Balkan Insight.* 5 October. Available at: https://balkaninsight.com/2018/10/05/bosnians-to-stage-protests-over-youngsters-deaths-10-05-2018/.

Lakic, Mladen. 2018c. Dodik Wins Presidency Seat in Bosnia Election. *Balkan Insight.* 7 October. Available at: http://www.balkaninsight.com/en/article/first-unconfirmed-results-of-bosnia-s-elections-10-07-2018.

Lakic, Mladen. 2018d. Dodik to Shun Bosnian Presidency HQ in Sarajevo. *Balkan Insight.* 11 October. Available at: http://www.balkaninsight.com/en/article/bosnian-serb-leader-insists-on-avoiding-sarajevo-10-11-2018.

Lakic, Mladen. 2018e. Bosnian Croats Protest against Komsic's Election Victory. *Balkan Insight.* 12 October. Available at http://www.balkaninsight.com/en/article/bosnian-croats-stage-protest-against-new-presidency-member-10-12-2018.

Liberman Peter. 2014. War and Torture as 'Just Deserts'. *Public Opinion Quarterly* 78(1): 47–70.

Lippman, Peter. 2015. Setbacks and Coalition-Building after October Elections in Bosnia-Herzegovina. *Washington Report on Middle East Affairs.* Special Report. January/February: 36–37.

Little, Adrian. 2003. The Problems of Antagonism: Applying Liberal Political Theory to Conflict in Northern Ireland. *The British Journal of Politics and International Relations* 5(3): 373–92.

Little, Adrian. 2004. *Democracy and Northern Ireland: Beyond the Liberal Paradigm?* London: Palgrave MacMillan.

Lundy, Patricia. 2009. Exploring Home-Grown Transitional Justice and its Dilemmas: A Case Study of the Historical Enquiries Team, Northern Ireland. *International Journal of Transitional Justice* 3(3): 321–40.

Lundy, Patricia. 2011. Paradoxes and Challenges of Transitional Justice at the 'Local' Level: Historical Enquiries in Northern Ireland. *Contemporary Social Science* 6(1): 89–105.

Mac Ginty, Roger. 2008. Indigenous Peace-Making Versus the Liberal Peace. *Cooperation and Conflict* 43(2): 139–63.

Mac Ginty, Roger. 2009. The Liberal Peace at Home and Abroad: Northern Ireland and Liberal Internationalism. *The British Journal of Politics and International Relations* 11(4): 690–708.

Mac Ginty, Roger. 2010. Hybrid Peace: The Interaction Between Top-Down and Bottom-Up Peace. *Security Dialogue* 41(4): 391–412.

Mac Ginty, Roger. 2011. *International Peacebuilding and Local Resistance: Hybrid Forms of Peace*. Basingstoke: Palgrave MacMillan.

Mac Ginty, Roger. 2016. Lockout: Peace Formation in Northern Ireland. In *Post-Liberal Peace Transitions: Between Peace Formation and State Formation*, edited by Oliver P. Richmond and Sandra Pogodda, 27–46. Edinburgh: Edinburgh University Press.

Mac Ginty, Roger and Oliver P Richmond. 2013. The Local Turn in Peace Building: A Critical Agenda for Peace. *Third World Quarterly* 34(5): 763–83.

Mac Ginty, Roger and Oliver P. Richmond. 2016. The Fallacy of Constructing Hybrid Political Orders: A Reappraisal of the Hybrid Turn in Peacebuilding. *International Peacekeeping* 23(2): 219–39.

Mac Giolla Bhéin, Ciarán. 2019. Time for an Irish Language Act. *The Irish News*. 14 January. Available at: http://www.irishnews.com/paywall/tsb/irishnews/irishnews /irishnews//opinion/2019/01/11/news/ciara-n-mac-giolla-bhe-in-time-for-an-irish -language-act-1527187/content.html.

Maguire, Mairead Corrigan. 2010. *The Vision of Peace: Faith and Hope in Northern Ireland*. Eugene, OR: Wipf and Stock.

Major, John. 1999. *The Autobiography*. London: Harper Collins.

Malik, John. 2000. The Dayton Agreement and Elections in Bosnia: Entrenching Ethnic Cleansing through Democracy. *Stanford Journal of International Law* 36(2): 303–54.

Manning, Carrie. 2004. Elections and Political Change in Post-War Bosnia and Herzegovina. *Democratization* 11(2): 60–86.

McBride, James. 2017. Vote Transfers: Breaking the Mould of Northern Ireland Politics. *RTÉ News*. 23 March. Available at: https://www.rte.ie/news/analysis-and -comment/2017/0312/859168-vote-transfers-north/.

McCann, Maria. 2019. Stormont: Protesters urge Politicians to 'Get Back to Work'. *BBC News*. 26 January. Available at: https://www.bbc.co.uk/news/uk-northern-ireland-47016521.

McCausland, Nelson. 2014. Irish Language is Still Undoubtedly a Weapon in Sinn Fein's Cultural War. *Belfast Telegraph*. 27 November. Available at: https://ww w.belfasttelegraph.co.uk/opinion/columnists/nelson-mccausland/irish-language-is-still-undoubtedly-a-weapon-in-sinn-feins-cultural-war-30777361.html.

McCormack, Jayne. 2019. General Election 2019: Pacts and Political Goodbyes. *BBC News*. 9 November. Available at: https://www.bbc.co.uk/news/uk-northern-ireland -50333803.

McCrudden, Christopher, John McGarry, Brendan O'Leary, and Alex Schwartz. 2016. Why Northern Ireland's Institutions Need Stability. *Government and Opposition* 51(1): 30–58.

McDonald, Henry. 2010. General Election 2010: Peter Robinson Loses Seat to Alliance Party. *The Guardian*. 7 May. Available at: https://www.theguardian.com/ politics/2010/may/07/general-election-peter-robinson-loses-seat.

McEvoy, Joanne. 2015. *Power-Sharing Executives: Governing in Bosnia, Macedonia, and Northern Ireland*. Philadelphia, PA: University of Pennsylvania Press.

McEvoy, Lesley, Kieran McEvoy, and Kirsten McConnachie. 2006. Reconciliation as a Dirty Word: Conflict, Community Relations and Education in Northern Ireland. *Journal of International Affairs* 60(1): 81–106.

McGarry, John and Brendan O'Leary. 1995. *Explaining Northern Ireland: Broken Images*. Oxford: Blackwell Publishers.

McGarry, John and Brendan O'Leary. 2004. *The Northern Ireland Conflict: Consociational Engagements*. Oxford: Oxford University Press.

McGarry, John and Brendan O'Leary. 2016. Power-Sharing Executives: Consociational and Centripetal Formulae and the Case of Northern Ireland. *Ethnopolitics* 15(5): 497–519.

McGlynn, Catherine, Jonathan Tonge, and Jim McAuley. 2014. The Party Politics of Post-Devolution Identity in Northern Ireland. *British Journal of Politics and International Relations* 16(2): 273–90.

McGrattan, Cillian. 2010a. *Northern Ireland 1968-2008: The Politics of Entrenchment*. Basingstoke: Palgrave MacMillan.

McGrattan, Cillian. 2010b. Learning From the Past or Laundering History? Consociational Narratives and State Intervention in Northern Ireland. *British Politics* 5(1): 92–113.

McGrattan, Cillian. 2010c. Explaining Northern Ireland: The Limitations of the Ethnic Conflict Model. *National Identities* 12(2): 181–97.

McKittrick, David and David McVea. 2012. *Making Sense of the Troubles: A History of the Northern Ireland Conflict*. London: Penguin Books.

McRobie, Heather. 2014. Listen to Bosnia's Plenums. *Open Democracy*. 25 March. Available at: https://www.opendemocracy.net/5050/heather-mcrobie/listen-to-bos nias-plenums.

McVeigh, Robbie. 2002. Between Reconciliation and Pacification: The British State and Community Relations in the North of Ireland. *Community Development Journal* 37(1): 47–59.

McVeigh, Robbie and Bill Rolston. 2006. From Good Friday to Good Relations: Sectarianism, Racism and the Northern Ireland State. *Race and Class* 48(4): 1–23.

Meagher, Kevin. 2017. Arlene Foster has led Northern Ireland into Crisis – and Westminster is Strangely Quiet. *New Statesman*. 11 January. Available at: https://www.newstatesman.com/politics/staggers/2017/01/arlene-foster-has-led-northern -ireland-crisis-and-westminster-strangely.

Meredith, Robbie. 2018. East Belfast May Get Irish-Medium School. *BBC News*. 19 December. Available at: https://www.bbc.co.uk/news/uk-northern-ireland-466 25962.

Milanovic, Marko. 2010. Sejdić & Finci v. Bosnia and Herzegovina. *American Journal of International Law* 104(4): 636–41.

Mitchell, David. 2018. Non-Nationalist Politics in a Bi-National Consociation: The Case of the Alliance Party of Northern Ireland. *Nationalism and Ethnic Politics* 24(3): 336–47.

Mitchell, George. 1999. *Making Peace*. Berkley, CA: University of California Press.

Mitchell, Paul, Geoffrey Evans, Brendan O'Leary. 2009. Extremist Outbidding in Ethnic Party Systems is Not Inevitable: Tribune Parties in Northern Ireland. *Political Studies* 57(2): 397–421.

Mowlam, Mo. 2002. *Momentum: The Struggle for Peace, Politics and the People.* London: Hodder and Stroughten.

Mujkic, Asim. 2007. We, the Citizens of Ethnopolis. *Constellations* 14(1): 112–28.

Mulaj, Klejda. 2005. On Bosnia's Borders and Ethnic Cleansing: Internal and External Factors. *Nationalism and Ethnic Politics* 11(1): 1–24.

Murtagh, Cera. 2016. Civic Mobilization in Divided Societies and the Perils of Political Engagement: Bosnia and Herzegovina's Protest and Plenum Movement. *Nationalism and Ethnic Politics* 22(2): 149–71.

Nardelli, Alberto, Denis Dzidic and Elvira Jukic. 2014. Bosnia and Herzegovina: The World's Most Complicated System of Government? *The Guardian.* 8 October. Available at: https://www.theguardian.com/news/datablog/2014/oct/08/bosnia-herzegovina-elections-the-worlds-most-complicated-system-of-government.

Oberschall, Anthony and L. Kendall Palmer. 2005. The Failure of Moderate Politics: The Case of Northern Ireland. In *Power Sharing: New Challenges for Divided Societies*, edited by Ian O'Flynn and David Russell, 77–91. London: Pluto Press.

O'Callaghan, Margaret. 2008. Genealogies of Partition: History, History-Writing, and 'the Troubles'. In *Intervening in Northern Ireland: Critically Re-Thinking Representations of the Conflict*, edited by Marysia Zalewski and John Barry, 141–56. London: Routledge.

Ó Caoindealbháin, Brian. 2006. Citizenship and Borders: Irish Nationality Law and Northern Ireland. *Institute for British-Irish Studies* Working Paper No. 68.

O'Duffy, Brendan. 2004. British and Irish Conflict Regulation from Sunningdale to Belfast. Part II: Playing for a Draw 1985–1999. *Nations and Nationalism* 6(3): 399–435.

Office of the High Representative. 1998. Decision on the Flying of the Flag of BiH. 4 April 1998. Available at: http://www.ohr.int/?p=67196.

Office of the High Representative. 1999. Decision Imposing the Law on the National Anthem of BiH. 25 June. Available at: http://www.ohr.int/?p=67164.

Office of the High Representative. 2002. Decision Suspending all Judicial and Prosecutorial Appointments in BiH (except to the BiH and the Entity Const. Courts, the BiH H. Rights Chamber, the BiH Court, and all Courts in the Brcko District) Pending the Restructuring of the Judicial System. 4 April. Available at: http://www.ohr.int/?p=66801.

Office of the High Representative. 2015a. Peace Implementation Council. Available at: http://www.ohr.int/?page_id=1220.

Office of the High Representative. 2015b. Election Legislation. Available at: http://www.ohr.int/?page_id=68222.

Office of the High Representative. 2015c. Constitutions. Available at: http://www.ohr.int/?page_id=68220 .

O'Halloran, Patrick J. 2005. Post-Conflict Reconstruction: Constitutional and Transitional Power-Sharing Arrangements in Bosnia and Kosovo. In *From Power*

*Sharing to Democracy: Post-Conflict Institutions in Ethnically Divided Societies*, edited by Sid Noel, 104–19. Montreal: McGill-Queen's University Press.

O'Leary, Brendan and John McGarry. 1996. *The Politics of Antagonism: Understanding Northern Ireland*. London: Continuum International Publishing Group.

O'Leary, Brendan. 1997. The Conservative Stewardship of Northern Ireland, 1979–97: Sound-Bottomed Contradictions or Slow Learning? *Political Studies* 45(4): 663–76.

Orentlicher, Diane. 2018. *Some Kind of Justice: The ICTY's Impact in Bosnia and Serbia*. Oxford: Oxford University Press.

Orford, Anne. 2003. *Reading Humanitarian Intervention: Human Rights and the Use of Force in International Law*. Cambridge: Cambridge University Press.

Organisation for Security and Co-operation in Europe. 1995. Dayton Peace Agreement. 14 December. Available at: https://www.osce.org/bih/126173.

Organisation for Security and Co-operation in Europe. 2000. OSCE Releases Final Results from Bosnia and Herzegovina Elections. 27 November. Available at: https://www.osce.org/bih/53160.

Organisation for Security and Co-operation in Europe. 2003. Bosnia and Herzegovina, General Elections, 5 October 2002: Final Report. 9 January. Available at: https://www.osce.org/odihr/elections/bih/14001.

Osland, Kari M. 2004. The EU Police Mission in Bosnia and Herzegovina. *International Peacekeeping* 11(3): 544–60.

Owen, David. 1995. *Balkan Odyssey*. San Diego, CA: Harcourt Brace.

Page, Chris. 2019. Northern Ireland Abortion and Same-Sex Marriage Laws Change. *BBC News*. 22 October. Available at: https://www.bbc.co.uk/news/uk-northern-ireland-50128860.

Pasic, Lana. 2014. Protests, Floods, Anniversaries and Arrests: Reflecting on Bosnia's Main Events of 2014. *Balkan Analysis*. 14 January. Available at: http://www.balkanalysis.com/bosnia/2015/01/14/protests-floods-elections-anniversaries-and-arrests-reflecting-on-bosnias-main-events-of-2014/.

Patterson, Henry. 2012. Unionism after Good Friday and St Andrews. *The Political Quarterly* 83(2): 247–55.

Perry, Valery. 2015. The 2013 Bosnia and Herzegovina Census: Waiting for Results and Counting the Questions. *Contemporary Southeastern Europe* 2(2): 50–64.

Perry, Valery. 2019. Frozen, Stalled, Stuck, or Just Muddling Through: The Post-Dayton Frozen Conflict in Bosnia and Herzegovina. *Asia Europe Journal* 17(6): 107–27.

Petritsch, Wolfgang. 2014. Bosnians are Hungry in Three Languages: Bosnia Must Escape From its Dead End through Complete Reform of its Failed Political System – With the Aid of a New EU Marshall Plan. *Balkan Insight*. 19 February. Available at: http://www.balkaninsight.com/en/article/bosnians-are-hungry-in-three-languages.

Pinkerton, Patrick. 2012. Resisting Memory: The Politics of Memorialisation in Post-Conflict Northern Ireland. *British Journal of Politics and International Relations* 14(1): 131–52.

Powell, Jonathan. 2008. *Great Hatred, Little Room: Making Peace in Northern Ireland.* London: The Bodley Head.

Prince, Simon. 2018. *Northern Ireland's '68: Civil Rights, Global Revolt and the Origins of the Troubles* (Revised Edition). Newbridge: Irish Academic Press.

Radin, Andrew. 2014. The Misunderstood Lessons of Bosnia for Syria. *The Washington Quarterly* 37(4): 55–69.

Reilly, Benjamin. 2001. *Democracy in Divided Societies: Electoral Engineering for Conflict Management.* Cambridge: Cambridge University Press.

Reynolds, Albert and John Major. 1993. Joint Declaration on Peace. 15 December. Available at: http://cain.ulst.ac.uk/events/peace/docs/dsd151293.htm.

Richmond, Oliver P. 2010. Resistance and the Post-Liberal Peace. *Millennium: Journal of International Studies* 38(3): 665–92.

Richmond, Oliver P. 2012. A Pedagogy of Peacebuilding: Infrapolitics, Resistance, and Liberation. *International Political Sociology* 6(2): 115–31.

Richmond, Oliver P. and Audra Mitchell. 2012. *Hybrid Forms of Peace: From Everyday Agency to Post-Liberalism.* Basingstoke: Palgrave MacMillan.

Richmond, Oliver P. and Sandra Pogodda. 2016. Introduction: The Contradictions of Peace, International Architecture, the State, and Local Agency. In *Post-Liberal Peace Transitions: Between Peace Formation and State Formation*, edited by Oliver P. Richmond and Sandra Pogodda, 1–26. Edinburgh: Edinburgh University Press.

Rolston, Bill. 1998. What's Wrong with Multiculturalism? In *Rethinking Northern Ireland: Culture, Ideology and Colonialism*, edited by David W. Miller, 253–74. Boston, MA: Addison Wesley Longman.

Ruane, Joseph and Jennifer Todd. 1996. *The Dynamics of Conflict in Northern Ireland: Power, Conflict and Emancipation.* Cambridge: Cambridge University Press.

Ruane, Joseph and Jennifer Todd. 1998. Irish Nationalism and the Conflict in Northern Ireland. In *Rethinking Northern Ireland: Culture, Ideology and Colonialism*, edited by David W. Miller, 55–69. Boston, MA: Addison Wesley Longman.

Ruane, Joseph and Jennifer Todd. 1999. The Belfast Agreement: Context, Content, Consequences. In *After the Good Friday Agreement: Analysing Political Change in Northern Ireland,* edited by Joseph Ruane and Jennifer Todd, 1–29. Dublin: University College Dublin Press.

Sarajevo Times. 2019. Long Delays in the Judiciary's Handling Cases are Unacceptable for a Country Seeking Membership in the EU. 30 June. Available at: https://www.sarajevotimes.com/long-delays-in-the-judiciarys-handling-cases-are-unacceptable-for-a-country-seeking-membership-in-the-eu.

Sebastián, Sofía. 2007. Leaving Dayton Behind: Constitutional Reform in Bosnia and Herzegovina. *FRIDE.* Working Paper 46. November.

Sebastián, Sofía. 2010. Statebuilding in Divided Societies: The Reform of Dayton in Bosnia and Herzegovina. *Journal of Intervention and Statebuilding* 4(3): 323–44.

Shirlow, Peter and Kieran McEvoy. 2008. *Beyond the Wire: Former Prisoners and Conflict Transformation in Northern Ireland.* London: Pluto Press.

Silber, Laura and Allan Little. 1996. *The Death of Yugoslavia* (Revised Edition). London: Penguin Books.

Simms, Brendan. 2002. *Unfinest Hour: Britain and the Destruction of Bosnia*. London: Penguin Books.

Smale, Alison. 2014. Roots of Bosnian Protests Lie in Peace Accords of 1995. *The New York Times*. 14 February. Available at: http://www.nytimes.com/2014/02/15/world/europe/roots-of-bosnian-protests-lie-in-peace-accords-of-1995.html?_r=2.

Søberg, Marius. 2008. The Quest for Institutional Reform in Bosnia and Herzegovina. *East European Politics and Societies* 22(4): 714–37.

Spivak, Gayatri Chakravorty. 2016. Translator's Preface. In *Of Grammatology, 40th Anniversary Edition*, xxvii–cxi. Baltimore, MD: John Hopkins University Press.

Stjepanović, Dejan. 2015. Territoriality and Citizenship: Membership and Sub-State Polities in Post-Yugoslav Space. *Europe-Asia Studies* 67(7): 1030–55.

Stojanović, Nenad. 2018. Political Marginalization of 'Others' in Consociational Regimes. *Zeitschrift für Vergleichende Politikwissenschaft* 12(2): 341–64.

Stravidis, James. 2015. Syrian Ghosts: What the Balkans Can Teach us about How to End the Conflict in the Levant. *Foreign Policy*. 6 November. Available at: http://foreignpolicy.com/2015/11/06/lessons-from-the-balkans-for-Syria/?utm_content=buffer8ab7b&utm_medium=social&utm_source=twitter.com&utm_campaign=buffer.

Stroschein, Sherrill. 2014. Consociational Settlements and Reconstruction: Bosnia in Comparative Perspective (1995-present). *Annals, The American Academy of Political and Social Science* 656(1): 97–115.

Swann, Robin. 2017. SF are Using Irish Language as Weapon in a Cultural War. *News Letter*. 27 July. Available at: https://www.newsletter.co.uk/news/opinion/sf-are-using-irish-language-as-weapon-in-a-cultural-war-1-8074215.

Taylor, Peter. 1999. *Loyalists: War and Peace in Northern Ireland*. London: Bloomsbury.

Tennyson, Eóin. 2018. If Sinn Féin are Serious about Rights and Equality, they Must Prioritise Petition of Concern Reform. *Slugger O'Toole*. 4 August. Available at: https://sluggerotoole.com/2018/08/04/if-sinn-fein-are-serious-about-rights-and-equality-they-must-prioritise-petition-of-concern-reform/.

The Electoral Office for Northern Ireland. 2019a. Elections 2019. Available at: http://www.eoni.org.uk/Elections/Election-results-and-statistics/Election-results-and-statistics-2003-onwards/Elections-2019.

The Electoral Office for Northern Ireland. 2019b. Election Results and Statistics 2003 Onwards. Available at: http://www.eoni.org.uk/Elections/Election-results-and-statistics.

The Guardian. 2014. Time for Another Dayton: Bosnia. 16 February. Available at: http://www.theguardian.com/world/2014/feb/16/bosnia-another-dayton-editorial.

The Guardian. 2017. Police and Public Attacked in Derry Bonfire Violence. 15 August. Available at: https://www.theguardian.com/uk-news/2017/aug/15/police-public-attacked-derry-bonfire-violence-northern-ireland.

The Irish News. 2019. Bonfire Insult to Ballymurphy Victims. 11 July. Available at: https://www.irishnews.com/news/northernirelandnews/2018/07/11/news/calls-for-removal-of-offensive-ballymurphy-massacre-bonfire-slogans-1380288/.

The Irish Times. 2011. Ervine Relative Speaks up for Irish. 1 September. Available at: https://www.irishtimes.com/news/ervine-relative-speaks-up-for-irish-1.882766.

The Orange Order. 2018. Welcome to the Grand Orange Lodge. Available at: http://www.grandorangelodge.co.uk/What-is-the-orange-order#.W8cGrfZryUk.

Thompson, Simon. 2003. The Politics of Culture in Northern Ireland. *Constellations* 10(1): 53–74.

Toal, Gerard and Carl T. Dahlman. 2011. *Bosnia Remade: Ethnic Cleansing and its Reversal*. Oxford: Oxford University Press.

Todorova, Maria. 1997. *Imagining the Balkans*. Oxford: Oxford University Press.

Tonge, Jonathan and Jocelyn Evans. 2015. Another Communal Headcount: The Election in Northern Ireland. *Parliamentary Affairs* 68(1): 117–32.

Tonge, Jonathan and Jocelyn Evans. 2017. Northern Ireland: Double Triumph for the Democratic Unionist Party. *Parliamentary Affairs* 71(1): 139–54.

Tonge, Jonathan. 2002. *Northern Ireland: Conflict and Change* (Second Edition). Harlow: Pearson Education Limited.

Tonge, Jonathan. 2016. Plus Ça Change? The 2016 Devolved Elections in the UK. *Political Insight* 7(2): 12–15.

Tonge, Jonathan. 2017. Supplying Confidence or Trouble? The Deal Between the Democratic Unionist Party and the Conservative Party. *The Political Quarterly* 88(3): 412–16.

United Nations. 1991. Security Council Resolution 724. 15 December. Available at: https://undocs.org/S/RES/724(1991).

United Nations. 1992a Security Council Resolution 752. 5 May. Available at: https://undocs.org/S/RES/752(1992).

United Nations. 1992b. Security Council Resolution 758. 8 June. Available at: https://undocs.org/S/RES/758(1992).

United Nations. 1992c. Security Council Resolution 764. 13 July. Available at: https://undocs.org/S/RES/764(1992).

United Nations. 1992d. Security Council Resolution 776. 14 September. Available at: https://undocs.org/S/RES/776(1992).

United Nations. 1992e. Security Council Resolution 798. 18 December. Available at: https://undocs.org/S/RES/798(1992).

United Nations. 1993a. Security Council Resolution 819. 16 April. Available at: https://undocs.org/S/RES/819(1993)

United Nations. 1993b. Security Council Resolution 824. 6 May. Available at: https://undocs.org/S/RES/824(1993).

United Nations 1993c. Security Council Resolution 836. 4 June. Available at: https://undocs.org/S/RES/836(1993).

United Nations. 1995. Security Council Resolution 1016. 21 September. Available at: https://undocs.org/S/RES/1016(1995).

United Nations. 2020. Security Council Resolutions. Available at: https://www.un.org/securitycouncil/content/resolutions-0.

Vaughan-Williams, Nick. 2008. Towards a Problematisation of the Problematisations that Reduced Northern Ireland to a 'Problem'. In *Intervening in Northern Ireland: Critically Re-Thinking Representations of the Conflict*, edited by Marysia Zalewski and John Barry, 35–48. London: Routledge.

Viggiani, Elisabetta. 2014. *Talking Stones: The Politics of Memorialization in Post-Conflict Northern Ireland*. Oxford: Berghahn Books.

Weber, Bodo. 2014. The Limits of the EU's Transformative Power in Bosnia-Herzegovina: Implications for Party Politics. In *EU Integration and Party Politics in the Balkans*, edited by Rosa Balfour and Corina Stratulat, 95–106. European Policy Centre Issue Paper No. 77. Available at: http://www.epc.eu/documents/uploads/pub_4716_eu_integration_and_party_politics_in_the_balkans.pdf.

Weller, Marc and Stefan Wolff. 2006. Bosnia and Herzegovina Ten Years after Dayton: Lessons for Internationalized State Building. *Ethnopolitics* 5(1): 1–13.

White, Timothy J. 2014. Lessons from the Northern Ireland Peace Process: An Introduction. In *Lessons from the Northern Ireland Peace Process*, edited by Timothy J. White, 1–33. Madison, WI: University of Wisconsin Press.

Whyte, John. 1990. *Interpreting Northern Ireland*. Oxford: Oxford University Press.

Wilford, Rick. 2010. Northern Ireland: The Politics of Constraint. *Parliamentary Affairs* 63(1): 134–55.

Wilson, Robin. 2010. *The Northern Ireland Experience of Conflict and Agreement: A Model for Export?* Manchester: Manchester University Press.

Wolff, Stefan. 2001. The Road to Peace? The Good Friday Agreement and the Conflict in Northern Ireland. *World Affairs* 163(4): 163–70.

Woodward, Susan. 1995. *Balkan Tragedy: Chaos and Dissolution after the Cold War*. Washington D.C.: The Brookings Institute.

Young, Robert J.C. 1995. *Colonial Desire: Hybridity in Theory, Culture and Race*. London: Routledge.

Zahar, Marie-Joëlle. 2005. The Dichotomy of International Mediation and Leader Intransigence: The Case of Bosnia and Herzegovina. In *Power Sharing: New Challenges for Divided Societies*, edited by Ian O'Flynn and David Russell, 123–37. London: Pluto Press.

Zalewski, Marysia. 2008. Intervening in Northern Ireland: Critically Re-Thinking Representations of the Conflict. In *Intervening in Northern Ireland: Critically Re-Thinking Representations of the Conflict*, edited by Marysia Zalewski and John Barry, 1–19. London: Routledge.

Zarkov, Dubravka. 1995. Gender, Orientalism and the History of Ethnic Hatred in the former Yugoslavia. In *Crossfires: Nationalism, Racism and Gender in Europe*, edited by Helma Lutz, Ann Phoenix and Nira Yuval-Davis, 105–20. London: Pluto Press.

# Index

*Index*

# About the Author

**Patrick Pinkerton** is Associate Lecturer in the Department of Political Science at University College London.

www.ingramcontent.com/pod-product-compliance
Lightning Source LLC
Chambersburg PA
CBHW022317280326

41932CB00010B/1127